LANGUAGE AND COGNITIVE PROCESSES
2009, 24 (5), 625–630

Sublexical, lexical and supralexical information in speaking: Current insights and directions in language production research

Jens Bölte

Psychologisches Institut II, Westfälische Wilhelms-Universität Münster, Germany

Matthew Goldrick

Department of Linguistics, Northwestern University, Evanston, IL, USA

Pienie Zwitserlood

Psychologisches Institut II, Westfälische Wilhelms-Universität Münster, Germany

We summarise research on language production that is based on presentations given at the *Fourth International Workshop on Language Production* (Münster, Germany, September 2007). The individual contributions to this special issue cover language production in its full width: from processes and information types involved in formulation (Ziegler, Cholin & Levelt; Damian & Dumay), via lexical competition and selection (Abdel Rahman & Melinger; Mahon & Caramazza) to the interplay between conceptualisation and gesturing (Kita).

This special issue of Language and Cognitive Processes is dedicated to language production research. It comprises a subset of papers presented at

Correspondence should be addressed to Jens Bölte, Psychologisches Institut II, Westfälische Wilhelms-Universität Münster, Fliedner Str. 21, 48149 Münster, Germany. E-mail: boelte@psy.uni-muenster.de

The *Fourth International Workshop on Language Production*, held from September 3–5, 2007, in Münster, Germany, was sponsored by the German Scientific Research Council (DFG). In addition to the authors, the scientific committee consisted of F.-Xavier Alario, Albert Costa, and Victor Ferreira. We thank Ann-Kathrin Bröckelmann, Maren Hulisz, and Claudia Schulz for their hands-on help before and during the event.

http://www.psypress.com/lcp   DOI: 10.1080/01690960902767829

the *Fourth International Workshop on Language Production*, organised by the Psycholinguistic Research Group of the Department of Psychology at the University of Münster, Germany. It is the fourth in a series of special issues resulting from similar workshops (see Alario, Costa, Ferreira, & Pickering, 2006; Goldrick, Costa, & Schiller, 2008; Schiller, Ferreira, & Alario, 2007). The fact that four special issues have emerged within four years' time corroborates what has been evident for the last two decades: Language production is a fast-growing field of research, with researchers dedicated to experimentally fleshing out the models on the market, and to methodological innovation of the field. Clearly, the initiative taken by the organisers of the first workshop in Marseille in 2004 was timely, the turnover has been fast, and important findings have emerged.

All papers in this volume profited from the productive atmosphere at the workshop meeting, was the case for earlier workshops. The workshop series typically brings together researchers from various disciplines within psycholinguistics, from phonetics, and from other related disciplines. Equipped and trained with their specific methodologies, techniques and research questions, participants contribute their specific perspectives and know-how such that an interdisciplinary and integrative approach to language production research emerges. The contributions to this special issue exemplify this approach. A wide range of topics is covered in this special issue, including the non-linear structure of the phonetic code, the position-nonspecific activation of segments during phonological encoding, and the existence of a mental syllabary, all at the 'lower end' of language production. Further themes concern the interaction between gestures and conceptualisation and – a classic and hotly debated issue – lexical selection in language production. All contributions provide interesting overviews of the issues under debate and offer novel empirical and theoretical insights. Below, we briefly introduce each contribution, keeping to their order of appearance in the special issue, which is organised from articulation to conceptualisation.

The contribution by Ziegler (2009 this issue) offers interesting insights from patients with apraxia into the organisation of the phonetic code. Ziegler states that current models of language production by Dell and colleagues (Dell, 1986; Dell, Schwartz, Martin, Saffran, & Gagnon, 1997) or by Levelt and colleagues (Levelt, Roelofs, & Meyer, 1999) are, at best, underspecified with respect to the processes involved in the construction of phonetic or articulatory plans. The minimal assumption shared by both models is that discrete sound units are generated, which are then processed further at phonetic and articulatory stages. Ziegler argues that these conceptions miss out on relevant properties of language production, such as coarticulatory phenomena or the generation of prosody. These shortcomings have been taken up by, for instance, Goldrick and Blumstein (2006) and Goldstein, Pouplier, Chen, Saltzman, and Byrd (2007). Goldrick and Blumstein proposed that phonological planning processes and the articulatory-phonetic stage interact. Goldstein et al. suggest that invariant motor patterns (gestural scores) are stored at an abstract word-form level, such that a linear order of phonetic representations is lost. Ziegler's proposal shares with Goldstein et al. the assumption of a non-linear setup of articulatory gestures, and adds a probabilistic component to this. He tests this proposal against word-production-accuracy data from patients with apraxia of speech. The success of this approach supports his claim that phonetic plans cannot be conceived as linearly ordered sequences of discrete phonetic units. Clearly, this paper adds to the limited evidence available for the nature of late processes involved in speech production.

The role of the syllable as a unit in speech production is as interesting as it is elusive. Cholin and Levelt (2009 this issue) address the existence and the locus of syllabic units in speaking. Syllables are taken to mediate between phonological and phonetic representations, at least those syllables that are stored, because they occur frequently in the language (Levelt et al., 1999). A number of authors (e.g., Aichert & Ziegler, 2004; Carreiras & Perea, 2004; Levelt & Wheeldon, 1994) have argued for stored syllabic representations based on syllable-frequency effects in speaking (such that common syllables are produced more quickly/accurately than infrequent syllables). Levelt et al. proposed that syllables are accessed at the interface of phonological and phonetic encoding, but Cholin and Levelt argue that unequivocal evidence for this assumption is lacking. They therefore set out to test whether stored syllables are indeed relevant at a post-lexical level in speech planning. For this, they combine the implicit priming paradigm, with its proven sensitivity to post-lexical effects, with the manipulation of syllable frequency. Frequency effects, as Cholin and Levelt argue, can only come about when syllables are stored as units, because only stored units are assumed to exhibit frequency effects. So, the logic is that if frequency effects and the effects of post-lexical form similarity interact in implicit priming, this is evidence for a post-lexical locus of stored syllables. Cholin and Levelt indeed report an interaction and conclude that this implies that syllable processing is located at a post-lexical, pre-articulatory processing level. Given that languages differ with respect to the role of syllables as units of speech, it would be interesting to see whether the results for Dutch, as reported here (and elsewhere), generalise to other languages.

The paper by Damian and Dumay (2009 this issue) addresses a level above phonological-phonetic encoding. They investigate the activation of phonemes during multiple-word productions. It is well know that phonologically related distractors facilitate word production (Damian & Dumay, 2007; Meyer & Schriefers, 1991). A shared onset can, however, result in inhibition in certain paradigms (O'Seaghdha, Dell, Peterson, & Juliano, 1992). To further explore the discrepancy in results, Damian and Dumay used adjective-noun phrases (e.g., *green goblin*) to realise phoneme repetition. Would shared segments result in facilitation, as the picture-word interference data suggest, or in inhibition, as, for example, the paired-syllable paradigm would suggest? In an earlier study, Damian and Dumay (2007) had shown that word-initial overlap in adjective-noun phrases resulted in a facilitated production. In their current work, they replicate and extend this result, by comparing within- and between-utterance repetition effects. Shared segments produced facilitation within an utterance, but inhibition between utterances. Given that the position in the word of the repeated segment did not affect the strength of facilitation, Damian and Dumay suggest that the effect arises at a processing level, at which phonemes are activated in a position-unspecific manner.

Moving beyond sound-based representations in speech production, the contribution by Abdel Rahman and Melinger (2009a this issue) addresses a core issue of lexical processing in language production: lexical competition and selection. Spoken word production research, particularly within the chronometric tradition, has focused mainly on interference effects with categorically related stimuli (e.g., the increased latency for naming the picture of a CAT when DOG is present as distractor word). This interference effect was taken to indicate competition between coactivated lexical entries (e.g., < CAT > and < DOG >). However, recent studies have challenged this view, either by reporting the absence of interference effects or, even more convincing, the presence of facilitatory effects. For instance, Mahon, Costa, Peterson, Vargas, & Caramazza (2007) observed facilitation when distractor words are from a different grammatical class. They suggested that facilitation results from lexical priming whereas interference is a consequence of a bottleneck in a post-lexical articulatory buffer. In contrast, Kuipers, La Heij, and Costa (2006) assume that a response-congruency checking mechanism, located at the preverbal level, is at play. It generates both facilitatory and inhibitory effects, depending on the task. In their contribution to this volume, Abdel Rahman and Melinger (2009a this issue) propose a lexical-network account for semantic context effects that rests on two assumptions. (1) The context provided by the distractor modulates the generation of a lexical competitor cohort. The target response enters into a competition with the cohort competitors and must exceed the cohort-competitors' summed activation in order to be selected for production. (2) Whether facilitation or interference will be observed depends on a trade-off between semantic/conceptual priming and lexical competition. Interference will be observed only when both a competitor cohort is sufficiently activated and conceptual facilitation is slight or absent; facilitation is observed in all other cases. Abdel Rahman and Melinger sketch how their proposal could be applied to picture-word interference and semantic blocking paradigms (noting, however, that the precise computational dynamics are still to be determined). In their rejoinder, Mahon and Caramazza (2009 this issue) criticise elements of this proposal. Abdel Rahman and Melinger (2009b this issue) respond to this rejoinder and clarify their arguments. These debates – concerning the nature and locus of lexical selection in speaking, the diverse interpretations of available results and their model implementation – are still far from resolved. The presentation of different viewpoints within one issue certainly is a valuable contribution to this ongoing discussion.

The final contribution to this special issue by Kita (2009 this issue) moves beyond lexical processing to investigate what determines the frequency of representational gestures during speaking. Kita proposes that representational gestures (including iconic gestures, such as the hands moving in a circle when describing a circle, and deictic gestures, for example, indicating a location) are coordinated with message generation. Kita (2000) has shown that more difficult speaking tasks result in more gestures. This finding suggests that representational gestures facilitate conceptualisation for speaking. In his contribution to this special issue, he tests his prediction that the frequency of representational gestures depends on the presence of competing representations in the conceptualisation process. His participants had to describe diagrams that differed only in the way certain lines were highlighted. In the easy diagrams, the highlighted lines were congruent with the target conceptualisation. In the hard condition, they elicited a competing conceptualisation. His participants indeed showed more representational gestures when the diagrams elicited competing conceptualisations than when not. These data add to a growing body of evidence on the way speech and speech-accompanying gestures are interleaved at various stages of (conceptualisation for) speech production.

The research as presented here in this special issue nicely illustrates how the field of language production research has expanded over the last two decades. This holds with respect to the overall number of studies, but, more importantly, to the range of phenomena and processes that have been subjected to rigorous experimental scrutiny. We are certain that the research presented in this issue will advance language production research and, more generally, research into the cognitive processes underlying language.

REFERENCES

Abdel Rahman, R., & Melinger, A. (2009a, this issue). Semantic context effects in language production: A swinging lexical network proposal and a review. *Language and Cognitive Processes, 24*, 714–735.

Abdel Rahman, R., & Melinger, A. (2009b, this issue). Dismissing lexical competition does not make speaking any easier: A rejoinder to Mahon and Caramazza. *Language and Cognitive Processes, 24*, 750–761.

Aichert, I., & Ziegler, W. (2004). Syllable frequency and syllable structure. *Brain and Language, 88*, 148–159.

Alario, F.-X., Costa, A., Ferreira, V. S., & Pickering, M. J. (2006). Architectures, representations and processes of language production. *Language and Cognitive Processes, 21*, 777–789.

Carreiras, M., & Perea, M. (2004). Naming pseudowords in Spanish: Effects of syllable frequency in production. *Brain and Language, 90*, 393–400.

Cholin, J., & Levelt, W. J. M. (2009, this issue). Effects of syllable preparation and syllable frequency in speech production: further evidence for syllabic units at a post-lexical level. *Language and Cognitive Processes, 24*, 662–685.

Damian, M. F., & Dumay, N. (2007). Time pressure and phonological advance planning in spoken production. *Journal of Memory and Language, 57*, 195–209.

Damian, M. F., & Dumay, N. (2009, this issue). Exploring phonological encoding through repeated segments. *Language and Cognitive Processes, 24,* 686–713.

Dell, G. S. (1986). A spreading-activation theory of retrieval in sentence production. *Psychological Review, 93*, 283–321.

Dell, G. S., Schwartz, M. F., Martin, N., Saffran, E. M., & Gagnon, D. A. (1997). Lexical access in aphasic and nonaphasic speakers. *Psychological Review, 104*, 801–838.

Goldrick, M., & Blumstein, S. E. (2006). Cascading activation from phonological planning to articulatory processes: evidence from tongue twisters. *Language and Cognitive Processes, 21*, 649–683.

Goldrick, M., Costa, A., & Schiller, N. O. (2008). Situating language production within the matrix of human cognition: the state of art in language production research. *Language and Cognitive Processes, 23*, 489–494.

Goldstein, L., Pouplier, M., Chen, L., Saltzman, E., & Byrd, D. (2007). Dynamic action units slip in speech production errors. *Cognition, 103*, 386–412.

Kita, S. (2000). How representational gestures help speaking. In D. McNeil (Ed.), *Language and gesture* (pp. 162–185). Cambridge, UK: Cambridge University Press.

Kita, S. (2009, this issue). Competing conceptual representations trigger co-speech representational gestures. *Language and Cognitive Processes, 24,* 762–776.

Kuipers, J.-R., La Heij, W., & Costa, A. (2006). A further look at semantic context effects in language production: the role of response congruency. *Language and Cognitive Processes, 21*, 892–919.

Levelt, W. J. M., & Wheeldon, L. (1994). Do speakers have access to a mental syllabary? *Cognition, 50*, 239–269.

Levelt, W. J. M., Roelofs, A., & Meyer, A. S. (1999). A theory of lexical access in speech production. *Behavioral and Brain Sciences, 22*, 1–75.

Mahon, B. Z., & Caramazza, A. (2009, this issue). Why does lexical selection have to be so hard? Comment on Abdel Rahman and Melinger's Swinging Lexical Network Proposal. *Language and Cognitive Processes, 24*, 736–749.

Mahon, B. Z., Costa, A., Peterson, R., Vargas, K. A., & Caramazza, A. (2007). Lexical selection is not by competition: A reinterpretation of semantic interference and facilitation effects in the picture–word interference paradigm. *Journal of Experimental Psychology: Learning, Memory, and Cognition, 33*, 503–535.

Meyer, A. S., & Schriefers, H. (1991). Phonological facilitation in picture-word interference experiments: Effects of stimulus onset asynchrony and types of interfering stimuli. *Journal of Experimental Psychology: Learning, Memory, and Cognition, 17*, 1146–1160.

O'Seaghdha, P. G., Dell, G. S., Peterson, R. R., & Juliano, C. (1992). Models of form-related priming in comprehension and production. In R. G. Reilly & N. E. Sharkey (Eds.), *Connectionist approaches to natural language processing* (pp. 373–408). Hillsdale, NJ: Lawrence Erlbaum Associates.

Schiller, N. O., Ferreira, V. S., & Alario, F.-X. (2007). Words, pauses, and gestures: New directions in language production research. *Language and Cognitive Processes, 22*, 1145–1150.

Ziegler, W. (2009, this issue). Modelling the architecture of phonetic plans: evidence from apraxia of speech. *Language and Cognitive Processes, 24*, 631–661.

LANGUAGE AND COGNITIVE PROCESSES
2009, 24 (5), 631–661

Modelling the architecture of phonetic plans: Evidence from apraxia of speech

Wolfram Ziegler

EKN – Clinical Neuropsychology Research Group, Neuropsychological Clinic, City Hospital München, Germany

In theories of spoken language production, the gestural code prescribing the movements of the speech organs is usually viewed as a linear string of holistic, encapsulated, hard-wired, phonetic plans, e.g., of the size of phonemes or syllables. Interactions between phonetic units on the surface of overt speech are commonly attributed to either the phonological encoding stage or the peripheral mechanisms of the speech apparatus. Apraxia of speech is a neurogenic disorder which is considered to interfere with the mechanisms of phonetic encoding. Analyses of apraxic speech errors have suggested that phonetic representations have a non-linear, hierarchically nested structure. This article presents a non-linear probabilistic model of the phonetic code, which embraces units from a sub-segmental level up to the level of metrical feet. The model is verified on the basis of accuracy data from a large sample of apraxic speakers.

Keywords: Apraxia of speech; Non-linear phonology; Phonetic planning; Speech production.

Correspondence should be addressed to PD Dr. Wolfram Ziegler, EKN, Dachauer Str. 164, D-80992 München, Germany. E-mail : wolfram.ziegler@extern.lrz-muenchen.de

This research was supported by DFG-grants Zi 469/4–1, 4–2, 6–1, 6–2, 8–1, 10–2. The speech therapy team from our clinical department is acknowledged for long-lasting and friendly collaboration. Michaela Liepold, Bettina Brendel, and Marco Mebus have contributed to many of the auditory analyses reported here. Some of the patients in this sample have thoroughly and extensively been examined by Ingrid Aichert and Anja Staiger, to both of whom I am also indebted for many fruitful discussions of the issues covered here. The final version of this article profited from the insightful comments of two anonymous reviewers and of Matthew Goldrick. I would also like to express my thanks to all the patients whose speech data ended up in the large database presented in this article.

http://www.psypress.com/lcp   DOI: 10.1080/01690960802327989

INTRODUCTION

When the mathematician Leonhard Euler, in the 18th century, thought about building a talking machine, he conceived of it like a piano or an organ, the keys of which represented the instructions for the generation of the speech sounds. Pressing the keys in an orderly sequence would orchestrate the mechanisms of the speaking apparatus for the production of meaningful words (cited after Dolar, 2007). A century later, a German immigrant to America, Joseph Faber, actually constructed a talking head of this kind: its mechanical speech organs were made from ivory and rubber and were connected to a board of 17 keys. To the amusement of the audience, the proud inventor played on the keyboard, pressing the keys in a linear order to produce strings of sounds for words or short phrases (Riskin, 2003).

Modern ideas about the functioning of the machinery of spoken language production have become a lot more elaborate than the mechanical approaches of these days. However, the linear sound pattern principle conceived by Euler and implemented in Faber's machine is still alive in contemporary speech production models, since some of these models rely fundamentally on the principle that the motor apparatus for speech sound production is driven by linear strings of phonetic representations.

Dell's account of word retrieval, for instance, which is based on an interactive model of phonological encoding, ends up with an ordered set of discrete phonemes as the input to an unspecified speech motor component (Dell, 1986). Even though the model is not concerned with the phonetic and articulatory stages of speech production, the idea is that each of the selected phonemes is translated into an articulatory code for the control of the speech muscles (Dell et al., 1997, p. 806). Any interaction that may occur between the constituents of a word is attributed to an interactive network dealing with discrete *phonological* units (Dell, 1986, p. 294), and no mechanism is recognisable that would be able to account for an interaction of *phonetic* units or articulatory codes, as for instance in co-articulation.

The model proposed by Levelt, Roelofs, and Meyer (1999) differs from Dell's account in many respects, but it shares with it the idea of a linearly ordered string of speech motor plans. In the Levelt model, the 'keys' of the speaking machinery are represented by the entries in the 'mental syllabary', i.e., by a collection of ready-made, holistic programs for syllables (see also Cholin, Levelt, & Schiller, 2006). For the production of a multi-syllabic word, each single syllable is downloaded from this mental store and is then translated, one by one, into vocal tract movements (Levelt et al., 1999, p. 32). In this theory, any interaction between units smaller than the syllable is 'pre-wired' in the syllabic motor program, and any potential interaction between syllables is attributed to a more peripheral stage of speech motor execution. Levelt's theory also postulates a second, sub-syllabic mechanism for the production of low frequency syllables, and Levelt et al. (1999, p. 32) moreover concede that units larger than the syllable could play a role in phonetic encoding as well. Yet, whatever the size of such units may be, the idea is that they are arranged to a string of gestural scores, each of which prescribes a separate portion of the speech gestures for words or phrases. Any interaction between these units is peripheral.

These theories suffer from the weakness that they constrain the processes of speech motor planning to discrete, local fragments of the speech stream. If the fragments are small, like in Dell's theory (where they are the size of phonemes), they provide no account of the motor planning aspects of *prosody*. The larger the fragments are, on the other hand, the less can they account for a motor planning of the fine texture of speech. Levelt's theory, for instance, is underspecified on the issue of how speakers organise the articulation of new syllables.

Several theoretical accounts have proposed alternatives to such a strictly segmental view by postulating a more permeable interface between the stage of post-lexical phonological processing and the phonetic/articulatory stage. One such account was proposed by Goldrick and Blumstein (2006), who hypothesised that information from higher phonological levels may cascade down to influence the lower processes of speech motor planning. In such a view, the complex organisation of phonological representations, as embodied, for instance, in Dell's network (Dell, 1986), may also permeate into the phonetic organisation of speech.

Another account, which avoids any explicit distinction between phono-logical and phonetic representations, is the dynamic action approach of *Articulatory Phonology* (e.g., Goldstein, Pouplier, Chen, Saltzman, & Byrd, 2007). In this theory, the units constituting abstract word forms are conceived of as gestural scores which are represented by invariant dynamic properties of the evolving motor patterns. In this approach, phonetic representations have lost their linear-string property, since the temporal extension and overlap of speech gestures and the potential of speech movements to interact are already implemented on the most abstract level of word form representations.

The study presented here deals with the question of whether the architecture of speech motor plans can be considered as a linearly ordered string of units, each of which represents a local prescription for the articulators to move. The approach is based on an investigation of a specific clinical condition, i.e., apraxia of speech. Apraxia of speech is an articulatory impairment resulting from lesions to anterior perisylvian or sub-sylvian cortex of the left hemisphere. Apraxic speakers produce many speech errors, phonemic and phonetic, and their speech is laborious, halting, with false starts and with trial-and-error groping movements (see Ziegler, 2008, for an overview). The syndrome is considered different from aphasic phonological impairment, on the one hand, and from dysarthria, on the other (e.g., Croot, 2002). The most prevalent view of apraxia of speech is that it constitutes an impairment of the speech motor programming or the phonetic encoding stage of spoken language production (Code, 1998; Ziegler, 2002). If this assumption is valid, the errors made by apraxic speakers may inform us about the architecture of phonetic representations, or, more specifically, about the sites of fraction within this architecture that become visible under conditions of impaired phonetic planning.

However, regarding the question of which units play a role in phonetic encoding, evidence from apraxic speech errors is inconsistent. Varley and Whiteside (2001) proposed, on the basis of Levelt's theory, that apraxic patients have lost access to the holistic speech motor programs stored in the mental syllabary and are therefore forced to assemble the phonetic plans for syllables from smaller elements. However, several investigations have demonstrated that accuracy of apraxic speech is influenced by syllable frequency. This was interpreted as evidence that syllabic units must still play a role in apraxic speech, even though the presence of strong syllable structure effects suggests that the holistic nature of syllabic motor routines must be questioned (Aichert & Ziegler, 2004; Laganaro, 2008; Romani & Galluzzi, 2005; Staiger & Ziegler, 2008).

In a recent study we examined a corpus of speech errors from ten apraxic speakers to more directly scrutinise the assumption that phonetic plans for words are linear strings of discrete, sublexical phonetic representations and to identify the primitives of linear representations (Ziegler, Thelen, Staiger & Liepold, 2008). The assumption was that if, for instance, syllables were the units of phonetic encoding, as suggested by Levelt et al. (1999), syllable-based error counts should yield stable estimates of a patient's impairment over a large range of materials of different phonological structures. A similar assumption can also be formulated for phonemes or for any other sublexical unit. In a series of linear models we tested this assumption by postulating phonemes, syllable constituents, syllables, metrical feet, or whole words, respectively, as the 'beads' of the supposed phonetic strings, and by counting apraxic speech errors by each of these units separately. It turned out that there was no single error unit which explained the error patterns for different word forms in the predicted way, and each of the different error counts was influenced by structural factors above and/or below the level of the assumed critical units. For instance, syllable-based errors were influenced by sub-syllabic variables and by the foot-structure of words, phoneme-based error counts were modulated by metrical parameters etc. We concluded from these data that the domain of phonetic encoding extends over several levels of a hierarchically organised architecture of spoken words and phrases (Ziegler et al., 2008).

More direct evidence for this view was obtained in another study of apraxic speech errors, in which the architecture of phonetic plans for words was modelled by a tree-like, non-linear metrical structure extending from the phoneme- to the word level (Ziegler, 2005). The idea was that in a linear account the likelihood of accurate production of a complex unit, e.g., a syllable or a word, solely depends on the likelihood of accurate production of each of its sub-units. If, on the contrary, certain units are more adhesive than others, the probability of accurate production of a complex 'phonetic molecule' not only depends on the number of its atoms, but also on the strengths of the bonds between them. This idea was tested by collapsing the speech error data from a large sample of apraxic patients (N = 100 data sets) over a broad range of words with varying phonological structures, in order to obtain a stable estimate of the probability of accuracy for each single word. These accuracy scores were then predicted by a nonlinear regression model, the regressors of which represented the phonological structure of words. As a result of this study it was found that the phonemes in a syllabic rime and the syllables of a trochaic foot contributed less to word production failure than was predicted on purely combinatorial grounds. One interpretation of this finding is that rimes and trochees are particularly adhesive motor units in apraxia of speech, whereas combinations of onset consonants with their rimes or of two metrical feet are less stable molecules of the phonetic plans for words. As an example, in a word like [knɛçt] (*Engl.* farm labourer), assembly of the coda [çt] with the nucleus [ɛ] appeared to contribute much less to error rates than assembly of the rime [ɛçt] with the onset [kn] for [knɛçt] – hence there seems to be less programming load in the former process than in the latter. Likewise, expansion of the stressed syllable [blu:] by an unstressed syllable [mə] to form the trochee [blu:mə] (*Engl.* flower) decreased accuracy much less than one would predict from the fact that an additional syllable or two additional phonemes have to be produced in [blu:mə] as compared with [blu:]. As an interpretation, the motor programs of syllabic rimes or of trochaic feet obviously contain some natural 'glue' by which their constituents are conjoined to form a higher-order phonetic unit, which is less complex than the sum of its parts.

A paradox of the model proposed in Ziegler (2005) was that it started at a level of *phonemes* to explain the mechanisms of a *phonetic* impairment. Both in this account and in the linear modelling account of Ziegler et al. (2008), phonemes were the smallest units considered in the analyses, and this may explain why in both approaches segmental phonemic units had a strong influence on the occurrence of apraxic speech errors.

The approach presented here tries to overcome this limitation by proposing a non-linear model based on sub-segmental units termed 'gestures'. The term 'gesture' is used here to describe the transitions between neighbouring segments, as defined by the phonetic features of these segments. It expands the concept of distinctive features insofar as it relates to *feature gradients* between adjacent segments rather than to static properties of discrete phonemes. Admittedly this is a very discrete, categorical conception of phonetic gestures, as compared, for instance, to the understanding of gestures in dynamic control theories (Goldstein et al., 2007). Gestures as considered here are simplifications to the extent that they have no extension in time, no overlap, and no gradation or damping. Nonetheless, with this tool the model allows us to more specifically characterise the articulo-motor requirements defined by the phonological structure of a word.

Similar to the model proposed earlier (Ziegler, 2005), a core assumption of the present model was that the workload of phonetic planning depends strongly on the structural properties of a word, and that these properties are inherently non-linear. Starting with a variable describing the likelihood of a gesture to be produced accurately, the model accounts, in a series of hierarchically nested steps, for the modulation of the probability of accurate production by the factors *synchrony of gesture production*, *consonant clustering*, *nucleus-coda affiliation*, *onset-rime-affiliation*, *syllabic prominence* (within a metrical foot), and *foot prominence* (between two feet in a word).

METHODS

A non-linear, gesture-based model of articulatory accuracy

Vocal tract gestures.   The model proposed here is based on binary units describing the transitions between two adjacent phonemes. Since these units represent changes in vocal tract configurations from one segment to the next, they will be referred to as 'gestures'. As mentioned in the introduction, this term is used in a figurative sense, since, unlike the gestures considered in Articulatory Phonology (Goldstein et al., 2007), the gestural units of the present model have no temporal extension, are not graded, and do not overlap in time, even though certain combinations of them may occur simultaneously.

Gestural units are assigned to three tiers, as described in Figure 1a. The gestures that form the basis of the present model include *lip gestures*, *tongue-tip gestures*, and *tongue-body gestures*. In the framework of Figure 1a these types of gestures pertain to a tier of *oral gestures*. For the sake of parsimony, the model proposed here will not distinguish between different degrees of constriction, i.e., between gestures for plosives, fricatives, liquids, etc.

A transition from one segment to the next usually involves two oral gestures, one pertaining to the falling edge of the left segment and the other pertaining to the rising edge of the right segment (Figure 1a). As an example, the transition from [ʃ] to [m] in the word [ʃmuk] (*Engl.* jewellery) is

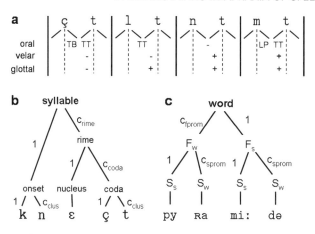

Figure 1. Hierarchical structure of word forms used in the model proposed here. (a) Gestural modelling of four different consonant-consonant transitions. Note that the gestures towards the consonant [t] depend on the distinctive features of the preceding consonant. Two gestures each are involved in [Xτ], [λτ], and [vτ], four gestures in [μτ]. In [λτ], and [vτ], synchronisation of two gestures is required, in [μτ] the tongue-tip gesture must be synchronised with a glottal (abduction) and a velar (elevation) gesture. (b) Sub-syllabic modelling of the word 'knecht' (*Engl.* farm labourer). (c) Supra-syllabic modelling of the word 'pyramide'. TB: tongue body, TT: tongue tip, LP: lips. For details see text.

accomplished by a lingual gesture for the release of [ʃ] and a labial gesture for the bilabial closure of [m]. Note that the overlap that occurs between these movements in articulation is not part of the model. Transitions between two consonants differing only by *manner of articulation* are considered to involve only a single oral gesture, as for instance the transitions from [n] to [s] or from [s] to [t] in the word [kʊnst] (*Engl.* art), or from [l] to [t] in the word [valt] (*Engl.* wood; see Figure 1a). If the same articulator is involved in the production of two subsequent consonants and the degree of constriction is not altered, as in the [nt]-cluster in [vant] (*Engl.* wall), the transition is considered to include no oral gesture at all (Figure 1a).

Oral gestures can be combined, on a supralaryngeal tier, with velar gestures distinguishing between oral and nasal consonants, and with glottal gestures, distinguishing betwen voiced and voiceless sounds (Figure 1a). In the example [ʃmʊk] mentioned above, the transition from [ʃ] to [m] involves a velar lowering gesture and a glottal adduction gesture in addition to the two oral gestures. Likewise, the [n]-to-[s] transition in [kʊnst] requires a velar (narrowing-) gesture parallel to a glottal opening gesture for the devoicing of [s] and to a tongue-tip gesture for the fricative.

Figure 1a presents further examples illustrating the gestural analysis introduced here. More specifically, these examples explicate the relationship between the 'gestures' used in the present model and the concept of distinctive features: In each of the four examples, a transition towards the plosive [t] (with the 'static' features *plosive, alveolar, oral, voiceless*) occurs, yet different combinations of binary gestures are involved at the rising edge of the transition towards [t], depending on the features of the preceding segment.

Gestures at word onsets are defined as transitions from a 'neutral state' to the initial segment of the word. The neutral state is characterised as [-lips], [-tongue-tip], [-tongue-body], [-velum], and [-glottis]. Hence, a word like [fas] (*Engl.* barrel) starts with only a labial gesture, [valt] (*Engl.* forest) with a labial and a glottal gesture, and [mo:nt] (*Engl.* moon) with a labial, a velar, and a glottal gesture.

Since the assumption of discrete gestural units appears particularly unnatural for vowel gestures, a specific convention for vowels is introduced. Transitions from a consonant to a vowel are modelled like transitions between consonants, i.e., by a release gesture for the pre-vocalic consonant and a tongue-body gesture towards the vowel, with the idea that the target configuration for the vowel must actually be reached at this point, even though the gesture may have been anticipated several segments earlier. Vowel-to-consonant transitions, on the contrary, are not specified for the vowel gesture component, in order to compensate for the fact that vowel gestures overlap with consonant gestures. The rationale here is that achievement of the target configuration of the post-vocalic consonant usually does not require a complete resetting of the vowel gesture. In the word [dam] (*Engl.* dam), as an example, the [da]-transition is characterised by a tongue-tip gesture for the release of [d] and a tongue body gesture for [a], whereas the [am]-transition involves only the labial and velar gestures for [m], but no gesture specifically related to the right flank of the vowel segment.

Rounded vowels are specified for an additional lip gesture. If a rounded vowel is preceded by a labial consonant, the labial consonant release gesture and the lip rounding gesture for the vowel are considered as a single gesture (analogous to the case of a transition between two homorganic consonants, as specified above). If two rounded vowels occur in two successive syllables with no labial consonant in-between (e.g., in [ʃokola:də], *Engl.* chocolate), no extra lip rounding gesture is assumed for the second vowel. Diphthongs are modelled by an additional oral gesture in the nucleus-position of a syllable (see below).

Probability of accurate production.   In the following it is assumed that a speaker's probability of producing an accurate gesture is some real number $p_{gest} \in]0, 1[$. In healthy adult speakers this number must be close to 1, since healthy adults rarely produce errors. In a patient with apraxia of speech, on the contrary, p_{gest} may be substantially lower than 1, depending on the patient's severity of apraxic impairment.

Assuming that production of a word involves n gestures and that their probabilities of being accurate are mutually independent, the probability p_w that the whole word is produced accurately can, in a first approximation, be determined as

$$p_w = p_{gest}^n. \tag{1}$$

If, as an example, $p_{gest} = 0.95$, production of an utterance involving 10 gestures would, according to this equation, be accurate with a probability of only $0.95^{10} = 0.60$.

Modelling the sound patterns of words.   The major assumption underlying the non-linear model proposed here is that the likelihood of a vocal tract gesture to be accurate may vary depending on its phonological context. Hence, for each gesture the probability of correct articulation is modified by a multiplicative, context-dependent factor c, yielding

$$p'_{gest} = c * p_{gest}, \quad p'_{gest} \in]0, \ 1[. \tag{2}$$

If the context in which a gesture occurs facilitates its production, c will assume a value > 1, hence $p'_{gest} > p_{gest}$. If, on the contrary, the context of a gesture is particularly demanding, c will be < 1, hence $p'_{gest} < p_{gest}$.

A non-linear structure of words with hierarchically embedded units, following the principles of metrical phonology, is assumed (e.g., Clements & Kayser, 1983). Words are always considered in their citation forms. The model postulated here includes one sub-segmental, three sub-syllabic, and two supra-syllabic, binary-branching, tiers (Figure 1a–c). Gestures within the different branches of this tree-structure are attributed different weights for their probabilities of accurate production. Without loss of generality, oral gestures in the onset of a syllable carrying primary stress are considered as default and are weighted by the factor 1. All other weighting coefficients are considered relative to this. On the higher nodes of the metrical tree, right branches are weighted by variable model coefficients while left branches, without loss of generality, are given constant weight 1. An exception to this rule is the weighting of foot prominence in a word, where always the more prominent foot receives the default weight 1 (Figure 1c).

In a first step, the likelihood of accurate word production is modified by taking into account that velar and laryngeal gestures can be produced in synchrony with oral gestures (Figure 1a). The synchrony condition may either decrease or increase the likelihood of accuracy p_G of a combination of two synchronised gestures. This is modelled by a synchronisation factor c_{sync} yielding

$$p_G = p_{or} * p_{vel} * c_{sync}, \tag{3a}$$

or

$$p_G = p_{or} * p_{glo} * c_{sync}, \tag{3b}$$

or

$$p_G = p_{or} * p_{vel} * p_{glo} * c_{sync}^2, \tag{3c}$$

with p_{or}, p_{vel}, and p_{glo} denoting the likelihood of correct production of oral, velar, and glottal gestures, respectively. As an example, equation (3a) might describe the [m]-gesture in [lam] (*Engl.* lamb), which requires synchronisation of lip closure with a velar lowering gesture. The [l]-gesture in [kl], to make another example, is modelled by (3b), since the tongue-tip movement for [l] has to be synchronised with a glottal adduction gesture. Equation (3c) models, for instance, the transition towards the nasal consonant [n] from an oral [k], as in the consonant cluster [kn], since the tongue-tip gesture for [n] has to be synchronised with both a velar lowering and a glottal narrowing gesture (for further examples see Figure 1a).

If the synchronisation of two gestures requires extra programming effort, c_{sync} will assume a value < 1 and thereby increase the likelihood of an error to occur, over and above the mere fact that two gestures instead of only one have to be made. If, on the contrary, the synchronisation of oral gestures with glottal or velar articulations is largely 'hard-wired', c_{sync} will assume a value > 1, meaning that synchronised gestures may reinforce each other or that the 'cost' of a gesture is low when another gesture occurs in synchrony with it.

For the sake of parsimony and since we have no a priori reasons to assume otherwise, the likelihood of accurate production will be considered the same across all types of gestures, hence $p_{or} = p_{vel} = p_{glo} = p_{gest}$, $0 < p_{gest} < 1$. With this convention, equation (3c) describing the [n]-transition of the [kn]-cluster is simplified to

$$p_G = p_{gest}^3 * c_{sync}^2, \tag{3d}$$

In the next three steps, the phonological context of a gesture is determined relative to the structural architecture of the syllable in which it occurs. On a first sub-syllabic tier, transitions between the consonants of an onset- or a coda-cluster are weighted by a cluster-factor c_{clus}. In the example of the word [knɛçt] (*Engl.* farm labourer) depicted in Figure 1b, this applies to the four gestures at the transition from [k] to [n] (tongue-back release, tongue-tip closure, velar lowering, and glottal closure) and to the two gestures defining the transition from [ç] to [t] (tongue-back release and tongue-tip closure). Formally we get, for the [ç] to [t] transition,

$$p\,([ç] \rightarrow [t]) = p_{gest}^2 * c_{clus}^2, \tag{4}$$

where p_{gest} represents the probability of accuracy of each of the two oral gestures implied in this transition. In a few rare cases of the materials used in this study, ternary-branching clusters occur (e.g., the example [kʊnst] mentioned above). In these cases, the cluster-weight c_{clus} is applied to the transitions from the first to the second and from the second to the third cluster consonant.

On a second sub-syllabic tier, gestures are weighted for being part of the coda of a syllabic rime by introducing a multiplicative coda factor c_{coda}. This factor weights the consonantal gestures of the coda position relative to the nucleus gestures, which receive weight 1 by default. The factor c_{coda} is applied to all coda gestures, including the gestures at the rising edge of the first coda consonant. In the example of Figure 1b we obtain, together with (3b) and with (4) above,

$$p(\lfloor\varepsilon\rfloor \rightarrow [\varsigma]) = p_{gest}^2 * c_{sync} * c_{coda}^2, \text{ and} \tag{5a}$$

$$p([\varsigma] \rightarrow [t]) = p_{gest}^2 * c_{clus} * c_{coda}^2, \tag{5b}$$

where c_{clus} and c_{coda} denote the cluster- and the coda-factors, c_{sync} the synchronisation factor introduced above. As a technical detail, schwa-syllables with an [r]-coda (e.g., in [laɪtər], *Engl.* ladder) are treated as open syllables with an a-schwa ([laɪtɐ]). This convention conforms to modern standards of German citation-form pronunciation (e.g., Duden-Redaktion, 2001). It might be mentioned that in an earlier model the [ər] – variant was used (Ziegler, 2005).

On a third sub-syllabic tier, the gestures pertaining to the rime of a syllable are weighted by a rime-factor c_{rime}. Again, this factor is applied to all rime-gestures, including the gestures leading from the (final) onset consonant to the vocalic nucleus of a syllable, and to all coda-gestures. In particular, the terms in (5a) and (5b) above, referring to the coda consonants of the word [knɛçt], are expanded by a multiplication of each gesture factor with the factor c_{rime}. Recall that the rime-factor also extends to the lip gesture related to vowel rounding, if the nucleus is a rounded vowel, and to the oral gestures in diphthongs. Note also that the rime-weighting must be considered relative to the default weighting of the onset gestures (see Figure 1b).

In two further steps, the vocal tract gestures introduced in this model are weighted for supra-syllabic, metrical factors. First, the gestures pertaining to the weak syllable(s) of each metrical foot in a word are weighted by a syllable prominence factor c_{sprom}. Since the metrical theory of German used here postulates left-headed binary and ternary stress patterns (Venneman, 1988), syllabic weighting by c_{sprom} is applied to the ultimate syllables of trochees and dactyls and to the penultimates of dactyls, while the head of a foot receives default weight 1. Figure 1c contains an example of a word comprising two trochees, [py.ʀʌ.mi:.də] (*Engl.* pyramid), with a

c_{sprom}-weighting of the gestures pertaining to the two weak syllables [ʀa] and [də]. An example of a dactyl is the word [zɛ[l]ɐʀiː] (*Engl.* celery; [l] denotes ambisyllabicity), where the gestures of the two unstressed syllables [lɐ] and [ʀiː] are weighted by the syllable factor c_{sprom}, while the gestures of [zɛl] are weighted by 1. Syllable prominence weighting is also applied to anacruses, as for example to the first syllable of the word [ma.ʃiː.nə] (*Engl.* engine), which is parsed into a right-aligned trochee [ʃiː.nə] and an 'upbeat' [ma]. Like in the cases discussed before, the gestures at the left edge of unstressed syllables and all gestures pertaining to a weak syllable's onset and rime are included in this weighting. Note that in syllables linked by an ambisyllabic consonant no gestures occur at the between-syllable boundary.

As a second suprasyllabic factor, a foot-based weighting is introduced at the word-node level (Figure 1c). In German words consisting of two metrical feet, one of the two feet is usually the more prominent one. The gestures of the more prominent foot in a word are weighted by the constant 1, whereas those of the less prominent foot are weighted by a model coefficient c_{fprom} (see Figure 1c for an example). Unlike the tiers discussed so far, the word-tier allows for a parametric weighting of the left *or* the right branch, depending on which of two feet is more prominent. In the example depicted in Figure 1c, the leftmost foot is the less prominent one, hence its gestures are weighted by the foot coefficient c_{fprom}. In a number of German three- and four-syllabic words, metrical parsing leaves an unparsed syllable. Parsing of the word [tomaːtə], for instance, yields the trochee [maːtə] and an unparsed remainder [to]. In the model proposed here, unparsed syllables are treated like weak metrical feet, i.e., probabilities of accuracy of their gestures are weighted by c_{fprom}.

Modelling of nonwords.   Since the materials used in this study comprise both words and nonwords, the lexical status of an item has to be considered in the model as well. It is postulated that the likelihood of a gesture to be accurate depends on whether the gesture occurs in a word or in a nonword. Hence, a lexicality coefficient c_{lex} is introduced by which each gesture of a nonword is weighted. Without loss of generality, gestures in existing words are weighted by the default constant 1.

The full model.   To summarise the features of the model presented here, the likelihood of accurate production of a word is computed as a weighted product of the probabilities of accurate gesture production. The weighting coefficients are selected in a way that the integration of phonetic gestures into increasingly larger units can be analysed. The probabilistic model is based on eight coefficients:

p_{gest}:   likelihood of accuracy of a vocal tract gesture (oral, velar or glottal, respectively),

c_{sync}:   weighting for synchronous production of oral with velar and/or glottal gestures,

c_{clust}:   weighting of within-cluster gestures (relative to onset of first cluster consonant),

c_{coda}:   weighting of coda gestures (relative to nucleus gestures),

c_{rime}:   weighting of rime gestures (relative to syllable onset gestures),

c_{sprom}:   weighting of gestures of weak syllable(s) in a foot (relative to head of foot),

c_{fprom}:   weighting of gestures of a weak foot in a word (relative to a more prominent foot),

c_{lex}:   weighting of nonword gestures relative to word gestures.

These coefficients are arranged in a hierarchically nested, recursive way, which reflects the non-linear architecture of word forms illustrated in Figure 1 a–c.

Examples.   To illustrate the model by further examples, accuracy of the monosyllabic word [knɛçt] depicted in Figure 1b is determined by

$$p([knɛçt]) = p_{gest}^{12} * c_{sync}^{4} * c_{clus}^{6} * c_{coda}^{4} * c_{rime}^{6}. \tag{6a}$$

Equation (6a) reflects that the word is composed of 12 gestures (according to the conventions discussed above). In four cases, glottal and/or velar gestures have to be synchronised with oral gestures, hence the term c_{sync}^{4}. Six gestures (including velar and glottal gestures) occur between clustered consonants, six within the syllabic rime, and four in the coda. Since [knɛçt] is monosyllabic, c_{sprom} and c_{fprom} are both $= 1$. Likewise, since it is a real word, $c_{lex} = 1$.

The corresponding equation for the word [py.ʀa.mi:.də] (Figure 1c) is

$$p([py.ʀa.mi:.də]) = p_{gest}^{14} * c_{sync}^{3} * c_{rime}^{6} * c_{sprom}^{5} * c_{fprom}^{6}. \tag{6b}$$

Even though the number of syllables is much higher here than in the example of (6a), the number of gestures is increased by only 2. The coefficients of equation (6b) reflect that [py.ʀa.mi:.də] has no clusters and no coda consonants. Instead it consists of two trochaic feet, hence the weightings by syllable-prominence and foot-prominence factors.

Sample

Empirical testing of the non-linear model described above was based on a total of 120 data samples.

Forty carefully selected patients (15 women, 25 men) with a clinical diagnosis of apraxia of speech were examined over a period of several years. All patients were right-handed native speakers of German (mean age 51.7 years, $SD = 8.4$). Thirty-seven of the patients had suffered ischemic infarction of the left middle cerebral artery (MCA) and three had a cerebral haemorrhage in the left anterior MCA-territory. Time since onset varied between less than a month and more than two years. The diagnosis of apraxia of speech was based on the following criteria: presence of phonemic errors and of phonetic distortions, dysfluent speech with intersyllabic pauses and irregular phoneme lengthenings, visible groping, and initiation difficulties, such as false starts and restarts. The observed errors were inconsistent in the sense that a phoneme might be produced accurately in one instant and with different types and degrees of phonetic or phonemic distortion in other instances.

All patients had been clinically diagnosed as apraxic before referral to the EKN research unit. The clinical diagnoses were made by experienced therapists who had seen the patients for several weeks. Diagnoses were verified by the author on the basis of the patients' clinical records and by independent analyses of videotaped speech samples from an interview. In all cases, the clinical diagnosis of apraxia of speech agreed with the judgements of the taped interviews, and apraxia of speech was always diagnosed as the primary deficit.

All patients except five had mild or moderate aphasic impairments as verified by the Aachener AphasieTest (AAT; Huber, Poeck, Weniger, & Willmes, 1983), five patients were not aphasic. All patients had good comprehension and their writing was better than their speech. In all patients, significant dysarthria could be excluded by auditory speech analyses, based on the criterion that dysarthric impairment leads to constant phonetic distortion.

Most of the patients enrolled in this study had also participated in other research projects (Aichert & Ziegler, 2008; Brendel & Ziegler, 2008; Staiger & Ziegler, 2008; Ziegler et al., 2008) and had therefore been scrutinised for apraxic symptoms several times and by different experts. Half of the patients from this study had already been included in an earlier non-linear modelling study (Ziegler, 2005).

In order to obtain a high resolution of the accuracy scale, the database was inflated by entering multiple examinations of several of these patients. Thirteen of the patients, who had been enrolled in a therapy study conducted in our department, were examined multiple times over a period of *ca.* five months (Brendel & Ziegler, 2008). Inclusion of these multiple examinations resulted in a complete set of 120 samples, with an average of 3 examinations per patient (maximum: 8). Mean time since lesion was 6.4 months ($SD = 5.8$). The 120 data sets were pooled and no further account was taken of the fact that they had been obtained from only 40 patients. Nonetheless, the consistency of the data corpus was examined empirically (see Results section).

Materials

As described in Ziegler (2005), all patients were administered a word repetition test including 48 words and 48 nonwords (Liepold, Ziegler, & Brendel, 2003). Most of the words were monomorphemic, uninflected, frequent, concrete nouns. Nonwords were derived from the words by exchanging one or more vowels. In order to avoid lexical interference effects caused by undue similarities of derived nonwords with their original words, one or more consonants were also exchanged in some of the longer words.

The applied word- and nonword lists were grouped into 8 sublists varying by syllable number (1 to 4 syllables) and by the structure of the involved syllables (simple vs. complex). In order to balance the sublists for syllabic complexity (number of phonemes per syllable), three words and three nonwords with the highest phoneme densities were eliminated from the 1- and 2-syllabic items, and the same number of words and nonwords with the lowest phoneme densities were eliminated from the 3- and 4-syllabic lists. As a consequence, the computations that follow are based on a balanced list consisting of 36 words and 36 nonwords of 1–4 syllables length.

Table 1 contains, in each cell, the average number of phonemes per syllable (p/s) and of gestures per syllable (g/s) over the 9 items of a cell. A two-way ANOVA for p/s failed to reveal main effects of syllabic length, $F(3, 64) = 2.05$, $p > .05$, and of lexicality, $F(1, 64) = 0.01$, $p > .05$, and there was no interaction between these two factors, $F(3, 64) = 0.01$; $p > .05$. For gestures, the same ANOVA revealed a weak main effect of syllable number, $F(3, 64) = 3.06$, $p = .04$, which was due to a slightly higher gesture density of monosyllabics as compared to polysyllabic words. There was no lexicality effect, $F(1, 64) = 0.09$, $p > .1$, and no interaction between the two factors,

TABLE 1
Architecture of the word list. N: number of items; p/s: phonemes per syllable; g/s: gestures per syllable

| | *Number of syllables* | | | |
	1	*2*	*3*	*4*
Words	N = 9	N = 9	N = 9	N = 9
	p/s = 3.0	p/s = 2.6	p/s = 2.6	p/s = 2.6
	g/s = 7.8	g/s = 6.5	g/s = 6.6	g/s = 6.3
Nonwords	N = 9	N = 9	N = 9	N = 9
	p/s = 3.0	p/s = 2.6	p/s = 2.6	p/s = 2.6
	g/s = 8.0	g/s = 6.5	g/s = 6.8	g/s = 6.4

$F(3, 64) = 0.03$; $p > .1$. A more detailed description of the materials can be found in Ziegler (2005) and in Liepold et al. (2003).

Procedure

Patient examinations were performed in a quiet room and were recorded on video tape. An external microphone (Sony, ECM-MS957) was used to optimise the quality of the audio recording.

Auditory analysis

The recordings were analysed by six experienced examiners who were unaware of the goals of the present study. Each recording was judged by at least two examiners, a large proportion was rated by four listeners (see below). Listening sessions were performed in a quiet room. The videotapes were analysed word-by-word, according to the protocol described in Liepold et al. (2003). When a patient made more than one attempt at responding, the first complete response was selected for auditory evaluation. Upon presentation of a word like *Knecht* (*Engl.* farm labourer), a patient might for instance produce something like kin .. kne .. ke ... kecht. In such a case, the last trial (i.e., kecht) was evaluated. Fragmentary responses were not considered.

Each word was judged for phonemic and phonetic errors, and for fluency, with the fluency variable not being considered any further in this article. The following pass-fail-rating procedure was applied: (1) A phonemic error was registered if one or several phonemes of the word were substituted, exchanged, or omitted, or if one or more segments were added. (2) A word was counted as phonetically distorted when one or several of its segments were mis-articulated, i.e., when they differed from the regular phonetic form of Modern Standard German or from the patient's individual dialectal variant thereof. In the following cases a patient's response was rated as a null response: the patient (a) made no attempt at responding, (b) perseverated on one of the preceding words, (c) produced a semantic paraphasia, (d) produced a phonetically undifferentiated vocal utterance, i.e., an utterance which could not be analysed segmentally, or (e) produced only a small fraction of the target word. Null responses, which occurred in 2.9% of all 8640 observations, were excluded from further analysis.

Phonetic and phonemic errors were combined to form a 'segmental error'. A segmental error was assigned to words containing either a phonemic or a phonetic error, or both. Calculation of a combined segmental error score was justified by a significant correlation of phonetic and phonemic errors over the 120 data samples examined here ($r = .73$, $p < .01$).

Significant between-rater agreement values were reported for ratings of segmental errors, with an average Kendall's τ of 0.80 (four listeners, 576 items; $p < .01$; Liepold et al., 2003). Further examinations of the validity and reliability of the error analysis underlying this study were reported in Liepold et al. (2003).

Statistics

The model introduced above was tested by a non-linear regression analysis (SPSS 15.0). For each of the 72 test items, an empirical estimate of its error probability was calculated by averaging segmental error scores (either 0 or 1) over the pool of 120 data sets described above. The resulting scores were considered to represent an index of the relative error susceptibility of each test item to apraxic impairment. Since the model is based on likelihood of *accurate production*, error scores were transformed into accuracy scores by subtracting them from 1. Hence the accuracy scale ranged between 0 and 1, with a resolution of 0.0083.

The accuracy scores of the 72 test items were stored in an SPSS data base and each item was marked by variables indicating the numbers of oral, velar, and laryngeal gestures in each of the constituents distinguished in the model (see Figure 1). With these variables, a recursive procedure implementing the multiplicative terms described above (equations 6a, b) was prepared in the non-linear regression module of the SPSS package, with accuracy scores as the dependent variable, and the eight variables introduced above as regressors.

RESULTS

The average accuracy scores of the 120 patient recordings varied over a large range of severity of apraxic impairment, i.e., between .01 and .92 (mean = .39, $SD = .25$; median value = .41). For the analyses to be reported here the data were pooled by item, yielding a normally distributed sample of accuracy scores over the 72 words/nonwords included in this study (Kolmogorov-Smirnov, $Z = .49$, $p = .97$; mean = 0.39, $SD = 0.17$). The highest accuracy score (0.78) was obtained for the word [a͡ʊgə] (*Engl.* eye), i.e., 78% of the 120 samples of this word were accurate. The most difficult nonword obtained an accuracy score of 0.10, hence only 12 out of 120 samples of this item were accurate. Mean accuracy scores for the words included in Figure 1b, c were 0.328 for [knɛçt] (Figure 1b, equation 6a) and 0.356 for [py.Ra.mi:.də] (Figure 1c, equation 6b), respectively. There was a significant difference in accuracy between words (.46 ± .16) and their associated nonwords (.33 ± .16), matched-pairs t-test; $t(35) = 10.7$, $p < .001$.

Consistency of data set.   The accuracy scores of word-nonword pairs were highly correlated ($r = .90$, $N = 36$), showing that the structural parameters varied here had stable effects on accuracy in apraxic speakers, irrespective of the lexical status of an item. The consistency of the data set was further examined by collapsing accuracy scores separately over four equal subsamples of 60 patients each, with each subsample having a similar average degree of severity as the full sample. To this end, patients were ordered by their overall accuracy scores. First, two mutually exclusive subgroups of patients with odd and even rank numbers, respectively, were selected (mean accuracy scores: 0.39 and 0.40, respectively). Item-wise accuracy scores of the two subgroups were highly correlated ($r = .91$, $p < .001$; $N = 72$). Second, two further mutually exclusive subgroups were formed by selecting patients with severity ranks 31–90 ('mid-rank'; mean accuracy score 0.39) and severity ranks 1–30 and 91–120 ('extreme-rank'; mean accuracy score 0.41). Again, accuracy scores averaged over each of the 72 items were correlated significantly ($r = .87$, $p < .001$; $N = 72$). Moreover, correlations between all other pairs of subgroups (odd-rank with mid-rank, even-rank with extreme-rank etc.) were higher than $r = .92$ and correlations between each subgroup and the full sample were higher than $r = .94$. As a conclusion, different partitions of the patient sample yielded highly similar distributions of accuracy scores across items, provided that average severity of impairment was kept constant.

Further tests of the internal consistency of a data set resulting from a subgroup of the sample examined here were reported in Ziegler (2005).

Non-linear regression.   A nonlinear regression analysis was calculated over the 72 items, as described in the Methods section. To avoid instabilities, the model coefficients were constrained to $> .2$ for all parameters. The initial value of the variable p_{gest} was set to an arbitrary value of .5. Initial values for all other model coefficients were set to 1, which conforms to a null-hypothesis of no influence of these variables.

The model converged after 70 major iterations and explained 84.5% of the variance in the data. Figure 2 illustrates the goodness-of-fit of the model, Table 2 presents the estimated values of all parameters with their 95% confidence intervals, and the goodness-of-fit statistics. The coefficients deviating significantly from 1 are marked by asterisks.

As can be inferred from Table 2, the average likelihood of accurate gesture production, according to the model formulated here, turned out slightly below .90. The synchronisation factor was significantly higher than 1, indicating that the co-production of oral with velar and/or glottal gestures was boosted relative to the base score. Further, the probability of accurate gesture production was strongly modulated by the structural properties of words. Gestures within a cluster were weighted significantly more vulnerable

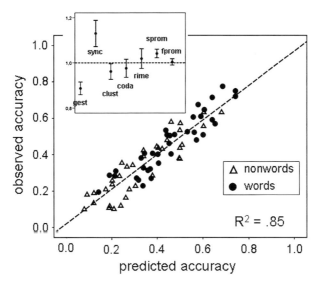

Figure 2. Scatter-plot of predicted vs. observed accuracies of 72 words and nonwords, after non-linear regression with 8 independent variables. The insert displays the estimates of the model coefficients and the 95% confidence intervals of these estimates (cf. Table 2).

than cluster onset gestures, and gestures within the unstressed syllables of metrical feet received a significant boost relative to the gestures in the head of a foot. There was a tendency of gestures in the coda-position to be more vulnerable than in the nucleus, and of gestures in the rime to be less vulnerable than in the onset. Production of more than one metrical foot caused neither facilitation nor inhibition of the gestures in the less prominent foot.

TABLE 2
Coefficients of the non-linear regression model ($R^2 = .845$, df1 $=8$, df2 $=64$); residual sum of squares: 0.3; regression sum of squares: 13.2

Coefficient	Estimate	Standard error[1]	95% confidence interval[1]
p_{gest}	0.887*	0.014	[0.859, 0.915]
c_{sync}	1.131*	0.029	[1.073, 1.189]
c_{clus}	0.962*	0.017	[0.927, 0.996]
c_{coda}	0.976	0.020	[0.936, 1.016]
c_{rime}	1.019	0.022	[0.975, 1.063]
c_{sprom}	1.042*	0.009	[1.023, 1.061]
c_{fprom}	1.004	0.007	[0.990, 1.018]
c_{lex}	0.979*	0.004	[0.927, 0.986]

Note: [1]asymptotic values; *95% confidence interval excludes 1 (where 1 indicates no influence).

Re-considering, on the basis of these coefficients, the examples plotted in Figure 1b-c, the predicted accuracy score of [knɛçt] (Figure 1b, equation 6a) was .313, while the score predicted for [py.Ra.mi:.də] (Figure 1c, equation 6b) was slightly higher, namely .380. Hence, the model obviously weighted the structural properties of the two words in a way that [py.Ra.mi:.də], despite having more gestures, more phonemes, and more syllables than [knɛçt], was attributed a lower programming load. Recall that the *observed* scores of these two items were .328 and .356, respectively, which is in close agreement with the predicted values and confirms that the longer word was indeed less difficult than the shorter one.

Validity of the model.   In order to test the validity of the model, initial values for all independent variables were varied between 0.2 and 3.0, in steps of 0.2. Ten pseudo-random samples of initial values were drawn within these limits. With all these combinations of initial values the model converged to exactly the same vector of parameters, as displayed in Table 2, and to exactly the same goodness-of-fit value.

In order to test if the high goodness-of-fit obtained here simply resulted from the fact that as many as 8 regressors were used to fit 72 data points, the same model was applied to 10 random data samples generated by an SPSS routine. The random samples were normally distributed, with the same mean and standard deviation as the original data. In all cases, the non-linear modelling of random data sets resulted in R^2-values lower than 0.02, indicating that any random contribution to the fitting obtained here was negligible.

A further validation of the model can be seen in the fact that all parameters were within a plausible range and that the confidence intervals were rather small. Finally, the residual error of the regression analysis was Gaussian (mean $= 0.001$, $SD = 0.97$; Kolmogorov–Smirnov, $Z = 1.03$, exact $p = .22$), which counts as a further criterion for the validity of the model obtained here (Draper & Smith, 1998).

Consistency of the model.   The model discussed so far reflects the accuracy pattern of an 'ideal' apraxic patient, i.e., a pattern averaged over a large patient sample with a broad range of severity of apraxic impairment. Therefore, the shape of the model seen here might be an artifact, i.e., might be representative of only the average, but not of any single subsample or even a single apraxic patient.

Since the accuracy scores presented here were based on pass-fail ratings, the non-linear model described above cannot be applied to single subjects or to small samples. The consistency problem was therefore addressed by calculating separate models for each of the four split-half subsamples mentioned earlier, i.e., the odd- and even-rank subgroups and the mid- and

TABLE 3
Comparison of non-linear regression models calculated for four subsamples of 60 patients each (split-half methods, see text)

Selection	Odd ranks	Even ranks	Mid ranks	Extreme ranks
R^2	.77	.73	.80	.66
p_{gest}	0.880*	0.900*	0.889*	0.891*
c_{sync}	1.124*	1.114*	1.138*	1.097*
c_{clus}	0.958*	0.959*	0.935*	0.985$^+$
c_{coda}	0.990	0.993	0.977	1.002
c_{rime}	1.030	1.001	1.029	1.005
c_{sprom}	1.044*	1.045*	1.029*	1.059*
c_{fprom}	1.000	1.007	0.993	1.014
c_{lex}	0.981*	0.978*	0.973*	0.985*

Note: *95% confidence interval excludes 1.0; $^+$close to significance (95%CI: [.941, 1.001]).

extreme-rank subgroups. Recall that the average severity of impairment was similar for these subselections and the full sample (0.39–0.41).

The coefficients of the four subsample models are presented in Table 3. In all cases, the model coefficients were very similar to those of the full-sample model (Table 2). More importantly, the same coefficients were significantly different from 1.0 in all five models (full sample, odd-rank, even-rank, mid-rank, extreme-rank), with the exception that c_{clus} tightly missed significance in the extreme-rank model. As a conclusion, the model coefficients depicted in Table 2 are consistent in the sense that they are also representative for different subselections of patients, as long as average severity of impairment is kept constant.

Severity of apraxic impairment. To examine whether the shape of the linear model described in Table 2 depends on severity of impairment, the sample of 120 data sets was subdivided into two equal halves of mildly impaired (ranks 1–60, accuracy scores > .40; mean = 0.61, SD = 0.12) and severely impaired cases (ranks 61–120, accuracy scores < .40; mean = 0.17, SD = 0.11). The two data sets were modelled independently, as described above. Both models converged after 23 (mild) and 67 iterations (severe). In the severe subgroup, a much higher proportion of the variance in accuracy scores was explained than in the mild subgroup ($R^2 = .82$ vs. .74). The estimated accuracy of gestures, i.e., the magnitude of p_{gest}, was .94 in the high scorers vs. .79 in the low-scorers. The synchronisation bonus c_{sync} was significant in both groups ($c_{sync} > 1$), and both groups obtained similar weights for the influence of lexical status (mild: $c_{lex} = .98$, severe: $c_{lex} = .96$; both values significantly lower than 1).

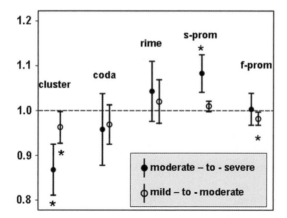

Figure 3. Estimates and 95% confidence intervals of the model coefficients describing the supra-segmental structure of words. Results are depicted for two subgroups of patients with moderate-to-severe (closed circles) and with mild-to-moderate apraxia of speech (open circles). Asterisks denote that coefficients were significantly different from default value 1. s-prom: syllable prominence coefficient; f-prom: foot prominence coefficient (see text).

Figure 3 depicts the estimates of the five remaining coefficients of the two models.

The overall shapes of the two models were similar, but there were differences in several details. First, the detrimental effect of clusters on gestural accuracy was much stronger in the severe than in the mild subgroup, and, second, the mitigating effect of intra-foot structure was also stronger in this group. Remarkably, a significant effect of foot prominence appeared in the subgroup of less severely impaired patients.

Prediction of novel data.   From the original set of 96 items, 24 had been discarded, in order to account for large differences in syllable complexity between monosyllabic and multisyllabic words (see Methods section above). The items from this set were now used to make a prediction of their accuracies on the basis of the model coefficients of Table 2. Application of the model yielded a significant prediction of the accuracy scores of items not included in the original modelling sample, $F(1, 22) = 15.3$, $p < .001$; $R^2 = .41$), even though these items represented two extreme poles of German word form architecture, i.e., three-to-four-syllabic words with very low phoneme densities and mono- and disyllabic words with very high phoneme densities.

DISCUSSION

The major goal of this study was to unveil some of the factors influencing the occurrence of errors in patients with apraxia of speech. There are at least two good reasons to strive for this goal. One is clinical: Knowledge of the conditions that make a patient succeed or fail on a speech task is important to improve the diagnostic assessment of apraxia of speech and helps us find more efficient tools and more direct ways for the treatment of this disorder. The other reason is theoretical: Since apraxia of speech is considered as an impairment which interferes with a specific stage of spoken language production, i.e., phonetic encoding, knowledge of the factors influencing apraxic failure may inform us about the processes and representations of the phonetic encoding stage. More specifically, knowledge about what it is in a word that makes it easy or hard for an apraxic speaker to pronounce may help us to better understand the architecture of phonetic representations.

The idea of this approach was to model the likelihood of accurate word production in apraxic speakers by a non-linear description of the phonological structures of words. Taking only the structural properties of a given word as its input, the model tries to predict the probability of an apraxic speaker to succeed or fail. The pass/fail-probabilities of a total of 72 words and nonwords were empirically determined by collapsing the accuracy scores of 120 data samples from 40 apraxic speakers.

In a sense, this approach was a replication of an earlier study of word length effects in apraxia of speech (Ziegler, 2005). Like in this earlier account, the phonological structures of words were described in terms of a non-linear metrical theory of phonological representations, and a non-linear regression analysis was conducted to estimate the model coefficients.

As a major innovation, however, the new model started on a sub-segmental rather than the phoneme level. A natural assumption of any theory of apraxia of speech is that the patho-mechanism of this disorder interferes with the planning of speech gestures. As a consequence, models of apraxia of speech should include a level relating to the gestural organisation of speech. In the present approach, an extensively simplified concept of phonetic gestures was introduced, operationally defined as the transitions between the feature vectors of two neighbouring phonemes. The likelihood of such gestures being produced accurately was taken as the basic parameter of a computational model, and potential modifications of this magnitude through contextual factors were simulated by a series of recursive embeddings of gestures into increasingly larger phonological structures.

Application of this model to empirical accuracy scores converged to a stable solution, with a goodness-of-fit of almost .85. Hence, an extensive proportion of the variance in the accuracy scores of the 72 words was explainable by only the structural properties of these words. A number of tests were conducted to demonstrate that the solution of the non-linear regression was stable and valid. Moreover, largely isomorphic models were obtained for different sub-selections of patients, suggesting that the solution was not idiosyncratic to only the full-sample average of 120 data samples, but could be generalised to subpopulations with similar average accuracy scores. Furthermore, applications of the model to split-half subgroups of mild and severe patients revealed that the overall shape of the model remained largely invariant across degrees of severity, even though the model solutions for the two groups differed in a few details. Another remarkable result was that the model provided a significant prediction of the accuracy values of words not contained in the modelling sample.

Given the high goodness-of-fit and the high validity of the non-linear model, the coefficients obtained in the regression analysis may contribute to our understanding of how the different word form factors influence the accuracy of word production in apraxia of speech.

As a first result, the estimate of the likelihood of gestural accuracy in the resulting model was close to 0.9. This value may, at a first glance, appear rather high, considering that the mean accuracy for words in this sample was only 0.39. However, since a word bears many occasions to fail on any one of its gestural components, the likelihood of whole-word accuracy decreases rapidly with an increasing number of gestures, even if the base rate of gestural accuracy is high.

Gestural synchrony

Remarkably, the factor correcting for the synchronicity of oral with velar and/or laryngeal gestures turned out significantly higher than 1, indicating that two synchronised gestures were less expensive than one would predict on purely combinatorial grounds. At first sight this seems incompatible with what we have learned about apraxic speakers, namely that they have particular problems with the relative timing of two articulators, and especially with coarticulation (e.g., Itoh, Sasanuma & Ushijima, 1979; Ziegler & von Cramon, 1986). However, calculation of a concrete example reveals that phonological conditions known to be particularly demanding for apraxic speakers, i.e., consonant clusters requiring the synchronized co-ordination of several articulators, in fact received particularly low accuracy values in the model. The onset clusters [kn] and [kl], for instance, are modelled by

$$p([kn]) = p_{gest}^4 * c_{sync}^2 * c_{clus}^4 = .678, \text{ and} \tag{7a}$$

$$p([kl]) = p_{gest}^3 * c_{sync} * c_{clus}^3 = .703, \tag{7b}$$

respectively. Hence, the clinically motivated expectation that [kn] is more error-prone than [kl] is indeed represented in the model. The high value of c_{sync} ($= 1.131$) prevents predicted accuracy scores in situations like (7a) becoming excessively low.

On closer inspection it also becomes apparent that in many of the instances of gestural synchrony modelled here, the parallel execution of two independent gestures may indeed be boosted by other factors. For instance, there is an obligatory co-occurrence of certain phonetic gestures, such as glottal adduction and velar lowering (since German nasals are always voiced) or glottal adduction and vocal tract opening for vowels (since vowels are always voiced). Another obligatory motor pattern of German is final obstruent devoicing, i.e., the regular co-occurrence of a glottal devoicing gesture with complete or almost complete oral closure at the end of a syllabic cycle. Due to the high frequency of occurrence of such co-ordinated patterns, gestural synchrony may in these particular instances be a highly overlearned routine, which remains stable in apraxia of speech.[1] Such an explanation extends the domain of frequency-related effects from the syllabic level, where it has been discussed extensively (e.g., Aichert & Ziegler, 2004; Cholin et al., 2006), to the level of articulatory gestures. This suggests that effects of frequency of occurrence and motor skill learning penetrate several levels of phonetic representation and are not confined to the domain of the syllable. It also reinforces claims for a speech-specific organisation of vocal-tract gestures for speaking (Ziegler, 2006), since it demonstrates that the disintegration of phonetic gestures in apraxia of speech is not anarchic, but rather follows the regularities of the gestural organisation of a patient's native language.

Consonant clusters

Another remarkable result was that the *cluster factor* contributed to a decrease of the likelihood of accurate word production, even though the effect was not very strong, especially in the patients with mild apraxia of speech. According to a common clinical observation, the complexity of syllables, especially the presence of consonant clusters, has a strong influence on the occurrence of apraxic speech errors (Romani & Galluzzi, 2005; Staiger & Ziegler, 2008), but it has so far been unresolved if this observation cannot simply be explained by the larger number of phonemes in syllables with clusters. In an earlier study of word length effects in apraxia of speech (Ziegler, 2005) consonant clusters had only a nonsignificant tendency of decreasing speech accuracy over and above the amount expected on purely stochastic grounds. The fact that the gesture-based model revealed a severity-dependent cluster effect may suggest that this model is more sensitive to the pathomechanisms of apraxia of speech.

Regarding the modelling of consonant clusters, an important limitation of the present approach becomes apparent, since the model cannot distinguish between phonotactically legal and illegal clusters. This weakness may lead to

---

[1] As a matter of fact, violations of the final obstruent devoicing rule have, to my knowledge, not been reported in German apraxic speakers.

unexpected results. For instance, the accuracies of the two legal onset clusters [kl] and [kn] as predicted by the non-linear model were .703 and .678, respectively. For the two illegal clusters [tl] and [tn] the predicted accuracy score would be considerably higher, namely .823 in both instances. This result is counter-intuitive, since a higher programming load would be expected for illegal as compared to legal consonant clusters. The model developed here cannot account for such effects since its empirical basis did not comprise phonotactically illegal forms.

Moreover, since the model was primarily based on numbers of gestures in a word, factors like sonority change, which might also have an influence, are not represented either. For instance, [gn], which is a legal onset, would receive a higher accuracy score than [kn] (.703 vs. .678), although there are reasons to assume that [gn], due to its low frequency of occurrence, is more difficult. To overcome such limitations in future applications, the feature transitions between segments might be weighted by biphoneme-frequencies.

Syllable constituents

Two of the results reported here appear unexpected at first sight, i.e., the observations that the coda- and rime-coefficients were statistically not different from 1. The rime coefficient tended to be above 1, although not to a significant extent. The coda-effect was not significant either, meaning that the presence of a coda in a syllabic rime did not make any specific contribution to the accuracy of a word, except for the fact that the number of gestures increased and the likelihood of accuracy decreased accordingly. This differs from our earlier finding of a relative preservation of syllabic rimes in apraxia of speech (Ziegler, 2005). One explanation for this inconsistency might be that the present model attributed particularly low costs to the vowel-consonant transitions in the coda position, since no vocalic gesture was considered at this point (see Methods section above), whereas the phoneme-based length-model of Ziegler (2005) had attributed equal weights to all constituents of a syllabic rime. While the relative preservation of syllabic rimes in apraxia of speech showed up in the empirical solution to our former model, it was built into the gestural architecture of the present model from the very beginning. As a consequence, the model indeed predicts higher accuracy scores for nucleus-coda as compared to onset-nucleus combinations. For example, the demi-syllable [ta] would obtain a substantially lower accuracy score in the model than the rime [at] (.727 vs. .796), even though the same phonemes are involved. This is consistent with the assumption that nucleus-coda-combinations are stable programming units.

A second explanation for different outcomes in the two approaches is that schwa-syllables ending on vocalic /r/, which occur frequently in German nouns, were treated as open syllables in the present model and as closed syllables in our earlier account (Ziegler, 2005). When the syllable-final /r/ following a schwa is considered as a full consonant, the difficulty of a word might be over-estimated, since most speakers of German omit the /r/ and produce an a-schwa. In our earlier model, the empirical solution may have corrected for this divergence by assigning a facilitating weight to syllabic rimes.

Metrical structure

As a further result, the model coefficient obtained for the syllable prominence factor was significantly above 1. It should be noted that this does not necessarily imply that gestures in unstressed syllables are less error-prone than gestures in stressed syllables, since our approach does not allow us to allocate the observed effects to a specific fragment of a word's phonological form. However, from the combined weighting of the strong and weak syllables of metrical feet it can be inferred that (1) metrical feet were obviously not dissected into their syllabic parts, but were produced as cohesive units, and (2) the likelihood of accuracy of words containing a full trochaic or dactylic foot was higher than one would predict from the number of gestures that occur in the stressed and unstressed syllables of the foot. When, for instance, a monosyllabic word is compared with a disyllabic trochee, the number of gestures is usually larger in the latter than in the former, but the likelihood of accuracy does not decrease to the same extent. As an example, the words [dax] (*Engl.* roof) and [deke] (*Engl.* blanket) obtain almost identical accuracy scores in the model (.628 and .629, respectively), although the latter contains more gestures, more phonemes, and more syllables than the former. This amounts to saying that metrical feet are phonetic molecules with strong atomic bonds. The degree to which speech gestures are integrated within a metrical foot reduces the workload of phonetic planning and, as a consequence, the likelihood of apraxic failure. This interpretation is entirely compatible with what we had found in an earlier study of word-length effects in apraxia of speech (Ziegler, 2005).

On the level where two feet are combined to form a complex word, the situation was different from the within-foot level. The foot prominence factor was not different from 1, meaning that – in the sample of patients considered here – two feet in a word can indeed be viewed as two independent speech motor actions: when two metrical feet of a complex word are produced separately, the likelihood that the whole word comes out accurately is simply the product of the probabilities of accurate production of each single foot. Remarkably, in the subgroup of less severely impaired patients a detrimental effect of the foot prominence factor was found. An explanation for this result could be that the patients with milder apraxic impairment attempted to merge the two feet of a complex word into an overarching phonetic plan, which resulted – as a true word length effect – in a disproportionate increase of errors. The more severely impaired patients, on the contrary, broke these words apart into two manageable, foot-sized pieces.

The issue of metrical influences provides an opportunity to discuss the relationship between the locus of an observed segmental error and the locus of its source. The present study was based on a pass-fail evaluation of word production, and no attempt was made to allocate apraxic errors to a specific fragment of a word, i.e., a foot, a syllable, a phoneme, etc. One (technical) reason for this approach was that precise localisation of apraxic errors in a sample as large as this is laborious and probably not very reliable. A second, more important reason was that the locus of an observed error need not necessarily coincide with the locus of the error source. The problem a patient encounters in a consonant cluster, for instance, may cause distortions not only in the cluster itself, but also in the segments preceding or following it. Moreover, the finding that words with complex metrical patterns are more error-prone than words consisting of a single metrical foot is not compatible with the idea of a local error source, i.e., of a phoneme or a syllable constituent eliciting the observed error. The origin of segmental errors may rather be sought in the overall shape of a phonetic representation, including the rhythmical aspects of an utterance.

Lexical status

A final comment might be devoted to the modelling of lexical status by the coefficient c_{lex} ($= .979$). Analyses of the raw data underlying this study revealed that nonwords were consistently less accurate than words, with an average difference of 0.13. The finding that the accuracy scores of word–nonword pairs were highly correlated suggests that the influences of phonological structure on accuracy were largely homomorphous in the two item groups. The non-linear modelling of these data revealed that a weighting of the probability of accurate nonword gesture production by a coefficient of .98 yielded a good prediction of word- and nonword accuracy by a common structural model. Hence, the assumption that gestures occurring in real words are slightly more likely to be accurate than gestures occurring in nonwords (.887 vs. .869) explains the large overall effect on the accuracy of words and nonwords. In a series of exploratory pilot calculations not reported here, the best prediction was obtained when each single gesture was weighted for lexicality, as compared to, for instance, a syllable-based, foot-based, or word-based weighting. This suggests that lexical status exerted an influence at the lowest structural layer of phonetic representations.

In conventional theories, lexicality effects are attributed to lexical mechanisms or to a propagation of lexical properties to *phonological* representations, while phonetic representations are usually considered to be shielded from the cascading of lexical information (for a discussion of this issue see Goldrick & Blumstein, 2006). In their analyses of tongue twister errors, however, Goldrick & Blumstein (2006) found continuous acoustic 'traces' of discrete phonological targets, which they interpreted as an indication of cascading activation from the phonological to the articulatory level. In particular, weaker traces were found when the errors resulted in real words, which indicated that real-word outcomes at the articulatory level received a stabilising support from the lexical level.

In Goldrick and Blumstein's view, the source of phonetic distortions elicited by tongue twisters lies in the parallel activation of competing phonological forms, which exerts a graded influence on articulation. In contrast, in the apraxic speech corpus discussed here the origin of segmental errors was allocated to the level of speech gesture planning. Based on the hypothesis that lexical properties may cascade downstream to influence articulation, one might speculate that firm lexical representations have a stabilising effect on the phonetic encoding mechanism in apraxic speakers, relative to novel phonological forms. As we have seen, a small lexical status effect propagating to the gestural level may be sufficient to cause large differences in overall accuracy of words and nonwords. Hence, there is no conflict between the assumption of a phonetic-level deficit and a lexical modulation of this deficit in apraxic speakers.

CONCLUSION

To summarise, the model proposed here provides a comprehensive and integrative account of the structural factors influencing word production accuracy in patients with apraxia of speech. The model achieved a highly accurate fit to a corpus of empirical data, which demonstrates that the phonological structure of words has a major impact on apraxic failure. This supports the view that apraxia of speech interferes with speech-specific mechanisms of the organisation of vocal tract gestures.

As a major result it should be stressed that the architecture of phonetic plans, as far as it becomes transparent through the error patterns of apraxic speakers, cannot be conceived as a linear sequence of phonetic units of whatever size. The results presented here are rather suggestive of a complex, non-linear, hierarchically nested organisation of phonetic plans which extends from the level of articulatory gestures to the level of metrical feet.

REFERENCES

Aichert, I., & Ziegler, W. (2004). Syllable frequency and syllable structure in apraxia of speech. *Brain and Language, 88*, 148–159.

Aichert, I., & Ziegler, W. (2008). Learning a syllable from its parts: Cross-syllabic generalization effects in patients with apraxia of speech. *Aphasiology, 22*, 1216–1229.

Brendel, B., & Ziegler, W. (2008). Effectiveness of metrical pacing in the treatment of apraxia of speech. *Aphasiology, 22*, 77–102.

Cholin, J., Levelt, W. J. M., & Schiller, N. O. (2006). Effects of syllable frequency in speech production. *Cognition, 99*, 205–235.

Clements, G. N., & Keyser, S. J. (1983). *CV phonology: A generative theory of the syllable.* Cambridge, MA: MIT Press.

Code, C. (1998). Major review: Models, theories and heuristics in apraxia of speech. *Clinical Linguistics and Phonetics, 12*, 47–65.

Croot, K. (2002). Diagnosis of AOS: Definition and criteria. *Seminars in Speech and Language, 23*, 267–280.

Dell, G. S. (1986). A spreading-activation theory of retrieval in sentence production. *Psychological Review, 93*, 283–321.

Dell, G. S., Schwartz, M. F., Martin, N., Saffran, E. M., & Gagnon, D. A. (1997). Lexical access in aphasic and nonaphasic speakers. *Psychological Review, 104*, 801–838.

Dolar, M. (2007). *His Master's Voice. Eine Theorie der Stimme.* Frankfurt: Suhrkamp.

Draper, N. R., & Smith, H. (1998). *Applied regression analysis.* New York: Wiley.

Duden-Redaktion (2001). *Duden. Deutsches Universalwörterbuch* (4th ed.). Mannheim, Germany: Dudenverlag.

Goldrick, M., & Blumstein, S. E. (2006). Cascading activation from phonological planning to articulatory processes: Evidence from tongue twisters. *Language and Cognitive Processes, 21*, 649–683.

Goldstein, L., Pouplier, M., Chen, L., Saltzman, E., & Byrd, D. (2007). Dynamic action units slip in speech production errors. *Cognition, 103*, 386–412.

Huber, W., Poeck, K., Weniger, D., & Willmes, K. (1983). *Aachener Apasie Test (AAT).* Göttingen: Hogrefe.

Itoh, M., Sasanuma, E., & Ushijima, T. (1979). Velar movements during speech in a patient with apraxia of speech. *Brain and Language, 7*, 227–239.

Laganaro, M. (2008). Is there a syllable frequency effect in aphasia or in apraxia of speech or in both? *Aphasiology, 22*, 1191–1200.

Levelt, W. J. M., Roelofs, A., & Meyer, A. S. (1999). A theory of lexical access in speech production. *Behavioral and Brain Sciences, 22*, 1–38.

Liepold, M., Ziegler, W., & Brendel, B. (2003). *Hierarchische Wortlisten. Ein Nachsprechtest für die Sprechapraxiediagnostik.* Dortmund, Germany: Borgmann.

Riskin, J. (2003). Eighteenth-century wetware. *Representations, 83*, 97–125.

Romani, C., & Galluzzi, C. (2005). Effects of syllabic complexity in predicting accuracy of repetition and direction of errors in patients with articulatory and phonological difficulties. *Cognitive Neuropsychology, 22*, 817–850.

Staiger, A., & Ziegler, W. (2008). Syllable frequency and syllable structure in the spontaneous speech production of patients with apraxia of speech. *Aphasiology, 22*, 1201–1215.

Varley, R., & Whiteside, S. P. (2001). What is the underlying impairment in acquired apraxia of speech? *Aphasiology, 15*, 39–49.

Vennemann, T. (1988). Preference laws for syllable structure and the explanation of sound change. Berlin. Mouton.

Ziegler, W. (2002). Psycholinguistic and motor theories of apraxia of speech. *Seminars in Speech and Language, 23*, 231–243.

Ziegler, W. (2005). A nonlinear model of word length effects in apraxia of speech. *Cognitive Neuropsychology, 22*, 603–623.

Ziegler, W. (2006). Distinctions between speech and nonspeech motor control: A neurophonetic view. In J. Harrington & M. Tabain (Eds.), *Speech Production: Models, Phonetic Processes, and Techniques.* New York: Psychology Press.

Ziegler, W. (2008). Apraxia of speech. In G. Goldenberg & B. Miller (Eds.), *Handbook of Clinical Neurology* (pp. 269–285). London: Elsevier.

Ziegler, W., & Cramon, D. von (1986). Timing deficits in apraxia of speech. *European Archives of Psychiatry and Neurologic Science, 236*, 44–49.

Ziegler, W., Thelen, A. K., Staiger, A., & Liepold, M. (2008). The domain of phonetic encoding in apraxia of speech: Which sub-lexical units count? *Aphasiology, 22*, 1230–1247.

LANGUAGE AND COGNITIVE PROCESSES
2009, 24 (5), 662–684

Psychology Press
Taylor & Francis Group

Effects of syllable preparation and syllable frequency in speech production: Further evidence for syllabic units at a post-lexical level

Joana Cholin

University of La Laguna, Spain

Willem J. M. Levelt

Max Planck Institute for Psycholinguistics, Nijmegen, the Netherlands

In the current paper, we asked at what level in the speech planning process speakers retrieve stored syllables. There is evidence that syllable structure plays an essential role in the phonological encoding of words (e.g., online syllabification and phonological word formation). There is also evidence that syllables are retrieved as whole units. However, findings that clearly pinpoint these effects to specific levels in speech planning are scarce. We used a naming variant of the implicit priming paradigm to contrast voice onset latencies for frequency-manipulated disyllabic Dutch pseudo-words. While prior implicit priming studies only manipulated the item's form and/or syllable structure overlap we introduced syllable frequency as an additional factor. If the preparation effect for syllables obtained in the implicit priming paradigm proceeds beyond phonological planning, i.e., includes the retrieval of stored syllables, then the preparation effect should differ for high- and low-frequency syllables. The findings reported here confirm this prediction: Low-frequency syllables benefit significantly more from the preparation than high-frequency syllables. Our findings support the notion of a mental syllabary at a post-lexical level, between the levels of phonological and phonetic encoding.

Keywords: Phonological/phonetic encoding; Mental syllabary; Implicit priming; Syllable frequency.

Correspondence should be addressed to Joana Cholin, University of La Laguna, Department of Cognitive Psychology, Campus de Guajara s/n, 38205 La Laguna, Santa Cruz de Tenerife, Spain. E-mail: jcholin@ull.es

http://www.psypress.com/lcp   DOI: 10.1080/01690960802348852

The mental syllabary is thought to be a store for whole gestural scores for at least the high-frequency syllables of a given language. The mental syllabary is an inherent part of the Levelt, Roelofs, and Meyer (1999) theory of spoken word production and is assumed to be located between the levels of phonological and phonetic encoding. At this interface, previously generated, abstract phonological syllables retrieve their phonetic matches from the syllabary. The retrieval of stored syllables facilitates the transformation from abstract phonological into context-dependent phonetic syllables as it reduces the workload relative to a segment-by-segment conversion. These phonetic syllables or motor programs will then guide the subsequent steps, including articulation, to produce spoken language.

In recent years, more and more evidence suggesting that speakers in fact retrieve stored syllabic units has been gathered (Carreiras & Perea, 2004; Cholin, Levelt, & Schiller, 2006; Laganaro & Alario, 2006; Levelt & Wheeldon, 1994; see also Aichert & Ziegler, 2004). However, findings that can clearly pinpoint the level at which those units are retrieved are very scarce. The Levelt et al. (1999) theory makes clear claims about the level where access to stored syllable programs ought to occur, namely at the interface of phonological and phonetic encoding.

The current paper aims to test whether the retrieval of syllabic units in fact takes place at this hypothesised location. So far, the available evidence is consistent with the notion of a separate retrieval of phonetic syllables at the phonetic/phonological interface but there is no direct evidence to support this claim. The present experiment aims to provide this direct evidence by examining the interaction between two independently established effects, one of which is relevant to identifying the relevant stage of processing and the other of which is relevant to the notion of stored representations. By examining the interaction between these two effects, we should find direct support for the claim that pre-compiled syllable representations are retrieved at this post-lexical level. We combined the *implicit priming paradigm* that has been successful in detecting the emergence of syllables during word-form encoding with a material set that manipulated the syllable-frequency of its items to directly test *when* syllabic units are retrieved during speech planning. The implicit priming technique makes use of the fact that implicit knowledge of certain aspects of an action accelerates the execution of this action (Rosenbaum, Inhoff, & Gordon, 1984). In implicit priming studies, participants learn sets of prompt-response pairs in which the responses are phonologically related to one another (e.g., *lo.tus, lo.ner, lo.cal*).[1] The relatedness may consist in segmental overlap, in overlap of syllabic structure or both (see above). The overlap between the responses within one set

---

[1] Dots indicate syllable boundaries.

functions as an implicit prime. Depending on the amount/quality of overlap, it can be tested what kind of information speakers need in order to best prepare for an utterance (in comparison to sets where there is no overlap between set members). Speakers can prepare an utterance more successfully when more information is given implicitly, i.e., when segmental and syllabic structures are shared between responses (as shown in the example above; Cholin, Schiller, & Levelt, 2004; Meyer, 1990, 1991; Roelofs & Meyer, 1998). As will be discussed in more detail below, implicit priming studies have established that knowledge about the syllable structure of a (to-be-prepared) utterance is relevant only *after* the word form are already retrieved from memory, which points towards the conclusion that syllables play a separate role (from words) during speech planning. However, even though these results testify to the relevance of syllabic information at this post-lexical level, these findings do not provide incontrovertible evidence for the assumption that syllables are in fact accessed as independent, pre-compiled units. On the other hand, the finding that high-frequency syllables yield faster production times than low-frequency ones strongly supports the notion that syllables are retrieved as whole units because only stored units are expected to exhibit frequency effects, however, a syllable-frequency effect per se is not informative with respect to the location of the assumed storage. Thus, a combination of the paradigm that has previously been found to be sensitive to effects occurring at this post-lexical level and an experimental factor that implicates stored syllabic units (i.e., syllable frequency) seems to be most promising in the endeavour to locate the mental syllabary. The virtue of the present experiment is that it will test for the interaction of the independently observed effects of syllable preparation and syllable frequency within one single experiment to provide evidence for the location of the mental syllabary.

Before we introduce the current study in more detail and further explain its logic, we present theories of word production and discuss the relevant evidence for and against their assumptions of an involvement of syllables at specific levels.

THEORIES OF WORD PRODUCTION AND THE INVOLVEMENT OF SYLLABLES

Theories of word production generally agree that syllables play a role in speech production planning (e.g., Dell, 1986, 1988; Levelt et al., 1999; Shattuck-Hufnagel, 1979, 1983), however, there are contrasting assumptions regarding the level at which syllables come into play. While some researchers (Dell, 1986, 1988; Shattuck-Hufnagel, 1979, 1983) assume that syllables are an inherent part of the lexicalized word forms, others (e.g. Cholin, Levelt, &

Schiller, 2006; Levelt et al., 1999; Schiller & Costa, 2006) argue that syllables (as abstract phonological units) emerge during context-dependent online syllabification processes and are separately stored and retrieved as phonetic syllable programs.

Generally, it is assumed that word production starts with the activation (Dell, 1986) or the selection (Levelt et al., 1999) of a word entry, the so-called lemma which, in turn, activates its corresponding word form. The different theories make different assumption with respect to the quality of the word form, or rather with respect to the kinds of information that are released upon retrieval of the word form. Dell (1986, 1988) assumes that the word's phonemic code is syllabified. In his theory, word-form retrieval makes two kinds of information accessible, on the hand, phonological syllabic units (bundle of segments); and on the other hand, syllabic frames or word-shape headers, that specify the C(onsonant)-V(owel) (hereafter CV-)structure of the syllable and syllable-internal positions such as onset, nucleus, and coda (for similar assumptions see MacNeilage, 1998; Shattuck-Hufnagel, 1979, 1983). The frames or word-shape headers serve as placeholders in which the segmental content will be filled in during the process of segment-to-frame-association.

Contrary to Dell (1986, 1988), Levelt and colleagues (1999) assume that the phonological code of a word form merely consists of an ordered set of phonemic segments. Crucially, at the stage of phonological encoding, phonological segments are not yet assigned to syllabic positions, nor is the CV-structure for the word specified. Similarly, while the metrical structure is an inherent feature of the retrieved word-shapes in Dell's model, the Levelt et al. theory assumes that the stress pattern for a given word is only stored in case of a non-default stress pattern. For monosyllabic words and for all other polysyllabic words with a default stress pattern (i.e., which in Dutch is the first syllable that carries stress), it is not stored but computed (see also Schiller, Fikkert, & Levelt, 2004).

The main argument for not assuming pre-determined syllable internal positions in the lexically stored phonological codes is based on the phenomenon of resyllabification. In connected speech, syllable boundaries often differ from a word's or morpheme's canonical syllabification. The domain of syllabification is the phonological word, which can be smaller or larger than the lexical word due to morphophonological processes like inflection or cliticisation (Booij, 1995). The ubiquity of 'resyllabifications' in the normal use of Dutch (see Schiller, Meyer, Baayen, & Levelt, 1996), renders pre-specification of segments to syllable positions highly inefficient.[2]

---

[2] The claim that phonological codes are not pre-syllabified is, in part, a language-specific claim. For a language like Mandarin Chinese, which has a small set of syllables and limited resyllabification processes, the story might be different (see Chen, Chen, & Dell, 2002).

The alternative assumption, therefore, is that a word's syllabification is not retrieved but computed on-line depending on the context in which the word appears. During online-syllabification, retrieved segments are incrementally combined to form successive syllables. Also, these successive syllables are incrementally assigned the appropriate metrical properties, either following default stress, or otherwise the retrieved non-default stress marking feature. The incremental composition of syllables follows, on the one hand, universal syllabification constraints (such as maximisation of onsets and sonority gradations) and, on the other hand, language-specific rules, e.g., phonotactics. Together, these rules create easily pronounced syllables. The output of phonological encoding is a phonological word, specified for its metrical, syllabic, and segmental properties.

PHONETIC ENCODING AND ACCESS TO THE MENTAL SYLLABARY

The fairly abstract, syllabified phonological words are incrementally translated into articulatory-motor programs. The Levelt et al. theory assumes that as soon as a syllable emerges during incremental syllabification, the corresponding syllabic articulatory gesture will be selected from the repository possibly located in Broca's area or a pre-motor area (Dronkers, 1996; Indefrey & Levelt, 2000; Kerzel & Bekkering, 2000). The output of the mental syllabary in turn serves as input to phonetic encoding. During this latter step contextually driven phonetic fine-tuning of retrieved motor programs occurs: The motor programs are still rather abstract representations of the articulatory gestures which have to be performed at different articulatory tiers, for example, a glottal tier, a nasal tier, and an oral tier. The gestural scores are abstract in the sense that their execution is highly context-dependent (due to allophonic variation, coarticulation and, as a result of this, assimilation). The actual details of the movements in realising the scores, such as lip protrusion and jaw lowering, are within the domain of the articulatory system (Goldstein & Fowler, 2003). According to Levelt (1989), the stored syllable can be pronounced with more or less force, with shorter or longer duration, and different kinds of pitch movements. These are free parameters, which have to be set from case to case. For new or very low-frequency syllables it is proposed that articulatory plans are assembled using the segmental and metrical information specified in the phonological syllables. Finally, the articulatory network, a coordinative motor system that includes feedback mechanisms (Goldstein & Fowler, 2003; Saltzman, 1986; Saltzman & Kelso, 1987), transforms these articulatory plans into overt speech.

EVIDENCE FOR AND AGAINST THE INVOLVEMENT OF SYLLABLES AT SPECIFIC LEVELS

Syllable priming studies

Under the assumption that the syllable constitutes a relevant unit during speech planning, a series of studies in a number of different languages used a syllable priming task to identify syllabic units during word-form encoding (for Dutch: Baumann, 1995; Schiller, 1997, 1998; for Mandarin Chinese: Chen, Lin, & Ferrand, 2003; for French: Brand, Rey, & Peereman, 2003; Evinck, 1997; Ferrand, Segui, & Grainger, 1996; Schiller, Costa, & Colomé, 2002; for English: Ferrand, Segui, & Humphreys, 1997; Schiller, 1999, 2000; Schiller & Costa, 2006; for Spanish and an overview see Schiller et al., 2002). In all these studies, a syllabic prime was given which was either congruent with the target's syllabic structure (e.g., *ba* as a prime for *ba*.sis or *bas* as a prime for *bas*.ket) or incongruent (e.g., *ba* as a prime for *bas*.ket or *bas* as a prime for *ba*.sis). The majority of these studies found a segmental overlap effect rather than a syllable priming effect, i.e., phonologically related primes, whatever their syllabic relation to the target word was, facilitated the response relative to unrelated control primes. The original segmental overlap effect (Schiller, 1998) has recently been specified in more detail (Schiller, 2004).[3] Schiller and Costa (2006) specifically asked whether the syllable priming method might be insensitive to syllabic effects and included more visible, that is, unmasked primes with a longer stimulus-onset-asynchrony (SOA) to allow for a longer and more explicit exposure of the prime. However, even this unmasked prime presentation did not lead to any syllable priming effects. Therefore, as Schiller and Costa concluded, we would like to deduce from these results that the reason why there was no syllable priming effect is that at the stage where the priming taps into speech planning there is only segmental but no syllabic structure available. The

---

[3] Much discussion has been given to the results of the apparent syllable priming effect in French (Ferrand et al., 1997, Experiment 5). However, Brand et al.'s (2003) failure to replicate the Ferrand effects suggests that this should not be taken as strong evidence for a syllable priming effect (see also Evinck, 1997; and for a review Schiller et al., 2002). The only study that showed a clear syllable priming effect was a study by Chen et al. (2003) conducted in Mandarin Chinese. Mandarin Chinese compared to the other languages under investigation consists of a low number of syllables. Mandarin Chinese has (not counting tone) a syllable inventory of 400 different syllables whereas languages as Dutch and English have more than 12,000 different syllables. Additionally, syllables in Mandarin Chinese are not resyllabified in connected speech. Thus, in languages with far less syllables that are not resyllabified the storage of syllables might be different. It might be the case that the syllable structure is in fact stored within the word-form that is retrieved from the mental lexicon. This would explain why a significant syllable priming effect could be found in Mandarin Chinese but not in Indo-European languages (see also O'Sheagdha, Chen, Shen, & Schuster, 2004). The issue of cross-linguistic differences has to be further investigated.

primes in the syllable-priming task never get overtly articulated; therefore, these syllabic primes may not reach the late stage where syllables are computed on-line. Instead, the primes are assumed to speed up the segmental retrieval from the mental lexicon. The finding that the magnitude of the priming effect increases with an increase in the number of shared segments, independent of a syllable match or mismatch with the target's first syllable, confirms the assumption that only shared segments can be primed.

It should be noted that some studies have found effects of abstract syllable structure supporting Dell's idea (Dell, 1986, 1988) of word shape headers (Costa & Sebastián-Gallés, 1998; Sevald, Dell, & Cole, 1995; but see Roelofs & Meyer, 1998 for counter-evidence). However, as already discussed, in the case of stored *phonological* syllables, the various syllable priming studies should have shown a syllable priming effect instead of the repeatedly found segmental overlap effect. This latter finding seriously challenges the notion of syllabified word forms and leads us to the conclusion that there – in fact – might not be any syllabic information within the entries in the mental lexicon.

Implicit priming studies

Another paradigm that uses a priming procedure is the already mentioned implicit priming paradigm. Here, the phonological overlap between responses within one set, the homogeneous set, is used to test what information speakers need in order to prepare for an utterance. In the Meyer (1990, 1991) studies, participants learned sets of semantically related prompt-response pairs in Dutch. In homogeneous sets, the overlap ranged from an overlap of the first segment (e.g., dijk [dike] – *pol.der* [polder]; nootje [nut] – *pin.da* [peanut]; tijger [tiger] – *pan.ter* [panther]) to an overlap of the first two (e.g., podium [platform] – *to*.neel [stage]; geheel [whole] – *to.taal* [total]; komkommer [cucumber] – *to.maat* [tomato]) and three segments (e.g., kruid [herb] – *ker.vel* [chervil]; specerij [spice] – *ker.mis* [fair]; gevangenis [prison] – *ker.ker* [dungeon]). Heterogeneous sets are created by regrouping the prompt-response pairs from the homogeneous sets; as a consequence, there is no shared phonological property among responses in those sets. Production latency (the time between onset of prompt and speech onset) is the dependent variable. The standard effect in the implicit priming paradigm is faster production latencies for homogeneous than for heterogeneous blocks. Meyer (1990, 1991) reported such an effect only when the response words in the homogeneous sets shared one or more word-initial segment(s). No effect was shown for shared word-final segments indicating that phonological encoding is a serial process that proceeds from the beginning to the end of a lexical item. Furthermore and more importantly, the preparation effect was found to increase with the number of shared segments.[4] That is, even though syllable structure was not directly manipulated in Meyer's experiments, the fact that the magnitude of the effect increases with the number of shared segments strongly points towards the same conclusion that we drew from the previously reported syllable priming studies: There is no syllable information stored within the word form retrieved from the mental lexicon. If word forms would already be chunked into syllables one would expect that syllables rather than shared segments would be sensitive to the preparation and accordingly there should be no difference whether there is an overlap of the first two or three segments.

But can we find evidence for the alternative assumption by Levelt and colleagues (1999) that syllables first surface during online-syllabification? In order to test whether the emergence of syllables during this stage of word-form encoding can be detected, the study by Cholin, Schiller, and Levelt (2004) directly manipulated syllable structure. An odd-man-out variant of the implicit priming technique (Janssen, Roelofs, & Levelt, 2002) was used to test whether speakers can benefit from a shared syllable structure. Two types of response sets were compared, namely constant and variable response sets: Constant sets had overlapping initial segments and a constant CV-structure (as in spui.en, [to drain]; spui.de, [drained]; spui.er, [person who drains]; spui.end, [draining]). Variable sets had an overlap of the first segments but did not have a constant syllable structure (e.g., spoe.len, [to rinse]; spoel.de, [rinsed]; spoe.ler, [person who rinses]; spoe.lend, [rinsing]). Note that the second item of this set shares the same initial segments but has a different initial syllable structure; it is the odd-man out for the set. The underlying hypothesis of this study was that – under the assumption that the syllable is a relevant processing unit in speech production – speakers need knowledge about the current syllabic structure in order to prepare for a target utterance. Thus, it was predicted that speakers can prepare their utterance more efficiently when they know what the structure of the initial syllable will be (as they do in constant sets) then when the initial syllable varies within the set of words (as they do in the variable sets). In other words, if syllables are encoded during online-syllabification and syllable structure is indeed a crucial piece of information then we should find a larger preparation effect for constant sets since speakers can proceed with their preparation beyond the level where syllables are encoded. Crucially, the deviant syllable structure was expected to

---

[4] For one experiment, Meyer (1991) reports that sets with open initial syllables (CV) that share only those two initial segments produced preparation effects that were equivalent to effects produced for sets with closed syllables (CVC) that shared three initial segments. This result was surprising because a pure segmental length effect would predict larger preparation effects in the CVC sets since they comprise one more shared segment. This finding supports the possibility of syllabic effects that are independent of segmental length. However, contrary to this result, Roelofs (1996), Experiment 6) showed that the size of the preparation effect depends on the length of the shared syllable in terms of number of segments.

spoil the preparation effect for the entire set, that is, even after removing the odd-man-out from the analysis of reaction times, the preparation effect for the remaining responses of an entire variable set should be reduced (see Cholin et al., 2004 for the details of the statistical analyses). Two different CV-structures (CVV, Exp. 1 and CCVV, Exp. 2) were investigated. The results in fact showed a significantly larger preparation effect for constant sets. The constant sets were on average 64 ms faster produced than the variable sets. Control studies showed that variable sets also yielded a preparation effect in comparison to a baseline condition where no phonological property was shared between members in a response set. Thus, responses in variable sets can also be prepared but to a lesser extent, indicating that syllables do play a functionally important role during speech planning. Of course, the crucial question is at what level. Recall that we attributed the segmental overlap effect that was replicated time and again in different languages and paradigms to the fact that those tasks do not tap into the level where syllables are retrieved or encoded. Since we find a graded preparation effect also for variable sets, we concluded that the segmental overlap in variable sets allows for a preparation of the shared segments but not for the syllable structure which is needed during online-syllabification. Thus, in variable sets, all stages preceding on-line syllabification contribute to the preparation effect. In contrast, in constant sets, the retrieval of stored syllabic units, phonetic encoding through articulation can contribute to the preparation effect. Thus, these results strongly support the assumption that syllables are computed online. However, they do not represent indisputable evidence for the notion of a separate retrieval of stored syllabic units. Effects that do represent strong evidence for the existence of the mental syllabary are effects of syllable frequency because only stored units are thought to exhibit frequency effects.

Syllable-frequency effects

In analogy to the findings of word frequency, that high-frequency words are retrieved and produced faster than low-frequency words (Jescheniak & Levelt, 1994; Oldfield & Wingfield, 1965), stored syllables should exhibit (syllable) frequency effects. If the mental syllabary consists of retrievable representations corresponding to syllables, than the retrieval process should be faster for high-frequency syllables than for low-frequency syllables. Syllable-frequency effects were found in a number of studies investigating syllable-frequency effects in different languages with words and pseudo-words (German: Aichert & Ziegler, 2004; Dutch: Cholin et al., 2006; Levelt & Wheeldon, 1994; Spanish: Carreiras & Perea, 2004; Perea & Carreiras, 1996; French: Brand, Rey, Peereman, & Spieler, 2002; Laganaro & Alario, 2006; but see also Croot & Rastle, 2004; Monsell, van der Lugt, & Jessiman, 2002). These studies strongly support the claim that syllables are retrieved as whole units that are separately stored from the word forms, most likely in a mental syllabary.[5] Two studies shall be mentioned in detail as they have further implications for the current study. Cholin et al. (2006) used a symbol-position association learning task to contrast the production of high- and low-frequency syllables in mono- and disyllabic pseudo-words. The material set was very carefully chosen to control for any potential confound. Since the materials from this study will provide a crucial piece for the material set of the current study it will be described in further detail. Quartets of four CVC-syllables, two of high- and two of low-frequency, were selected sharing the same nucleus (e.g., /ɛ/), two different onsets (e.g., /ʋ/ and /k/), and two different offsets (e.g., /m/ and /s/). The two syllables sharing the same onset were of different frequency (high vs. low) such as 'wem' (low-frequency) and 'wes' (high-frequency). The same holds for the two syllables sharing the same offset, such as 'wem' (low-frequency) and 'kem' (high-frequency). See Table 1 for a depiction.

The construction of those syllabic quartets guaranteed a control not only for onsets and offset within one quartet but also for CV structure (which had to be CVC for that matter), phoneme and biphone-frequency and also the transitional probabilities between the single phonemes of the syllables.

The participants' task was to respond as fast as possible with a previously learned associated target-word when a production cue was presented on the screen. In learning phases, participants were presented a symbol on one of two potential positions (the left or right position on a computer screen) and were simultaneously presented with the to-be-associated word via head-phones. In the test phase, the same symbol was shown on either the right or the left side of the computer screen to prompt the previously associated target utterance. The auditory presentation of the target ensured that potential confounds deriving from orthographic factors could be excluded. The results can be summarised as follows: A small but highly significant syllable-frequency effect of 9 ms was obtained in testing monosyllabic pseudo-words. This effect was replicated investigating disyllabic pseudo-words bearing the frequency-manipulation on the first syllable. Both effects strongly support the notion of stored syllables, especially because all potentially confounding factors have been carefully controlled for. The material that was used in this study will serve as the basis for constructing the material set in the current experiment.

Laganaro and Alario (2006) employed a different paradigm to investigate the assumption that stored syllables are retrieved during phonetic encoding. In six experiments involving immediate and delayed production, with or without an interfering task (articulatory suppression) they tested the

---

[5] Note that the idea of a mental syllabary is also in principle compatible with Dell's syllabified phonological code, the idea of syllabified word-forms itself does not deny the existence of a syllabary storing phonetic syllables.

TABLE 1
High- and low-frequency syllables within one quartet

High-frequency	Low-frequency
kem [kɛm]	kes [kɛs]
wes [ʋɛs]	wem [ʋɛm]

production of picture names and pseudo words that consisted of high- and/ or low-frequency syllables. They found syllable-frequency effects in immediate pseudo-word production and picture naming and in a delayed naming task with articulatory suppression but not in a delayed naming task without articulatory suppression. The authors' interpretation that the syllable-frequency effect has its origin at the level of phonetic encoding mainly stems from the comparison of the delayed naming experiments. In both experiments, participants had to name targets with high- and low-frequency syllables not upon target presentation but in response to a (delayed) cue. Syllable-frequency effects were only obtained when the delay was filled with an articulatory suppression task (repetition of the syllable 'ba'). The authors assume that the suppression task only disrupts phonetic processing but not phonological encoding and that the results therefore indicate that syllable-frequency effects are likely to arise at the level of phonetic encoding.

To summarise, the available evidence strongly points towards the conclusion that syllables play a role during later stages of word-form encoding and, most likely, in form of separately stored syllabic units.

The present study combines two factors, preparation (overlapping segments and syllabic structure) and syllable frequency (high- versus low-frequency), that have previously been used only in separate experiments to specifically investigate the involvement of syllables in speech production. The combination of these two factors might offer a verification of inferences that, so far, could only be drawn by pulling threads from different paradigms across experiments. An interaction of syllable-preparation and syllable-frequency effects would provide convincing support for the assumption that the retrieval of stored syllables directly follows phonological encoding. The virtue of the current experiment is that it tests the critical conditions as within-subject factors in a single experiment.

EXPERIMENT

We used a naming variant of the implicit priming paradigm (Roelofs, 2004) and contrasted production times for sets consisting of four Dutch disyllabic (pseudo-)words that had identical first syllables (i.e., the homogeneous sets), with sets consisting of four different Dutch disyllabic (pseudo-)words (i.e., the heterogeneous sets). Thus, the first factor is the standard preparation effect: Sets with syllabic overlap are predicted to be produced faster as speakers can prepare part of the utterance due to the implicit primes in homogeneous sets. The second factor is syllable frequency. The first syllables within both sets were either (all) high- or low-frequent. The critical prediction in this experiment is an interaction of these two factors: If speakers access stored syllable units at the level where syllables are prepared, and thus, the retrieval of those units contributes to the preparation effect, then we should find a difference in the preparation effects for high- and low-frequency syllables. In other words, low-frequency syllables should benefit more from the preparation that is possible in homogeneous sets than high-frequency syllables. As a result, the advantage that high-frequency syllables should have over low-frequency syllables should only be visible in hetero-geneous sets (where no preparation is possible). In homogeneous sets, however, the effect of syllable-frequency should be levelled out by the preparation effect. The frequency difference should no longer have an effect since high- and low-frequency syllables can be equally prepared for. The predicted interaction of the two effects would (a) indicate that the implicit priming paradigm entails syllabic processing and (b) support the assumption of a mental syllabary between the levels of phonological and phonetic planning levels.

Method

Participants.   Thirty-two native speakers of Dutch participated in the Experiment. They were randomly taken from the pool of participants of the Max Planck Institute in Nijmegen, the Netherlands and were paid for their participation. They had no known hearing deficit, and they had normal or corrected-to-normal vision.

Materials.   Four of the previously described and tested syllabic quartets from the Cholin et al. (2006) study (see section 'Syllable-frequency effects') were used as the basis for constructing the materials of the present experiment. By a very specific pairing, high- and low-frequency syllables within one quartet were controlled for the following factors: CV-structure, number of phonemes, phoneme frequency, bigram frequency and the transitional probabilities of phonemes within syllables. A full list of experimental quartets and their frequency counts is given in Appendix A. In order to create disyllabic pseudo-words out of these quartets, we chose four high-frequency CV syllables to serve as second syllables (li [li:], ta [ta:], wa [ʋɑ:], and jo [jo:]).[6] Each of these four CV syllables was combined with each member of the quartets thereby ensuring that the transitions (and the transitional probabilities) between first and second syllables were also controlled for, as in we**m.t**a [ʋɛm.ta], low-frequency, ke**m.t**a [kɛm.ta], high-frequency, and we**s.t**a [ʋɛs.ta], high-frequency, ke**s.t**a [kɛs.ta], low-frequency; see also Table 2 for a schematic depiction of the combination of all four CV syllables with one quartet.

All of the pseudo-words were phonotactically legal strings of Dutch but none of those words was an existing Dutch word. By pairing each quartet, i.e., all four members of one quartet with four different high-frequency syllables, 16 different disyllabic pseudo-words were created, that shared the first syllable.

Design. The 64 disyllabic pseudo-words were grouped into homogeneous (high- and low-frequency) and heterogeneous (high- and low-frequency) sets. Homogeneous sets consisted of four pseudo words sharing the first syllable (e.g., wemta, wemli, wemwa, and wemjo, low-frequency). There were homogeneous high-frequency sets as well as homogeneous low-frequency sets, the four pseudo-words again 'derived' from one base syllable (as in westa, wesli, weswa, and wesjo, high-frequency). Following this procedure, eight homogeneous high-frequency sets were created as well as eight homogeneous low-frequency sets, each of them containing four items. Sixteen heterogeneous sets were created by regrouping the items from the homogeneous sets, again – depending on the frequency of the first syllables – divided into eight low-frequency and eight high-frequency heterogeneous sets. Thus, the two high- and the two low-frequency syllables of each quartet appeared in a homogeneous as well as in a heterogeneous context; every item served as its own control. The experiment consisted of two crossed within-subject factors, the factor *Preparation* (two levels, homogeneous versus heterogeneous) and the factor *Frequency* (two levels, high versus low). In total, the experiment consisted of 32 different item sets, containing a total of 64 different items. For a full list of items and their distribution over the four conditions see Appendix B.

The presentation of blocks of homogeneous and heterogeneous sets alternated in blocks of four sets within the same frequency condition. The

---

[6] The four high-frequency syllables that were used to construct the second syllables in the disyllabic pseudo-words were among the first percentile of the most high-frequency Dutch syllables; for their frequency values see notes of Appendix A. We opted for these very high-frequency syllables because these syllables are most likely to be stored within the syllabary. The retrieval of those high-frequency syllables should be fast and least error-prone. Furthermore, we decided to have frequency-constant second syllable in order to keep this condition equal across items.

TABLE 2
Example for the learning sets in the four different conditions

| Homogeneous sets | | Heterogeneous sets | |
High-frequency	Low-frequency	High-frequency	Low-frequency
kem.ta [kɛm.ta]	kes.ta [kɛs.ta]	kem.ta [kɛm.ta]	kes.ta [kɛs.ta]
kem.li [kɛm.li]	kes.li [kɛs.li]	bin.li [bɪn.li]	bing.li [bɪŋ.li]
kem.wa [kɛm.ʋa]	kes.wa [kɛs.ʋa]	mer.wa [mɛr.ʋa]	meg.wa [mɛx.ʋa]
kem.jo [kɛm.jo]	kes.jo [kɛs.jo]	sup.jo [sʏp.jo]	suk.jo [sʏk.jo]
wes.ta [ʋɛs.ta]	wem.ta [ʋɛm.ta]	wes.ta [ʋɛs.ta]	wem.ta [ʋɛm.ta]
wes.li [ʋɛs.li]	wem.li [ʋɛm.li]	ning.li [nɪŋ.li]	nin.li [nɪn.li]
wes.wa [ʋɛs.ʋa]	wem.wa [ʋɛm.ʋa]	reg.wa [rɛx.ʋa]	rer.wa [rɛr.ʋa]
wes.jo [ʋɛs.jo]	wem.jo [ʋɛm.jo]	luk.jo [lʏk.jo]	lup.jo [lʏp.jo]

succession of the different sets was fully counterbalanced over 32 participants by applying a Latin-Square design.

Procedure and apparatus.   The participants were seated in a quiet room in
front of a 17-inch computer screen (iiyamaLM704UT). The distance between
participants and screen was approximately 50 cm. Before the experiment
started, participants received written instructions about the task. The
experiment consisted of alternating learning and test phases. In the learning
phase, participants were shown sets of four words on the computer screen.
The participants were instructed to look silently over the four target words.
Words were presented for 9 seconds with a vertical spacing in 24-points
lowercase Arial, white on a black screen; see Figure 1.

In the test phase, the words were presented one by one on the screen and
participants were instructed to read aloud the target words as fast and as
accurately as possible. A trial was structured as follows: participants saw a
warning signal (an asterisk) for 500 ms. Next, the screen was cleared for
500 ms, followed by the display of the target word for 1500 ms. Finally,
before the start of the next trial there was a blank interval of 500 ms.
Simultaneously with target onset the voice key was activated for 1500 ms.
The target word disappeared after the response with a delay of 500 ms. The
asterisk of the next trial appeared after 100 ms. All the items within each set
were repeated five times in a random order, resulting in 20 naming responses
per set. On average, an experimental session lasted about 30 minutes.

The presentation of the stimuli and the measuring of the reaction times
were controlled by the NESU2000 software package. The spoken reactions
were registered by a Sennheiser MD211N microphone, which fed into a
NESU-Box2 voice key device and a DAT recorder (Sony DTC-55ES). The
experimenter sat in the same room as the participant, separated by a

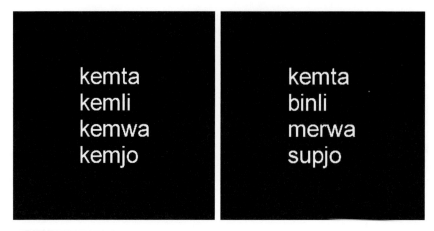

Figure 1. Example for a homogeneous (left) and heterogeneous (right) learning set.

partition-wall, and took note of hesitations, voice key errors, wrong or no naming responses.

Results and discussion

Test items leading to wrong or invalid responses (mispronunciations, voice key errors, or hesitations) were not included in the reaction time analysis. They were coded as errors. Reaction times above 800 ms and below 200 ms were considered as invalid and did not enter the reaction time analysis. Observations deviating from a participant's and an item's mean by more than 2 standard deviations were considered as outliers and also discarded from the reaction time analysis. 347 (1.7%) trials were treated as errors and 390 (1.9%) as outliers. Analyses of variance were run with *Preparation* (homogeneous versus heterogeneous) and *Frequency* (high versus low) as independent variables. Two complementary analyses were computed, one treating participants (F_1) and one treating item-quartets (F_2) as random factor (Clark, 1973).[7] The mean voice onset latencies, standard deviations and error rates are summarised in Table 3.

There is a significant effect of Preparation in the analysis of reaction times, $F_1(1, 31) = 122.99$, $MSE = 857.98$, $p < .001$; $F_2(1, 3) = 480.67$, $MSE = 27.48$, $p < .001$, reflecting faster naming latencies for homogeneous than for heterogeneous sets. Frequency did not show a significant main effect, F_1 $(1, 31) = 1.69$, $MSE = 317.90$, $p = .204$; $F_2(1, 3) = 5.22$, $MSE = 11.16$, $p = .106$. Most interestingly, a significant interaction between Preparation and

---

[7] Since the selection of one item determined the selection of three remaining items within one quartet, items cannot be considered a random factor in this design.

TABLE 3
Mean voice onset latencies (in ms), percentage errors, and standard deviations (in parentheses).

| | Frequency | | | | | | | |
| | High-frequency | | | | Low-frequency | | | |
	M	(SD)	% Err	(SD)	M	(SD)	% Err	(SD)
Homogeneous sets	386	(40)	2.0	(1.5)	386	(44)	1.7	(1.5)
Heterogeneous sets	439	(37)	1.5	(1.6)	447	(38)	1.5	(1.5)
Difference scores	−53		0.5		−61		0.2	

Frequency was obtained, $F_1(1, 31) = 5.21$, $MSE = 101.47$, $p < .05$; $F_2(1, 3) = 14.34$, $MSE = 4.66$, $p < .05$, reflecting a significantly larger preparation effect for the low-frequency condition (61 ms) than for the high-frequency condition (53 ms). t-tests revealed a significant difference between the high- and the low-frequency sets in the heterogeneous context, $t_1(31) = 2.701$, $p < .05$; $t_2(3) = 4.210$, $p < .05$. Here, no advanced preparation was possible as the four items within these sets had no initial syllable overlap. Thus, the effect of 8 ms reflects a clear syllable-frequency effect. Reaction times for the high- and low-frequency sets in the homogeneous context had identical values; the preparation effect wiped out the frequency effect (both $ts < 1$). The analysis of error rates yielded no significant effects.

An alternative explanation for the observed interaction could be that, in homogeneous sets, the first syllable of the disyllabic target word was repeated 20 times (five repetitions of each of the four target words) while in heterogeneous sets the same syllable was only repeated five times. The absence of a syllable-frequency effect in homogeneous sets might thus be attributed to the higher number of repetitions in those sets. In order to test for this possibility, an analysis including the factor Repetition was carried out. No interaction of Repetition, Frequency, and Preparation, $F_1(4, 124) = 1.55$, $MSE = 313.28$, $p = .193$; $F_2 < 1$, was found, indicating that the factor Repetition does not alternate the observed interaction of Frequency and Preparation. Additionally, inspection of the first item production only shows a data pattern similar to that of the overall data set: a significant syllable-frequency effect for heterogeneous blocks (10 ms, $p < .05$), while there was no frequency effect for homogeneous blocks (4 ms, $t < 1$).

GENERAL DISCUSSION

The aim of the present study was to gain further insights into the question where access to stored syllables occurs during speech planning. Two experimental paradigms that have previously been employed to investigate the role of the syllable in speech production were combined in a single experiment. The implicit priming paradigm provided an insight with respect to the level where syllables are encoded. The syllable-frequency effect provided evidence as to whether or not syllables constitute separate units. A naming variant of the implicit priming paradigm with a syllable-frequency manipulation was used to investigate whether or not access to the mental syllabary is involved and is thereby contributing to the syllable-preparation effect. We examined the voice-onset latencies for frequency-manipulated disyllabic pseudo-words in Dutch.

Disyllabic pseudo-words were named faster if presented in homogeneous sets consisting of items sharing the first syllable compared with hetero-geneous sets that consisted of non-overlapping items. The classic preparation effect for shared versus non-shared phonological properties (Meyer, 1990, 1991) was replicated: the homogeneous sets were on average 57 ms faster produced than the heterogeneous sets. Moreover, the difference between homogeneous and heterogeneous item sets was larger for item sets consisting of low-frequency first syllables than for item sets consisting of high-frequency first syllables. The replication of the syllable-frequency effect within the implicit priming paradigm indicates not only that the observed preparation effect includes access to the mental syllabary but also supports the assumption that the mental syllabary is to be located at a post-lexical level. In homogeneous sets high- and low-frequency syllables could be produced equally fast: The head start that high-frequency syllables have by a faster syllabary access compared with low-frequency syllables was annihi-lated by the advanced preparation in the present experiment.

Only heterogeneous sets yielded a syllable-frequency. Here, word-form encoding processes could first start with target presentation and thus, high-frequency syllables had an advantage over low-frequency syllables. From the former syllable-frequency studies (Cholin et al., 2006; see also Carreiras & Perea, 2004) we knew that a rather small effect had to be expected. In fact, the effect obtained in this study amounted to 8 ms, mirroring the syllable-frequency effect from the former syllable-frequency study (9 ms and 10 ms testing monosyllabic and disyllabic pseudo-words with the frequency-manipulation on the first syllable).

The outcome of the current experiment reveals two important findings: Firstly, the preparation effect in the implicit priming paradigm includes all stages of word-form encoding prior to articulation. Implicit primes that entail information that allow for the preparation of the full (first) syllable will prompt speakers to proceed with the item's preparation beyond on-line syllabification (see Cholin et al., 2004). This finding significantly contributes to our understanding of the implicit priming paradigm: It can serve as a task that can be used to investigate all stages of the word-form encoding process starting from the first stages of morpho-phonological encoding until and including syllabary access. Secondly, the results of this experiment provide further evidence for syllable-frequency effects and confirm thereby the notion of a mental syllabary using a different paradigm, a naming version of the implicit priming paradigm. Since this version of the paradigm does not require an intensive learning phase as well as a rehearsal of previously learned items, a memory effect as the basis for the syllable-frequency effect can be excluded. This result is particularly relevant as the other paradigms that have been used to investigate syllabic effects did involve memorisation of auditory or visual syllables (Cholin et al., 2004, 2006; Laganaro & Alario, 2006).

Furthermore, it can be excluded that the observed effects are due to grapheme frequencies because orthographic factors have been carefully controlled for by a specific pairing of high- and low-frequency onsets and offsets within one syllabic quartet. Moreover, syllable-frequency effects have been found with the very same material when it was presented exclusively auditorily (see Cholin et al., 2006).

Could the current findings possibly be explained within another account? In principle, the current data by itself do not speak against other theories. For example, Dell's model also assumes that syllabic nodes are sensitive to frequency (Dell, 1986, 1988). A larger gain for low-frequency syllables than for high-frequency syllables due to preparation would therefore be expected. As already stated, syllable-frequency effects as well as the notion of a mental syllabary are compatible with Dell's model. However, the repeated finding of a segmental overlap effect in more than a dozen of priming studies, while no syllabic-priming effect could be obtained, weakens the assumption of syllabified word forms at the phonological level. In this sense, the current results support the assumption that the retrieval of stored syllabic units occurs *after* phonological encoding is completed.

Our results corroborate the recent findings by Laganaro and Alario (2006) who found syllable-frequency effects in delayed naming conditions only when the delay was filled with an articulatory suppression task that prevented speakers from phonetically preparing the target utterances. These authors therefore concluded that syllabary access takes place during phonetic encoding.

It should be noted though, that whereas syllable-frequency effects provide evidence for independently stored syllable units that facilitate the late planning processes, these effects remain neutral as to the existence of other, alternative processes that assemble phonetic syllables segment by segment. Apparently, speakers are able to produce syllables they have neither heard nor produced before and that therefore cannot be part of the stored syllable inventory. The alternative assembly route might be limited to new syllables but it may also be the dominant operation for low-frequency syllables. It cannot be excluded that the assembly route is always active, running in parallel to the retrieval route. Speech latencies are then determined by whichever operation is fastest. The question of how we can envision different routes of phonetic encoding and how the alternative routes interact with one another remains subject to further research. The related question of whether, in fact, only the high-frequency syllables (of a given language) are stored within the syllabary or whether there are additional entries, for units that are larger and smaller than the syllable, must also remain open for the moment.

To conclude, the location of the mental syllabary at a post-lexical encoding level is strongly supported by these results. Further research will have to clarify the exact nature of retrieval mechanisms of stored syllables and how different planning procedures might interact during phonetic encoding.

REFERENCES

Aichert, I., & Ziegler, W. (2004). Syllable frequency and syllable structure in apraxia of speech. *Brain and Language*, *88*, 148–159.

Baumann, M. (1995). *The production of syllables in connected speech*. Ph.D. dissertation, Nijmegen University.

Booij, G. (1995). *The phonology of Dutch*. Oxford: Clarendon Press.

Brand, M., Rey, A., & Peereman, R. (2003). Where is the syllable priming effect in visual word recognition? *Journal of Memory and Language*, *48*, 435–443.

Brand, M., Rey, A., Peereman, R., & Spieler, D. (2002). Naming bisyllabic words: A large scale study. *Abstracts of the Psychonomic Society*, *7*, 94.

Carreiras, M., & Perea, M. (2004). Naming pseudowords in Spanish: Effects of syllable frequency in production. *Brain and Language*, *90*, 393–400.

Chen, J.-Y., Chen, T.-M., & Dell, G. S. (2002). Word form encoding in Mandarin Chinese as assessed by the implicit priming paradigm. *Journal of Memory and Language*, *46*, 751–781.

Chen, J.-Y., Lin, W.-C., & Ferrand, L. (2003). Masked priming of the syllable in Mandarin Chinese speech production. *Chinese Journal of Psychology*, *45*, 107–120.

Cholin, J., Schiller, N. O., & Levelt, W. J. M. (2004). The preparation of syllables in speech production. *Journal of Memory and Language*, *50*, 47–61.

Cholin, J., Levelt, W. J. M., & Schiller, N. O. (2006). Effects of syllable frequency in speech production. *Cognition*, *99*, 205–235.

Clark, H. H. (1973). The language-as-fixed-effect fallacy: A critique of language statistics in psychological research. *Journal of Verbal Learning and Verbal Behavior*, *12*, 335–359.

Costa, A., & Sebastián-Gallés, N. (1998). Abstract phonological structure in language production: Evidence from Spanish. *Journal of Experimental Psychology: Learning, Memory and Cognition*, *24*, 886–903.

Croot, K., & Rastle, K. (2004). Is there a syllabary containing stored articulatory plans for speech production in English? *Proceedings of the 10th Australian International Conference on Speech Science and Technology*, Macquarie University, Sydney, 8–10 December 2004.

Dell, G. S. (1986). A spreading-activation theory of retrieval in sentence production. *Psychological Review*, *93*, 283–321.

Dell, G. S. (1988). The retrieval of phonological forms in production: Tests of predictions from a connectionist model. *Journal of Memory and Language*, *27*, 124–142.

Dronkers, N. F. (1996). A new brain region for coordinating speech articulation. *Nature*, *384*, 159–161.

Evinck, S. (1997). *Production de la parole en français: Investigation des unités impliquées dans l'encodage phonologique des mots* [Speech production in French: Investigation of the units implied during the phonological encoding of words]. Unpublished Ph.D. dissertation, Brussels University.

Ferrand, L., Segui, J., & Grainger, J. (1996). Masked priming of word and picture naming: The role of syllable units. *Journal of Memory and Language, 35*, 708–723.

Ferrand, L., Segui, J., & Humphreys, G. W. (1997). The syllable's role in word naming. *Memory and Cognition, 25*, 458–470.

Goldstein, L., & Fowler, C. A. (2003). Articulatory phonology: A phonology for public language use. In N. O. Schiller & A. S. Meyer (Eds.), *Phonetics and phonology in language comprehension and production: Differences and similarities* (pp. 159–207). Berlin: Mouton de Gruyter.

Janssen, P. D., Roelofs, A., & Levelt, W. J. M. (2002). Inflectional frames in language production. *Language and Cognitive Processes, 17*, 209–236.

Jescheniak, J. D., & Levelt, W. J. M. (1994). Word frequency effects in speech production: Retrieval of syntactic information and of phonological form. *Journal of Experimental Psychology: Learning, Memory, and Cognition, 20*, 824–843.

Indefrey, P., & Levelt, W. J. M. (2000). The neural correlates of languages production. In M. Gazzaniga (Ed.), *The new cognitive neurosciences* (pp. 845–865). Cambridge, MA: MIT Press.

Kerzel, D., & Bekkering, H. (2000). Motor activation from visible speech: Evidence from stimulus-response compatibility. *Journal of Experimental Psychology: Human Perception and Performance, 26*, 634–647.

Laganaro, M., & Alario, F.-X. (2006). On the locus of the syllable frequency effect in speech production. *Journal of Memory and Language, 55*, 178–196.

Levelt, W. J. M. (1989). *Speaking: From intention to articulation*. Cambridge, MA: MIT Press.

Levelt, W. J. M., Roelofs, A., & Meyer, A. S. (1999). A theory of lexical access in speech production. *Behavioral and Brain Sciences, 22*, 1–75.

Levelt, W. J. M., & Wheeldon, L. (1994). Do speakers have access to a mental syllabary? *Cognition, 50*, 239–269.

MacNeilage, P. F. (1998). The frame/content theory of evolution of speech production. *Behavioral and Brain Sciences, 21*, 499–546.

Meyer, A. S. (1990). The time course of phonological encoding in language production: The encoding of successive syllables of a word. *Journal of Memory and Language, 29*, 524–545.

Meyer, A. S. (1991). The time course of phonological encoding in language production: Phonological encoding inside a syllable. *Journal of Memory and Language, 30*, 69–89.

Monsell, S., van der Lugt, A., & Jessiman, T. (2002, April). *In pursuit of the Syllabary: This Snark is a Boojum!* Paper presented at the Experimental Psychology Society Meeting, Leuven, Belgium.

Oldfield, R. C., & Wingfield, A. (1965). Response latencies in naming objects. *Quarterly Journal of Experimental Psychology, 17*, 273–281.

O'Sheagdha, P. G., Chen, J.-Y., Shen, Z. Y., & Schuster, K. (2004). The role of the syllable is distinctly different in Mandarin and English. Poster presented at *Architectures and Mechanisms for Language Processing (AMLaP)*, Aix-en-Provence, France.

Perea, M., & Carreiras, M. (1996). Efectos de frecuencia silábica en la tarea de pronunciación mixta ['Effects of syllable frequency in the mixed pronunciation task']. *Psicológica, 17*, 425–440.

Roelofs, A. (1996). Serial order in planning the production of successive morphemes of a word. *Journal of Memory and Language, 35*, 854–876.

Roelofs, A. (2004). Seriality of phonological encoding in naming objects and reading their names. *Memory and Cognition, 32*, 212–222.

Roelofs, A., & Meyer, A. S. (1998). Metrical structure in planning the production of spoken words. *Journal of Experimental Psychology: Learning, Memory and Cognition, 24*, 922–939.

Rosenbaum, D. A., Inhoff, A. W., & Gordon, A. M. (1984). Choosing between movement sequences: A hierarchical editor model. *Journal of Experimental Psychology: General, 113*, 372–393.

Saltzman, E. (1986). Task dynamic coordination of the speech articulators: A preliminary model. In H. Heuer & C. Fromm (Eds.), *Generation and modulation of action patterns* (pp. 129–144). New York: Springer-Verlag.

Saltzman, E., & Kelso, J. A. S. (1987). Skilled actions: A task-dynamic approach. *Psychological Review, 94*, 84–106.

Schiller, N. O. (1998). The effect of visually masked primes on the naming latencies of words and pictures. *Journal of Memory and Language, 39*, 484–507.

Schiller, N. O. (1997). *The role of the syllable in speech production. Evidence from lexical statistics, metalinguistics, masked priming, and electromagnetic midsagittal articulography.* PhD dissertation, Nijmegen University (MPI series; 2).

Schiller, N. O. (1999). Masked syllable priming of English nouns. *Brain and Language, 68*, 300–305.

Schiller, N. O. (2000). Single word production in English: The role of subsyllabic units during speech production. *Journal of Experimental Psychology. Learning, Memory and Cognition, 26*, 512–528.

Schiller, N. O. (2004). The onset effect in word naming. *Journal of Memory and Language, 50*, 477–490.

Schiller, N. O., & Costa, A. (2006). Activation of segments, not syllables, during phonological encoding in speech production. *The Mental Lexicon, 1*, 231–250.

Schiller, N. O., Costa, A., & Colomé, A. (2002). Phonological encoding of single words: In search of the lost syllable. In C. Gussenhoven & N. Warner (Eds.), *Papers in laboratory phonology 7* (pp. 35–59). Berlin: Mouton de Gruyter.

Schiller, N. O., Fikkert, P., & Levelt, C. C. (2004). Stress priming in picture naming: An SOA study. *Brain and Language, 90*, 231–240.

Schiller, N. O., Meyer, A. S., Baayen, R. H., & Levelt, W. J. M. (1996). A comparison of lexeme and speech syllables in Dutch. *Journal of Quantitative Linguistics, 3*, 8–28.

Sevald, C. A., Dell, G., & Cole, J. S. (1995). Syllable structure in speech production: Are syllables chunks or schemas? *Journal of Memory and Language, 34*, 807–820.

Shattuck-Hufnagel, S. (1979). Speech errors as evidence for a serial ordering mechanism in sentence production. In W. E. Cooper & E. C. T. Walker (Eds.), *Sentence processing* (pp. 295–342). New York: Halsted Press.

Shattuck-Hufnagel, S. (1983). Sublexical units and suprasegmental structure in speech production planning. In P. F. MacNeilage (Ed.), *The production of speech*. New York: Springer.

Appendix A

Experimental item-quartets

Quartet No.	High-freq. sets	Frequency counts		Low-freq. sets	Frequency counts	
		No. of occurrence	No. of summed frequency		No. of occurrence	No. of summed frequency
1	bin [bɪn]	6.4	127.26	bing [bɪŋ]	0.17	0.48
1	ning [nɪŋ]	23.5	1,192.57	nin [nɪn]	0.02	0.00
2	kem [kɛm]	1.48	62.24	kes [kɛs]	1.19	3.1
2	wes [ʋɛs]	3.24	162.60	wem [ʋɛm]	0.02	0.1
3	luk [lʏk]	1.74	209.14	lup [lʏp]	0.19	0.67
3	sup [sʏp]	4.17	82.55	suk [sʏk]	0.26	3.02
4	mer [mɛr]	5	313.12	meg [mɛx]	0.07	1.4
4	reg [rɛx]	8.19	339.86	rer [rɛr]	0.05	0.00

Note: All frequencies counts were obtained from the computer database CELEX (CEntre for LEXical Information), which has a Dutch lexicon based on 42 million word tokens. Syllable frequency was counted for phonetic syllables in Dutch. The phonetic script differentiates the reduced vowel schwa from full vowel forms, giving approximately 12,000 individual syllable forms. Syllable frequencies were calculated for the database from the word-form occurrences per million count. The syllable frequency ranges from 0 to approximately 90,000 per million words, with a mean frequency of 121. Two syllable frequency counts were calculated: The number of occurrences of each syllable (independent of the frequency of occurrence of the syllable in a particular word position, i.e., first or second syllable position within a word) and the number of the summed frequency of occurrence of each syllable (within words). Only instances that had in both scores comparable values were taken. The 8 high-frequency items ranged in the count for the number of occurrence (per one million words) from a value of 1.48 to 23.50 with an average of 6.72 ($SD = 7.15$) and for the count of the summed frequency of occurrence (per one million words) from a value from 62 to 1192.57 with an average of 311.18 ($SD = 369.99$). For the low-frequency-items the values in both counts were a follows: For the count number of occurrence (per one million words), low-frequency-items ranged from 0.02 to 1.19 with an average of 0.25 ($SD = 0.39$). For the count of summed frequency of occurrence (per million words), low-frequency items ranged from zero to 3.1 with an average of 1.1 ($SD = 1.3$). The four high-frequency syllables that served as second syllables had the following values in the two counts: li: 131 3476, ta: 89 2069, wa: 64 3254, jo: 54 1102. The first value gives the number of occurrence (per one million words), the second the summed frequency (per one million words).

Appendix B

Materials for experiment

Homogenous sets		Heterogeneous sets	
High-frequency	*Low-frequency*	*High-frequency*	*Low-frequency*
bin.ta [bɪn.ta]	bing.ta [bɪŋ.ta]	bin.ta [bɪn.ta]	bing.ta [bɪŋ.ta]
bin.li [bɪn.li]	bing.li [bɪŋ.li]	kem.li [kɛm.li]	kes.li [kɛs.li]
bin.wa [bɪn.ʋa]	bing.wa [bɪŋ.ʋa]	sup.wa [sʏp.ʋa]	suk.wa [sʏk.ʋa]
bin.jo [bɪn.jo]	bing.jo [bɪŋ.jo]	mer.jo [mɛr.jo]	meg.jo [mɛx.jo]
kem.ta [kɛm.ta]	kes.ta [kɛs.ta]	kem.ta [kɛm.ta]	kes.ta [kɛs.ta]
kem.li [kɛm.li]	kes.li [kɛs.li]	bin.li [bɪn.li]	bing.li [bɪŋ.li]
kem.wa [kɛm.ʋa]	kes.wa [kɛs.ʋa]	mer.wa [mɛr.ʋa]	meg.wa [mɛx.ʋa]
kem.jo [kɛm.jo]	kes.jo [kɛs.jo]	sup.jo [sʏp.jo]	suk.jo [sʏk.jo]
sup.ta [sʏp.ta]	suk.ta [sʏk.ta]	sup.ta [sʏp.ta]	suk.ta [sʏk.ta]
sup.li [sʏp.li]	suk.li [sʏk.li]	mer.li [mɛr.li]	meg.li [mɛx.li]
sup.wa [sʏp.ʋa]	suk.wa [sʏk.ʋa]	kem.wa [kɛm.ʋa]	kes.wa [kɛs.ʋa]
sup.jo [sʏp.jo]	suk.jo [sʏk.jo]	bin.jo [bɪn.jo]	bing.jo [bɪŋ.jo]
mer.ta [mɛr.ta]	meg.ta [mɛx.ta]	mer.ta [mɛr.ta]	meg.ta [mɛx.ta]
mer.li [mɛr.li]	meg.li [mɛx.li]	sup.li [sʏp.li]	suk.li [sʏk.li]
mer.wa [mɛr.ʋa]	meg.wa [mɛx.ʋa]	bin.wa [bɪn.ʋa]	bing.wa [bɪŋ.ʋa]
mer.jo [mɛr.jo]	meg.jo [mɛx.jo]	kem.jo [kɛm.jo]	kes.jo [kɛs.jo]
ning.ta [nɪŋ.ta]	nin.ta [nɪn.ta]	ning.ta [nɪŋ.ta]	nin.ta [nɪn.ta]
ning.li [nɪŋ.li]	nin.li [nɪn.li]	wes.li [ʋɛs.li]	wem.li [ʋɛm.li]
ning.wa [nɪŋ.ʋa]	nin.wa [nɪn.ʋa]	luk.wa [lʏk.ʋa]	lup.wa [lʏp.ʋa]
ning.jo [nɪŋ.jo]	nin.jo [nɪn.jo]	reg.jo [rɛx.jo]	rer.jo [rɛr.jo]
wes.ta [ʋɛs.ta]	wem.ta [ʋɛm.ta]	wes.ta [ʋɛs.ta]	wem.ta [ʋɛm.ta]
wes.li [ʋɛs.li]	wem.li [ʋɛm.li]	ning.li [nɪŋ.li]	nin.li [nɪn.li]
wes.wa [ʋɛs.ʋa]	wem.wa [ʋɛm.ʋa]	reg.wa [rɛx.ʋa]	rer.wa [rɛr.ʋa]
wes.jo [ʋɛs.jo]	wem.jo [ʋɛm.jo]	luk.jo [lʏk.jo]	lup.jo [lʏp.jo]
luk.ta [lʏk.ta]	lup.ta [lʏp.ta]	luk.ta [lʏk.ta]	lup.ta [lʏp.ta]
luk.li [lʏk.li]	lup.li [lʏp.li]	reg.li [rɛx.li]	rer.li [rɛr.li]
luk.wa [lʏk.ʋa]	lup.wa [lʏp.ʋa]	wes.wa [ʋɛs.ʋa]	wem.wa [ʋɛm.ʋa]
luk.jo [lʏk.jo]	lup.jo [lʏp.jo]	ning.jo [nɪŋ.jo]	nin.jo [nɪn.jo]
reg.ta [rɛx.ta]	rer.ta [rɛr.ta]	reg.ta [rɛx.ta]	rer.ta [rɛr.ta]
reg.li [rɛx.li]	rer.li [rɛr.li]	luk.li [lʏk.li]	lup.li [lʏp.li]
reg.wa [rɛx.ʋa]	rer.wa [rɛr.ʋa]	ning.wa [nɪŋ.ʋa]	nin.wa [nɪn.ʋa]
reg.jo [rɛx.jo]	rer.jo [rɛr.jo]	wes.jo [ʋɛs.jo]	wem.jo [ʋɛm.jo]

LANGUAGE AND COGNITIVE PROCESSES
2009, 24 (5), 685–712

Ψ Psychology Press
Taylor & Francis Group

Exploring phonological encoding through repeated segments

Markus F. Damian and Nicolas Dumay

University of Bristol, Bristol, UK

Five experiments explored the influence of repeated phonemes on the production of short utterances. In Experiment 1 coloured object naming showed faster latencies when colour and object started with the same phoneme ('green goat') than when they did not; the opposite was found when colour and object were named on consecutive trials ('green' – 'goat'). Experiments 2 and 3 focused on adjective-noun phrases and showed no effect of repeated phonemes on either acoustical duration of speeded responses, or latencies in a delayed variant of the task, suggesting a higher-level – rather than articulatory – locus of the effect. Experiments 4 and 5 demonstrated that the facilitation induced by repeated segments is not specific to word onset ('green chain') and is independent of whether or not the repeated phonemes occupy the same within-word position ('green flag'). These results indicate that in the production of multiple words, word forms are concurrently activated and evoke phonological segments represented in a position-nonspecific manner.

Keywords: Phonological encoding; Repetition priming; Spoken production.

Speaking involves the retrieval of phonological word forms, their conversion into phonological segments, and subsequent articulation. One way to make inferences as to the content of the involved representations is to manipulate the relationship between preceding or co-occurring context and the utterance to be spoken. For instance, in the picture-word interference paradigm speakers name objects while distractor words are visually or auditorily presented. Words which are form-related to the object name generally

Correspondence should be addressed to Markus F. Damian, University of Bristol, Department of Experimental Psychology, 12a Priory Road, Bristol BS8 1TU, UK. E-mail: m.damian@bristol.ac.uk

This research was supported by grant BB/C508477/1 from the Biotechnology and Biological Sciences Research Council (BBSRC) to the first author.

Nicolas Dumay is now at the University of Kent at Canterbury.

http://www.psypress.com/lcp   DOI: 10.1080/01690960802351260

accelerate response latencies, compared with an unrelated condition (e.g., Rayner & Posnansky, 1978), and this is whatever the position of the common portion, i.e., initial vs. final (e.g., Damian & Dumay, 2007; Meyer & Schriefers, 1991). The most likely account of this phenomenon is that the distractor word activates its corresponding phonological segments, which in the case of target-distractor overlap benefits target retrieval (see Starreveld, 2000, for a detailed discussion of several variants on this idea). Other facilitatory effects come from words presented prior to target onset (Collins & Ellis, 1992), from masked words (e.g., Ferrand, Segui, & Grainger, 1996), from ignored pictures superimposed upon target pictures (Meyer & Damian, 2007; Morsella & Miozzo, 2002), and phonological neighbours (e.g., Vitevitch, 2002; see also Gaskell & Dumay, 2002). In all these instances, the plausible explanation is that, in speaking, either the target word form or encoding of segments is accelerated by the redundant information.

However, there appear to be specific circumstances under which form overlap has been found to exert an inhibitory force in spoken production. For instance, Meyer and Gordon (1985) asked speakers to prepare to say a syllable pair (e.g., ub-ut). On a subset of the critical trials, they were cued to produce the pair in reverse order. Longer latencies and higher error rates were found when consonants of a syllable pair shared voicing or place of articulation than when they did not (see also Yaniv, Meyer, Gordon, Huft, & Sevald, 1990, using this technique to assess consonant and vowel similarity). O'Seaghdha, Dell, Peterson, and Juliano (1992) had speakers prepare for production one of two words ('cap-tin') presented on a computer screen. On two-thirds of the trials a cue prompted production of the prepared word ('cap'); on the other third of the trials another word was presented instead of the cue, which participants had to name as quickly as possible. Compared with an unrelated condition, latencies were longer when the new word ('can') started by the same sound as the prepared word, but not when it started by the same sound as the unprepared word ('till'). Sevald and Dell (1994) required participants to recite sequences of four CVCs as quickly as possible in eight seconds, and measured how many CVCs could be recited. Compared to a condition in which consonants were not repeated, repeated initial consonants (PICK-PUN-PUCK-PIN) decreased speech rate, whereas repeated final consonants (PICK-TUCK-PUCK-TICK) increased it. Sullivan and Riffel (1999) and Wheeldon (2003) investigated the effects of producing a word onto subsequent naming of a form-related or unrelated target picture. Both studies found an inhibitory effect on naming latencies in the case of initial overlap (CAT-CAP); in the case of final overlap (CAT-HAT), Sullivan and Riffel found reduced inhibition, whereas Wheeldon obtained significant facilitation.

Post-selective inhibition, i.e., the idea that segments enter a refractory period just after they are evoked, constitutes a potential mechanism accounting for the finding of inhibitory effects. However, this explanation does not account for the observed asymmetry between the effect of initial overlap (inhibitory) and final overlap (facilitatory, or at least not inhibitory to the same extent). To date, the most plausible account hinges on the mis-cueing of the target's final mismatching segments. According to Sevald and Dell's (1994) sequential cueing model (SCM), a variant of the interactive framework proposed by Dell (1986), attempting to say PIN having just said PICK involves activation of the constituent segments /p/, /i/, /n/, and because words and phonemes are bidirectionally connected (and hence induce feedback), the common phonemes will re-activate the still-active prime PICK. As a consequence, PICK will now mis-cue the final segment of the target, /n/, resulting in inhibition. As the model assumes that phonemes are sequentially activated, non-initial overlap has no such inhibitory effect: attempting to say TICK when having said PICK ensues no mis-cueing because by the time activation has fed back from the common segments to the word level and re-activated the prime PICK, nothing in the word remains to be mis-cued.

Recently Damian and Dumay (2007; Experiment 3) investigated potential effects of repeated phonemes within a coloured picture naming paradigm. Speakers produced adjective-noun phrases corresponding to the colour and object presented; the critical manipulation was whether the initial phonemes matched ('green goat') or not ('red goat'). The reasoning was that if this manipulation exerts an influence on the naming performance, it would imply that both phonological forms of the utterance were co-activated by the time articulation started, possibly yielding information about the extent of advance planning. Based on the evidence reviewed above, two effects were potentially at work in this situation: on the one hand, the redundancy in phonemes could render their selection easier; on the other, the word-initial overlap may cause a mis-cueing of the target's mismatching segments, as predicted by the SCM (Sevald & Dell, 1994). The results of this experiment showed a substantial facilitatory effect of phoneme repetition, suggesting that at the time a response was initiated, the phonological codes of the noun portion had already been activated.

The inference advocated in Damian and Dumay (2007) is that speakers plan an adjective-noun utterance in its entirety before initiating an articulatory response, an assertion consistent with the analysis of antici-patory speech errors (see Nooteboom & Quené, 2008, for a recent review). However, a similar facilitatory effect with coloured picture displays has recently been observed when participants named only the colour, but not the object (Janssen, Alario, & Caramazza, 2008; Navarrete & Costa, 2005), suggesting activation of word forms which are not part of the utterance. This possibility is compatible with similar recent studies in which one of two overlapping pictures are named, and phonological relatedness between target and distractor picture ('bed-bell') facilitates latencies (Meyer & Damian, 2007; Morsella & Miozzo, 2002). Roelofs (2008) also obtained this pattern, but found no effect of phonological relatedness when *both* pictures had to be named ('circle-circus'). Hence, the repeated phoneme effect shown in Damian and Dumay shows at minimum that the phonological content of the utterance is co-activated, but the implications for the issue of advance planning are less clear.

In the experiments reported below we capitalised on the effects of phoneme repetition in order to gain a more detailed insight into the nature of phonological encoding. The aim of the first experiment was to compare and contrast within- and between-utterance repetition effects with identical material. This allowed us to place the phenomenon observed by Damian and Dumay (2007) into broader perspective: as outlined above, Wheeldon (2003) and Sullivan and Riffel (1999) have shown between-trial inhibitory effects of repeated segments, and the mis-cueing of the target's final phonemes is the most plausible account of this phenomenon (Sevald & Dell, 1994). By contrast, in our previous study we found a facilitatory effect when the repeated phonemes occurred within the same utterance. Identifying the key factors responsible for this discrepancy is not straightforward, but two differences in the parameters of these experiments can be highlighted. First, the studies that reported inhibition looked at a perservatory phenomenon: namely, the ability to name a given word (e.g., CAT) having just named an onset-related word (e.g., CAP). This was not the case in our coloured picture naming task, where both instances of the repeated phoneme are part of the same response. The temporal interval between first and second occurrence of the critical segment was hence substantial in the trial-to-trial situation, and minimal in our paradigm. Second, and perhaps most important, in our task, the elements carrying the two instances of the repeated segments occur within the same utterance and therefore do not compete for the same temporal position within the prosodic frame. By contrast, in the trial-to-trial situation (and even in the segment blocking paradigm introduced by Sevald & Dell, 1994), every utterance contains a single word, and might compete for the same temporal position with the previous utterance. Hence, if this dimension is critical, within-trial situations should not give to rise to inhibitory effects.

In Experiment 2 and 3 our aim was to identify the processing level at which the facilitation induced by repeated segments within an utterance occurs. This effect could have at least two potential loci. First, it could be that the repeated instantiation of an abstract linguistic representation exerts a facilitatory effect on selection time. For instance, phonemes could be easier/faster to select if accessed more than once within a short period of time, or, assuming feedback connections from phonemes to word forms, access to word forms itself could benefit from the additional activation provided by the phonemic overlap. Second, the facilitatory effect could be due to lower-level processes: repeating a segment within the confines of a short utterance may incur articulatory consequences, simply because at the level of motor programming, the manipulation introduces a degree of redundancy.

We tackle this issue from two different angles. Experiment 2 capitalised on the acoustical durations of the utterances. The durational approach provides a measure of how articulatory execution unfolds over time, and investigating latencies and durations in conjunction allows insight into how response selection and execution relate to one another. This approach has been previously applied to investigations of rapid action sequences in spoken, manual or typed responses (e.g., Sternberg, Knoll, Monsell, & Wright, 1988; Sternberg, Monsell, Knoll, & Wright, 1978), and in tasks requiring the generation of linguistic or non-linguistic sequential keypresses (e.g., Fischman & Lim, 1991; Hulstijn & van Galen, 1983; Inhoff, Rosenbaum, Gordon, & Campbell, 1984; Pashler, 1994; Portier, van Galen, & Meulenbroek, 1990; Verwey, 1993). Specifically with regard to phono-logical encoding vs. articulation, it has been found that the acoustical durations of single-word (e.g., Damian, 2003) or multiple-word utterances (e.g., Schriefers & Teruel, 1999; Schriefers, de Ruiter, & Steigerwald, 1999, but see Ferreira & Swets, 2002) are generally unaffected by manipulations of semantic or phonological content. These findings suggest that in the production of short utterances, speakers plan the phonological code of the entire word, and subsequently translate it into articulatory programmes. Returning to the facilitatory influence of repeated segments, if this effect is due to co-activation of the adjective and noun phonology, then response durations should be unaffected. By contrast, a lower-level locus of the effect should manifest itself in parallel effects on response durations.

Investigating response durations in this task is of interest for a further reason. The trial-to-trial inhibitory effects documented in previous studies allow the possible prediction that encoding the adjective ('green') will inhibit, or mis-cue, encoding of a related subsequent noun ('goat'). In this case, while onset latencies of the utterance may be facilitated, response durations could plausibly be *prolonged*, simply because speakers might find it more difficult to encode the onset-related noun due to mis-cueing of the non-initial segments from the preceding adjective.

Experiment 3 investigates a possible articulatory locus of the effect of phoneme repetition by using a delayed naming task. In such a task participants are given ample time to prepare their response, and produce their answer – typically after variable delays – on presentation of a cue. This procedure is typically taken to allow speakers to complete all cognitive processes involved in identification and phonological encoding of the target prior to the onset of motor execution (e.g., Kemeny, Xu, Park, Hosey, Wettig, & Braun, 2006; Rastle, Croot, Harrington, & Coltheart, 2005). As a result, latencies in the delayed naming task should reflect only those components that occur subsequent to a speech motor plan having been compiled (e.g., Monsell, 1986; Sternberg et al., 1988).

We subsequently investigate whether the overlap effect is specific to the word-initial position, or whether it generalises to other positions. Previous studies investigating speech errors have revealed the so-called 'initialness effect'. Word-initial segments are more frequently involved in slips of the tongue and more prone to particular types of errors, such as exchanges (e.g., 'heft lemisphere', from Fromkin, 1971), than other parts of the word (Fudge, 1987; Garrett, 1975; MacKay, 1972; Shattuck-Hufnagel, 1987; Stemberger, 1985). As shown by Shattuck-Hufnagel (1987), this phenomenon is due to the word onset nature of segments, and as hypothesised by Dell, Juliano, and Govindjee (1993), it stems from the fact that, as a word is spoken, the uncertainty as to the identity of the segments gradually diminishes due to subsequent segments being cued by previous ones. Prominence of word onsets is also suggested by chronometric studies: as outlined above, Wheeldon (2003) showed inhibition from one trial to the next for initial overlap, but facilitation for rhyme overlap; Sullivan and Riffel (1999) showed substantially reduced inhibition for rhyming primes and targets, compared with the initial overlap condition. Damian and Dumay (2007) did not investigate whether in their coloured object naming paradigm, the facilitatory effect of phoneme repetition is specific to the initial position, or whether it can also be obtained for other positions. It may well be that initial segments are particularly susceptible to priming effects (in this case, by concurrently co-activated content of a subsequent word). Experiment 4 investigates this issue systematically by testing the effects of phoneme overlap in the initial, medial, or final condition.

Finally, Experiment 5 assesses whether the effect of phoneme repetition requires the two occurrences of the target phoneme to occupy the same within-word position, a question that directly relates to the way in which segment position is represented. The model of speech production brought forward by Dell and colleagues (e.g., Dell, 1986; Dell, Schwartz, Martin, Saffran, & Gagnon, 1997) implements a scheme in which phonemes are coded separately for within-word position; specifically, consonants are coded regarding whether they are pre- or postvocalic. In this framework, the facilitatory effect of phoneme repetition may be explained by hypothesising that the redundant phoneme receives activation from two sources – the adjective and the noun word form – resulting in more efficient selection. On the other hand, because segments are coded in a position-specific manner, a particular segment within the 'bank' of onset consonants (e.g., /g/ in 'green') will be entirely unrelated to the same segment occurring in the bank of coda consonants (/g/ in 'flag'). By contrast, the computational framework WEAVER (Levelt, Roelofs, & Meyer, 1999; Roelofs, 1997) only codes the sequential order of phonemes, but not directly their position within a word or syllable: a target word form activates in parallel all associated phonemes by means of numbered links which specify the sequential position within the word. In this model each segment is represented only once, but it can in principle be accessed more than once by means of multiple numbered links pointing to it (A. Roelofs, personal communication, November 2005). As far as we are aware, the situation of a particular phoneme appearing repeatedly within a word or utterance has not been explicitly modelled within this framework, however it appears plausible that the repeated segment will accrue additional activation compared with the unrelated case, resulting in faster phonological encoding. In sum, models which use position-specific coding predict that effects of repeated phonemes should be position-specific, i.e., they should only be observed if the critical segments occur within the same position in both words. By contrast, models which dispense with the assumption of CVC-specific coding predict that phoneme repetition should have a facilitatory influence even when repeated segments occupy different prosodic positions because the model exclusively encodes sequential position. We assessed this issue in a final experiment in which participants named, in the critical condition, objects which were paired with colours such that the first phoneme of the adjective, and the final phoneme of the name matched ('blue crab') or mismatched ('green crab').

EXPERIMENT 1

In the first experiment we directly contrasted within- and between-utterance phoneme repetition, using the same material. One group of participants named coloured objects with an adjective-noun phrase (cf. Damian & Dumay, 2007); another group used a modified procedure in which colour patches were named on prime trials, and black-and-white objects were named with bare nouns on target trials. Doing so allows us to gain insight into why segmental overlap has been previously shown to produce inhibitory effects in some cases, and facilitatory ones in others.

Method

Participants.   Twenty-four undergraduate students at the University of Bristol took part and received course credit. Twelve were randomly assigned to each utterance condition (adjective-noun vs. bare noun). All had normal or corrected-to-normal vision and were native speakers of English.

Materials.   Twenty line drawings of common objects with monosyllabic names were selected as targets, with an average length of 3.5 phonemes and a spoken CELEX (Baayen, Piepenbrock, & Gulikers, 1995) frequency of 18 per million. These were paired with the four colours blue, green, pink, and red. For the phonologically related condition, picture and colour names were paired such that the initial phoneme of colour and noun (and in two cases, also the following vowel) coincided (e.g., 'blue-bed'; the average overlap was 1.2 phonemes, or 34.8% of target length in phonemes). To form phonologically unrelated colour-object combinations, the colours and nouns were recombined such that the initial phoneme differed. In both conditions, care was taken to avoid obvious associations such as 'green-grass'. Appendix A shows a complete list of all combinations.

For the adjective-noun utterance group, target objects were presented with their lines coloured, and participants were instructed to name colour and object with an adjective-noun phrase (e.g., 'green bed'). For the bare noun group, the same colour and noun combinations were used, but trials alternated between prime trials on which a colour patch was named with an adjective, and target trials on which an object presented in black-on-white was named with a bare noun.

Design.   The experimental design included utterance format (adjective-noun vs. bare noun) as a between-participants and within-items variable, and colour-noun phonological relatedness (related vs. unrelated) as a within-participants and within-items variable. Each target object was presented under each of the two conditions once, yielding a total of 40 critical target trials per participant. Another 80 filler trials were created by pairing each picture twice with the two other phonologically unrelated colours, thereby ensuring a fairly low proportion (16.7%) of pictures paired with a phonologically related colour. Altogether, the experiment included 120 trials in the adjective-noun variant and 240 trials (120 primes and 120 target) in the bare noun variant.

Procedure.   Stimuli were presented from an IBM-compatible computer on a 17-inch monitor using DMDX 3.0 (Forster & Forster, 2003). The objects were digitised as line drawings to a size of approximately 8×8 cm and were presented on light grey background with their lines drawn in black in the bare noun group, or in blue, green, pink, or red in the adjective-noun group. Colour patches in the bare noun group were presented as squares of approximately 5×5 cm size. A headset (Sennheiser mb40) with attached microphone was connected to the computer, and DMDX determined the onset of each vocal response to the nearest millisecond.

Participants were first familiarised with the 20 target objects, followed by a first practice block in which each object was named once. Then, patches of the four target colours were shown on the screen. In the adjective-noun group participants were instructed that from now on the pictures would be presented with coloured lines, and they should name both with an adjective-noun utterance; 10 practice trials followed in which a random subset of the targets was shown in a colour phonologically unrelated to the target name. In the bare noun group participants were instructed that they would alternate between trials on which either the colour patches or the target pictures would have to be named. Twenty practice trials followed in which a random subset of ten targets alternated with colour patches. Then, the experimental trials were administered. A new pseudorandom trial sequence was generated for each participant such that neither the same colour nor the same object appeared on subsequent trials in the adjective-noun group, or trial pairs in the bare noun group.

On all trials, a fixation cross was presented for 500 ms. After a blank period of 500 ms, either the colour patch or the target object were shown for 1800 ms. Response latencies were measured relative to target onset. Following each naming response, the experimenter judged the response to be either correct or incorrect; incorrect responses consisted of responses other than the expected ones, repairs, stuttering, or mouth clicks. The intertrial interval was 1500 ms.

Results and discussion

Trials with responses judged to be incorrect by the experimenter for the reasons described above were excluded from the latency analysis (3.7%). Latencies faster than 250 ms or slower than 1500 ms were considered outliers and eliminated (3.4%). Table 1 displays the results, suggesting a facilitatory effect of Relatedness in adjective-noun utterances, contrasting with an inhibitory effect in bare noun utterances.

Analyses of variance (ANOVAs) conducted on the mean naming latencies, with utterance format and colour-noun phonological relatedness as variables, showed a main effect of Utterance Format, $F_1(1, 22) = 9.92$, $MSE = 342,524$, $p = .005$; $F_2(1, 19) = 198.53$, $MSE = 540,005$, $p < .001$, with latencies 169 ms slower in the adjective-noun than in the bare noun group.

TABLE 1

Results of Experiment 1. Response latencies (in ms) and error percentages (in per cent); standard deviations in parentheses

Utterance format	Related	Unrelated	Difference (Unrelated–Related)
Latencies			
Adjective-noun	774 (173)	811 (180)	+37
Bare noun	638 (64)	610 (70)	−28
Errors			
Adjective-noun	3.8 (4.8)	6.3 (6.1)	+2.5
Bare noun	2.1 (3.3)	2.5 (4.5)	+0.4

No main effect of Relatedness was found, both Fs < 1. Crucially, a significant interaction between Utterance Format and Relatedness was found, $F_1(1, 22) = 21.46$, $MSE = 12,690$, $p < .001$; $F_2(1, 19) = 5.26$, $MSE = 16,953$, $p = .033$. Simple effects of the factor Relatedness, assessed separately on each level of the factor Utterance Format, showed that for the adjective-noun group, the facilitatory effect of 37 ms was significant, $F_1(1, 11) = 10.94$, $MSE = 8,161$, $p = .007$; $F_2(1, 19) = 3.38$, $MSE = 10,570$, $p = .082$, and so was, for the bare noun group, the inhibitory effect of 28 ms, $F_1(1, 11) = 10.90$, $MSE = 4,757$, $p = .007$; $F_2(1, 19) = 4.40$, $MSE = 8405$, $p = .049$.

Similar ANOVAs conducted on the error scores showed a main effect of Utterance Format which was marginally significant in the analysis by participants, $F_1(1, 22) = 3.04$, $MSE = 88$, $p = .096$; and significant by items, $F_2(1, 38) = 4.44$, $MSE - 147$, $p = .042$, with more errors in the adjective-noun group (5.0%) than in the bare noun group (2.3%). No main effect of Relatedness was found, $F_1 = 1.50$, $p = .233$; $F_2 = 1.21$, $p = .286$, and no interaction between Utterance Format and Relatedness, both Fs < 1. It should be noted that for the adjective-noun group, error rates were numerically reduced by 2.5%, in the related condition compared with the unrelated condition, which closely mirrors the pattern reported by Damian and Dumay (2007, Experiment 3; a reduction of 2.7% in the group without a response deadline).

The results for the adjective-noun utterance group clearly replicate those previously reported in Damian and Dumay (2007): repetition of the initial phoneme of adjective and noun induces a substantial facilitatory influence. This effect implies that speakers had co-activated the two word forms of the utterance before initiating a response. By contrast, in the production of alternating adjectives and nouns, repetition of word-initial phonemes exerts a clear inhibitory influence on noun latencies. Hence repeated phonemes can cause both trial-to-trial perseveratory inhibition effects, and within-utterance anticipatory facilitation effects, thereby suggesting that occurrence of the repeated element within or outside an utterance is a key factor.

These findings raise the challenge of accommodating both types of forces in a computational framework of phonological encoding. Specifically, the perseveratory phoneme mis-cueing mechanism brought forward by Sevald and Dell (1994) to account for the inhibitory effect *prima facie* should also apply to the within-utterance constellation; in turn, the most likely explanation for the facilitatory within-utterance effect – segmental overlap benefiting word form or phoneme selection – may also emerge in the between-utterance situation. We will return to this issue in the General Discussion, and we will outline the constraints that our findings provide on existing computational models of speaking.

EXPERIMENT 2

In the second experiment, we tested the effects of repeated phonemes in coloured object naming, digitally recorded all responses, and manually determined adjective onset, noun onset, and offset. This procedure allowed us to derive individual duration measures for the adjective and the noun portion. To reiterate, finding that repeated phonemes affect latencies, but not durations would imply that this effect resides at an abstract linguistic level, rather than at the articulatory stage.

Method

Participants.   Twelve undergraduate students at the University of Bristol, none of whom had been in the first experiment, took part and received course credit. All had normal or corrected-to-normal vision and were native speakers of English.

Materials, design and procedure.   These were identical to the adjective-noun utterance condition of Experiment 1, except that DMDX digitally recorded each oral response for further analysis.

Results and discussion

For each trial, three latencies (adjective onset, noun onset, and response offset) were measured through audio-visual inspection of the waveform. Incorrect responses were excluded from the latency analysis (1.5%). Adjective onset latencies faster than 250 ms or slower than 1500 ms were considered outliers and eliminated (0.6%); the corresponding other measures for these trials were also deleted. Durations were computed as the difference between onset and offset latencies. Table 2 displays the results, showing a substantial effect of phoneme repetition which emerges in virtually identical strength in adjective onset, noun onset, and response offset; adjective, noun, and overall duration appear unaffected by the relatedness manipulation.

ANOVAs were conducted on the latencies, with Measure (adjective onset, noun onset, offset) and Relatedness as variables. The results showed an effect of Measure, $F_1(2, 22) = 367.03$, $MSE = 3{,}667{,}808$, $p < .001$; $F_2(2, 38) = 1742.60$, $MSE = 6{,}074{,}466$, $p < .001$, and of Relatedness, $F_1(1, 11) = 18.44$, $MSE = 35{,}277$, $p = .001$; $F_2(1, 19) = 8.75$, $MSE = 56{,}124$, $p = .008$, but crucially no interaction, both $Fs < 1$.

Further analyses were conducted on response durations, with Measure (adjective duration vs. noun duration) and Relatedness as variables. The results showed an effect of Measure, $F_1(1, 11) = 107.17$, $MSE = 369{,}217$, $p < .001$; $F_2(1, 19) = 103.42$, $MSE = 616{,}083$, $p < .001$, but neither an effect

TABLE 2
Results of Experiment 2. Adjective and noun onset and offset latencies (in ms),
adjective, noun and overall duration (in ms) and error percentages (in per cent);
standard deviations in parentheses

Measure	Related	Unrelated	Difference (Unrelated–Related)
Onset$_{adjective}$	823 (130)	870 (155)	+47
Onset$_{noun}$	1130 (167)	1170 (188)	+40
Offset	1599 (245)	1645 (269)	+46
Duration$_{adjective}$	301 (49)	300 (51)	−1
Duration$_{noun}$	475 (91)	477 (76)	+2
Duration$_{overall}$	775 (108)	775 (108)	0
Errors	0.8 (1.9)	2.2 (3.6)	+1.4

of Relatedness, nor an interaction between Measure and Relatedness, all $Fs < 1$.

Analyses conducted on the error scores showed no significant effect of Relatedness, $F_1 = 1.07$, $p = .322$; $F_2 = 1.97$, $p = .176$.

The results for utterance onset latencies again show a facilitatory effect of phoneme repetition. The durational analysis by contrast shows that the relatedness manipulation affected neither adjective, nor noun, nor overall duration. This is the outcome predicted under the assumption that speakers co-activate both word forms, and complete preparation of the response before initiating articulation. In turn, we are able to rule out the possibility that repeated articulation may have incurred a benefit at the motoric level, which should have resulted in shortened durations. Moreover, this finding makes it unlikely that evocation of the initial phoneme may have mis-cued selection of a subsequent matching segment, which should have resulted in prolonged durations. The absence of an effect on acoustical durations suggests that the latency effect of repeated segments resides exclusively at the level of phonological encoding.

EXPERIMENT 3

Experiment 3 tackled the same issue as Experiment 2 by using a version of the coloured picture naming task in which responses were fully prepared and produced upon presentation of a cue. If the effect of phoneme repetition found with immediate responses resides at the level of phonological encoding, it should be eliminated with delayed responses.

Method

Participants.   Twelve undergraduate students at the University of Bristol, none of whom had been in the experiments described above, took part and received course credit. All had normal or corrected-to-normal vision and were native speakers of English.

Materials, design and procedure.   These were identical to Experiment 2, except that on each trial the coloured object was presented for 500 ms, and speakers were asked to prepare the corresponding adjective-noun utterance and to produce it only upon visual presentation of an exclamation mark. The cue appeared at either 1 s, 2 s, or 3 s after target onset; all critical items were presented under the 2 s cue.

Results and discussion.   Incorrect trials were extremely rare (0.2%). Latencies faster than 200 ms or slower than 1000 ms were considered outliers and eliminated (1.2%). The results showed a mean of 487 ms for the related condition, and of 488 ms for the unrelated condition; the difference was not significant, both Fs < 1. Under the assumption that the delayed version eliminates lexical contributions and isolates articulatory components of spoken production, the results confirm the inference drawn from the second experiment, namely that the phoneme repetition effect can be safely attributed to the pre-articulatory level.

EXPERIMENT 4

Having established that the effects of phoneme overlap reside at the level of phonological encoding, Experiment 4 assessed the extent to which they are specific to word onsets, or can be obtained in non-initial positions. As summarised in the Introduction, some findings from speech errors and experimental studies suggest a special prominence for the word-initial position. To investigate whether this is also the case with the repeated segment effect, here we manipulated phoneme overlap in the initial, medial, or final positions.

Method

Participants.   Twenty-two undergraduate students at the University of Bristol, none of whom had been in the experiments described above, took part and received course credit. All had normal or corrected-to-normal vision and were native speakers of English.

Materials, design and procedure.   For the 'initial overlap' condition, 12 line drawings of common objects with monosyllabic names were selected as targets, with a spoken CELEX frequency of 13 per million and an average length of 3.2 phonemes. These were presented in either red, green, or black, such that the initial phoneme either matched ('black boat') or mismatched ('green boat'). For the 'medial overlap' condition, another 12 objects (spoken CELEX frequency: 12 per million; average length: 3.3 phonemes) were selected such that the central vowel of colour adjective and name matched ('black pan') or mismatched ('red pan'). Finally, for the 'final overlap' condition, 12 other objects (spoken CELEX frequency: 8 per million; average length: 3.6 phonemes) were selected such that the final consonant of colour adjective and name matched ('black monk') or mismatched ('red monk'). The design included Relatedness (related vs. unrelated) as a within-participants and within-items variable, and Overlap position (initial, medial, final) as a within-participants, but between-items variable. The combination of 3×12 targets and the Relatedness manipulation resulted in 72 critical trials. A further 36 filler trials were added in which objects were presented together with the remaining unrelated colour, resulting in a total of 108 trials per experimental session. The procedure was identical to Experiment 2.

Results and discussion

Incorrect responses were eliminated from the latency analysis (2.6%). Latencies faster than 250 ms or slower than 1500 ms were considered outliers and eliminated (2.3%). Table 3 shows the results, suggesting largely comparable effects for the three overlap conditions.

ANOVAs were conducted on the mean naming latencies, with Relatedness and Overlap position as variables. A significant effect of Relatedness was

TABLE 3
Results of Experiment 4. Response latencies (in ms) and error percentages (in per cent); standard deviations in parentheses

Position of overlap	Related	Unrelated	Difference (Unrelated–Related)
Latencies			
Initial	771 (133)	796 (122)	+25
Medial	740 (105)	762 (99)	+22
Final	755 (120)	775 (112)	+20
Errors			
Initial	6.1 (5.9)	4.5 (3.3)	−1.6
Medial	1.5 (3.3)	0.8 (2.5)	−1.7
Final	1.5 (3.3)	1.1 (2.9)	−0.4

found, $F_1(1, 21) = 8.39$, $MSE = 16,342$, $p = .009$, $F_2(1, 33) = 14.00$, $MSE = 8,915$, $p < .001$, with latencies being 22 ms faster in the related than in the unrelated condition. The effect of Overlap position was significant in the analysis by participants, $F_1(2, 42) = 4.71$, $MSE = 11,830$, $p = .014$, but not by items, $F_2 = 1.52$, $p = .234$. Note that the manipulation of overlap position involved three different sets of pictures only matched in terms of the spoken frequency and length in phonemes of the corresponding labels, hence a main effect is difficult to interpret. Importantly, the interaction between Relatedness and Overlap position was not significant, both $Fs < 1$.

ANOVAs on the errors indicated no effect of Relatedness, $F_1 = 1.63$, $p = .216$, $F_2 < 1$, and an effect of Overlap position that was significant by participants, $F_1(2, 42) = 13.02$, $MSE = 244$, $p < .001$; but not by items, $F_2 < 1$. The interaction between Relatedness and Overlap position was not significant, both $Fs < 1$.

The results clearly indicate that the facilitatory effect of phoneme repetition within an utterance is not confined to the word-initial position – a statistically equivalent benefit is obtained when the overlapping segments occupy the central or the final position within each word. Apparently, the properties of word-initial sounds which make them particularly error-prone do not affect their degree of susceptibility to priming from repeated instances.

EXPERIMENT 5

The experiment reported above demonstrates that the effect of phoneme repetition is not restricted to the initial position. The final experiment investigates whether the effect requires the two instances of the repeated phoneme to occupy the same within-word (or syllabic) position. Finding that the repeated phoneme effect is restricted to segments in matching positions would lend credibility to models which represent segments in a position-specific manner; by contrast, finding the effect even with mismatching segment positions would favour models which do not explicitly code segment position within a word or syllable.

Method

Participants. Twenty-four undergraduate students at the University of Bristol, none of whom had been in the experiments described above, took part and received course credit. All had normal or corrected-to-normal vision and were native speakers of English.

Materials, design and procedure. For the 'initial overlap' condition, 15 line drawings of common objects with monosyllabic names were selected as targets, with a spoken CELEX frequency of 23 per million and an average length of 3.2 phonemes. These were presented in either blue, green, or pink, such that the initial phoneme either matched ('green goat') or mismatched ('blue goat'). For the 'initial/final overlap' condition, 15 further objects (spoken CELEX frequency: 25 per million; average length: 3.1 phonemes) were selected such that the first phoneme of the adjective, and the final phoneme of the name matched ('blue crab') or mismatched ('green crab'). Due to severe constraints on stimulus selection, five pairs (four related and one unrelated) in the initial overlap and two unrelated pairs in the initial/final overlap condition also shared non-initial segments. A full list of the stimuli can be found in Appendix C. The design included Relatedness (related vs. unrelated) as a within-participants and within-items variable, and Overlap position (initial vs. initial/final) as a within-participants, but between-items variable. The combination of 2 × 15 targets and the Relatedness manipulation resulted in 60 critical trials. A further 30 filler trials were added in which objects were presented together with the remaining unrelated colour, resulting in a total of 90 trials per experimental session. The procedure was identical to Experiment 2.

Results and discussion

Incorrect responses were eliminated from the latency analysis (2.2%). Latencies faster than 250 ms or slower than 1500 ms were considered outliers and eliminated (2.3%). Table 4 shows the results. ANOVAs were conducted on the data, with Relatedness and Overlap position as variables. A significant effect of Relatedness was found, $F_1(1, 23) = 14.93$, $MSE = 15,069$, $p < .001$, $F_2(1, 28) = 6.91$, $MSE = 8,297$, $p = .014$. The effect of Overlap position was significant in the analysis by participants, $F_1(1, 23) = 12.33$, $MSE = 11,388$, $p = .002$, but not by items, $F_2(1, 28) = 2.36$, $p = .136$.

TABLE 4
Results of Experiment 5. Response latencies (in ms) and error percentages (in per cent); standard deviations in parentheses

Position of overlap	Related	Unrelated	Difference (Unrelated–Related)
Latencies			
Initial	768 (99)	801 (105)	+33
Initial/Final	798 (98)	815 (101)	+17
Errors			
Initial	2.5 (5.1)	2.2 (3.8)	−0.3
Initial/Final	1.7 (3.5)	2.2 (3.2)	+0.5

Importantly, there was no interaction between the two factors, $F_1(1, 23) =$ 1.10, $p = .305$, $F_2 < 1$.

Similar ANOVAs on the errors showed no significant effects, all $Fs < 1$.

These results suggest that the effect of phoneme repetition is largely independent of whether or not the involved segments occupy the same or different positions within the two words. The lack of an interaction between initial and initial/final condition suggests that statistically, the priming effect is equivalent in both cases. However, the repetition effect is numerically reduced in the initial/final, compared with the initial, condition. One explanation is that related stimulus pairs in the initial overlap condition had additional repeated segments whereas those in the initial/final overlap condition did not (see Materials), which could have inflated facilitation in the former case. An alternative account of this reduction hinges on the distance between the repeated phonemes: in the initial condition, an average of 2.7 phonemes separated the repeated segments, whereas in the initial/final condition, it was 4.8 phonemes (for comparison, in Experiment 1 and 2, the distance was 2.5; in Experiment 3 the distance was 2.6 for the initial condition, 2.0 for the medial condition, and 2.7 for the final position). Assuming sequential encoding of the segments, as in Sevald and Dell's (1994) model, and further assuming relatively rapid decay at the segmental level (see General Discussion), it is plausible to assume that the effects of phoneme repetition diminish with increasing sequential distance between the two instances. The crucial finding, however, is that the effect is not specific to segments which occupy the same position within adjective and noun.

The fact that priming can be obtained even when the two instances of the repeated element are acoustically quite distinct has important consequences for the way in which we conceive sublexical representations for spoken production. The received view is that segments constitute important phonological encoding units, i.e., that a speaker's memory explicitly represents abstract phonemes as such, and not merely bundles of features such as [+ voiced], [+ labial], etc. This view is largely based on the observation that most phonological speech errors consist of a single segment being anticipated, perseverated, shifted, exchanged, added, or deleted (e.g., Dell, 1986; Stemberger, 1982), and as a consequence most present psycholinguistic models (e.g., Dell, 1986; Levelt et al., 1999; Stemberger, 1982) postulate the existence of corresponding abstract phonemes (for an alternative view, see Dell et al., 1993). Evidence coming from experimental studies that would speak to the psychological reality of phonemes (e.g., Roelofs, 1999) is relatively scarce. In our Experiment 5, the repeated phonemes in utterances such as 'green flag' are positional allophones. Hence the observed facilitation constitutes strong evidence for the psychological reality of a segmental level which is rather abstract from the surface realisation of the corresponding sound. In our view, allophonic variation therefore must arise at a later processing stage, at which articulatory programmes are retrieved which take syllabic position into account (as assumed by, e.g., Levelt et al., 1999).

GENERAL DISCUSSION

In previous research (Damian & Dumay, 2007) we observed that when speakers name coloured objects with adjective-noun utterances, responses were faster when the initial segment of both words matched than when they mismatched. In the experiments reported in this article, we delineated the exact circumstances under which such an effect of phoneme repetition is obtained. In Experiment 1 we explicitly related this finding to previous reports which had shown inhibitory effects when spoken production of a word was preceded by a trial on which a response started by the same initial phoneme (e.g., Wheeldon, 2003). We demonstrated that when instead of coloured objects, colour patches and objects were named on consecutive trials, the effect of initial phoneme repetition was inhibitory. This raises the challenge – further expanded below – of accounting for both the facilitatory within-utterance effect, and the inhibitory trial-to-trial effect, within one and the same computational framework. The following experiments focused on the within-utterance case (i.e., adjective-noun phrases). The results indicate that under these circumstances both word forms are simultaneously co-activated, which is evidenced not only by the central observation that phoneme repetition exerts a facilitatory influence, but also by the finding from Experiment 2 that response duration is unaffected by the manipulation, and by the results from Experiment 3 demonstrating that the effect is eliminated in a delayed naming task. Finally, we investigated the extent to which the within-utterance phoneme repetition effect is specific to the word-initial position. Experiment 4 showed that the effect is essentially unchanged when the repeated phonemes occupy non-initial (but matching) positions within both words, and perhaps most interestingly, Experiment 5 demonstrated that repeated phonemes do not have to occupy congruent positions. These findings provide important constraints on how computational accounts of phonological encoding specify the representation of segments.

On the most general level, the observation that repetition of a phoneme within an utterance tends to have a facilitatory effect implies that at either the word form or the segment level, redundancy incurs a benefit. In a purely feedforward network, activated word forms transmit activation to corresponding segments. One possibility is that access to the repeated segment itself is facilitated, which would then reduce the overall time to encode the utterance. In the WEAVER framework (Roelofs, 1997) which has such feedforward properties, however, phonemes are not selected, but merely transmit activation to a subsequent syllabary level in which articulatory programmes corresponding to syllables are stored. These syllable programmes are assumed to engage in a competitive selection process, and it is possible that overlap at the phoneme level in a two-word utterance will increase activation levels of the corresponding syllables, implying faster response latencies. Alternatively, models of phonological encoding may specify feedback from segments to word forms, as is the case in Dell's (1986; Dell et al., 1997) framework. In this case, segmental overlap may facilitate the selection of word forms directly via backward spreading activation. Although Dell's model was not designed to account for latency data, it is easy to see how feedback from shared segments would increase the activation levels of both corresponding word nodes, which could cause reduced selection times if selection time was rendered activation-dependent. In sum, the general observation of a benefit from repeated phonemes can be accounted for by purely feedforward models, as well as those which specify feedback from segments to word forms.

A more specific issue arises from the finding that the repeated phoneme effect is apparently not confined to the redundant element occupying the same position within a word/syllable. This finding suggests that phonemes are not coded regarding their CVC position. WEAVER indeed codes phonemes in such a position-unspecific manner. Phonemes are activated in parallel via labelled links which specify only their sequential order. The activated phonemes then sequentially activate matching syllabic motor programmes. It is evident that the model principally makes the correct predictions – phoneme repetition effects should not be confined to matching word positions.

Dell's model by contrast stipulates a 'slot-based' scheme of segmental representation in which pre- and postvocalic consonants are coded by different banks of units. Consequently, two instances of the same phoneme occupying *different* positions within two words (e.g., /t/ in CAT vs. TIP) cannot benefit from the mutual co-activation that arises with matching segments occupying the same within-word position. Implementing a slot coding scheme in order to represent sequential order or spatial position is oftentimes characterised as a deliberately unrealistic simplification. For instance, several prominent models of visual word recognition have used such a scheme (e.g., McClelland & Rumelhart, 1981; Seidenberg & McClelland, 1989; see Plaut, McClelland, Seidenberg, & Patterson, 1996, for discussion), despite the fact that knowledge acquired through exposure and learning corresponding to one particular slot would not generalise to other slot positions. There also exists ample evidence which questions the underlying assumptions of slot coding in word reading (e.g., Frankish & Turner, 2007; Perea & Lupker, 2003, 2004; see Davis & Bowers, 2006, for a review).

In the case of Dell's model, restricting the exchange of activation to phonemes occupying the same slot within a word form is theoretically motivated, however: in speech errors, sounds almost always respect syllabic position when moving to a different syllable. To allow the model to produce sound errors which exhibit this characteristic, the model stipulates that consonants which can occur pre- or postvocalically are represented by two different instances. Dell (1986) states that 'This position encoding of consonants is an ad hoc mechanism that enables the model to handle the positional specificity of interference, the fact that initial and final consonants rarely substitute for one another' (p. 294). The results from our final experiment, however, suggest that the beneficial effect of within-utterance phoneme repetition does not rely on shared position within a word or syllable, which seems to contradict the principle instantiated in the model. In sum, the findings from Experiment 5 favour models which code segment position independently of their syllabic position.

A final issue is how to account for the inhibitory effects of phoneme repetition when occurring from a previous trial observed in the first experiment, in conjunction with the facilitatory effects of within-utterance phoneme repetition. The perhaps most obvious account of the inhibitory process – post-selective inhibition which may affect either word forms, or segments – does not hold because the effect differentially affects word-initial and word-final overlap (Sevald & Dell, 1994; Wheeldon, 2003). The only detailed account of this effect is provided by the SCM proposed by Sevald and Dell (1994), according to which phonemes get activated strictly in a sequential manner (cf. O'Seaghdha et al., 1992, for a similar account). When prime and target have the same onset, selection of the target's phonemes will re-activate the prime word due to feedback connections between the phonemic and the lexical level, and thereby will induce a mis-cueing of the target's final phonemes. By contrast, in the case of final overlap, the resonance induced between the target and its form-related words can only benefit the selection of the target's final segments.

Although this mechanism constitutes a plausible account of the specific empirical pattern that it was devised to explain, it achieves its goal by somewhat artificially restricting the selection process to just the word-final phoneme, with the assumption that selection of this phoneme controls much of the variance in responding (cf. O'Seaghdha et al., 1992, p. 392). Under this assumption, primes with word-initial overlap will indeed mis-cue selection of the critical target phoneme whereas primes with word-final overlap will facilitate its selection. But if all target phonemes are considered in conjunction, then phonemic overlap should have a generally beneficial effect on target selection. Compared to an unrelated sequence, both PICK-PIN and PICK-TICK should make retrieval of the *matching* segments easier because of feedforward activation. In addition, mis-cueing of word-final segments via feedback and re-activation of the prime may counteract the feedforward priming effect. In fact, the mis-cueing mechanism suggested by the SCM is likely to be less powerful than the feedforward priming due to overlap: the former requires three steps (from target word to corresponding segments, from shared segments to prime, from prime to mismatching target segments) whereas the latter requires only a single step (from primes/targets to their shared segments). The net result should hence be facilitation, not inhibition, in all cases.

A speculative account of the data reported here would assume that activation at the word and the segmental level undergoes different rates of decay. It is possible that activation at the segmental level is quite fleeting, and perhaps decays too quickly to show an effect from one trial to the next. The assumption that activation at the phoneme level undergoes rapid decay is in fact plausible, given that a rather small number of segment units must suffice to code all possible words, and persistent activation would hence favour segmental speech errors. On the other hand, lexical activation should arguably be more persistent because this is required for the generation of connected speech (note the 'episodic node' in O'Seaghdha et al.'s, 1992, simulation, which provides a temporary 'memory trace' of the priming episode). Assuming rapidly decaying segmental activation, but more persistent lexical activation, the principle advocated by the SCM could account for trial-to-trial effects that are inhibitory due to mis-cueing (the 'bare noun' condition in Experiment 1, as well as the inhibition shown in Wheeldon, 2003, arising from word-initial overlap with a previous response) or facilitatory (i.e., the priming effects shown by Wheeldon with word-final overlap with a previous response). By contrast, the activation of form-related items in close temporal proximity (as in the coloured picture naming task) would induce facilitation. The principle of differential decay rates for word forms and segments, although not currently part of the proposed computational models, could be implemented relatively easily. Such an account would be able to accommodate the results reported in this article, however, it would leave unexplained why Sevald and Dell (1994) found both decreased and increased speech rate in close temporal proximity.

An alternative account is based on the idea that sequential cueing and its potential inhibitory consequences can only apply if the two overlapping entities occupy the same position in the encoding (response) frame. This is clearly the case in the between-utterance condition of Experiment 1, where overlapping adjectives and nouns are produced as single-word responses on alternate trials, in Wheeldon's (2003) experiments in which nouns are produced on consecutive trials, and in Sevald and Dell's (1994) speeded repetition paradigm which involves the concatenation of single-word responses. Here, onset overlap would entail mis-cueing of the complementary segments and therefore would induce inhibition. By contrast, in the within-utterance situation, the two entities do not compete for the same portion of the encoding frame, as they are different parts of the same response. Here, with sequential mis-cueing disabled, there would be no obvious reason why onset overlap should induce inhibition. A problem with conceptualising this idea is that existing computational models of phonological encoding in their present form are blind as to whether or not activated lexical entities are part of the same utterance.

An interesting follow-up question based on our results is whether phoneme repetition also entails consequences when occurring within the same word, rather than within an utterance. In other words, is a picture of TRACTOR named faster than a picture of a TROLLEY, assuming a match on all other linguistic and non-linguistic variables? Based on our hypothesis that the repeated phoneme effect investigated above reflects accumulating activation between shared phonemes, we predict this to be the case. Furthermore, given our finding that the repeated phoneme priming is not primarily constrained by position within a word (or syllable), it should also be the case that CACTUS, in which the instances of the repeated phoneme occupy a different syllable position, is named faster than a matched control such as CARPET. Devising the corresponding experiments is unfortunately not trivial, due to the serious restrictions on stimulus selection with pictorial material. For instance, in the Snodgrass and Vanderwart (1980) picture set, less than 10% of those objects typically named with a single word (i.e., excluding responses such as 'frying pan') contain a repeated phoneme. Given that pictorial stimuli tend to have rather short labels in English, and in short words phonemes are typically not repeated, it will not be easy to identify the appropriate stimuli to address this issue empirically.

In summary, the results reported in this article suggest that the manipulation of phoneme redundancy in coloured picture naming constitutes a valuable vehicle for the investigation of phonological encoding in spoken production. This task provides information regarding the format of representations at the phonological level, the way in which position of these sublexical units is specified within a word, and how these interact with compatible word forms.

REFERENCES

Baayen, R. H., Piepenbrock, R., & Gulikers, L. (1995). *The CELEX lexical database* (Release 2) [CD-ROM]. Philadelphia, PA: Linguistic Data Consortium, University of Pennsylvania [Distributor].

Collins, A. F., & Ellis, A. W. (1992). Phonological priming of lexical retrieval in speech production. *British Journal of Psychology, 83*, 375–388.

Damian, M. F. (2003). Articulatory duration in single word speech production. *Journal of Experimental Psychology: Learning, Memory and Cognition, 29*, 416–431.

Damian, M. F., & Dumay, N. (2007). Time pressure and phonological advance planning in spoken production. *Journal of Memory and Language, 57*, 195–209.

Davis, C. J., & Bowers, J. S. (2006). Contrasting five different theories of letter position coding: Evidence from orthographic similarity effects. *Journal of Experimental Psychology: Human Perception and Performance, 32*, 535–557.

Dell, G. S. (1986). A spreading activation theory of retrieval in sentence production. *Psychological Review, 93*, 283–321.

Dell, G. S., Juliano, C., & Govindjee, A. (1993). Structure and content in language production: a theory of frame constraints in phonological speech errors. *Cognitive Science, 17*, 149–195.

Dell, G. S., Schwartz, M. F., Martin, N., Saffran, E. M., & Gagnon, D. A. (1997). Lexical access in aphasic and nonaphasic speakers. *Psychological Review, 104*, 801–838.

Ferrand, L., Segui, J., & Grainger, J. (1996). Masked priming of word and picture naming: The role of syllabic units. *Journal of Memory and Language, 35*, 708–723.

Ferreira, F., & Swets, B. (2002). How incremental is language production? Evidence from the production of utterances requiring the computation of arithmetic sums. *Journal of Memory and Language, 46*, 57–84.

Fischman, M. G., & Lim, C. H. (1991). Influence of extended practice on programming time, movement time, and transfer in simple target-striking responses. *Journal of Motor Behavior, 23*, 39–50.

Forster, K. I., & Forster, J. C. (2003). DMDX: A Windows display program with millisecond accuracy. *Behavior Research Methods, Instruments and Computers, 35*, 116–124.

Frankish, C., & Turner, E. (2007). SIHGT and SUNOD: The role of orthography and phonology in the perception of transposed letter anagrams. *Journal of Memory and Language, 56*, 189–211.

Fromkin, V. A. (1971). The nonanomalous nature of anomalous utterances. *Language, 47*, 27–52.

Fudge, E. C. (1987). Branching structure within the syllable. *Journal of Linguistics, 23*, 359–377.

Garrett, M. F. (1975). The analysis of sentence production. In G. H. Bower (Ed.), *The psychology of learning and motivation* (pp. 133–177). New York: Academic Press.

Gaskell, M. G., & Dumay, N. (2003). Effects of vocabulary acquisition on lexical competition in speech perception and production. In M. J. Solé, D. Recasens, & J. Romero (Eds.), *Proceedings of the 15th ICPhS Conference* (pp. 1485–1488). Adelaide, Australia: Causal Productions.

Hulstijn, W., & van Galen, G. P. (1983). Programming in handwriting: Reaction-time and movement time as a function of sequence length. *Acta Psychologica, 54*, 23–49.

Inhoff, A. W., Rosenbaum, D. A., Gordon, A. M., & Campbell, J. A. (1984). Stimulus response compatibility and motor programming of manual response sequences. *Journal of Experimental Psychology: Human Perception and Performance, 10*, 724–733.

Janssen, N., Alario, F. X., & Caramazza, A. (2008). A word-order constraint on phonological activation. *Psychological Science, 19*, 216–220.

Kemeny, S., Xu, J., Park, G. H., Hosey, L. A., Wettig, C. M., & Braun, A. R. (2006). Temporal dissociation of early lexical access and articulation using a delayed naming task – An fMRI study. *Cerebral Cortex, 16*, 587–595.

Levelt, W. J. M., Roelofs, A., & Meyer, A. S. (1999). A theory of lexical access in speech production. *Behavioral and Brain Sciences, 22*, 1–75.

MacKay, D. G. (1970). Spoonerisms: The structure of errors in the serial order of speech. *Neuropsychologia, 8*, 323–350.

MacKay, D. G. (1972). The structure of words and syllables: Evidence from errors in speech. *Cognitive Psychology, 3*, 210–227.

McClelland, J. L., & Rumelhart, D. E. (1981). An interactive activation model of context effects in letter perception: Part 1. An account of basic findings. *Psychological Review, 88*, 375–407.

Meyer, A. S., & Damian, M. F. (2007). Activation of distractor names in the picture-picture interference paradigm. *Memory and Cognition, 35*, 494–503.

Meyer, A. S., & Schriefers, H. (1991). Phonological facilitation in picture-word interference experiments: effects of stimulus onset asynchrony and types of interfering stimuli. *Journal of Experimental Psychology: Learning, Memory and Cognition, 17*, 1146–1160.

Meyer, D. E., & Gordon, P. C. (1985). Speech production: Motor programming of phonetic features. *Journal of Memory and Language, 224*, 3–26.

Monsell, S. (1986). Programming of complex sequences: Evidence from the timing of rapid speech and other productions. In H. Heuer & R. A. Schmidt (Eds.), *Generation and modulation of action patterns* (pp. 72–86). Berlin: Springer.

Morsella, E., & Miozzo, M. (2002). Evidence for a cascade model of lexical access in speech production. *Journal of Experimental Psychology: Learning, Memory and Cognition, 28*, 555–563.

Navarrete, E., & Costa, A. (2005). Phonological activation of ignored pictures: Further evidence for a cascade model of lexical access. *Journal of Memory and Language, 53*, 357–378.

Nooteboom, S., & Quené, H. (2008). Self-monitoring and feedback: A new attempt to find the main cause of lexical bias in phonological speech errors. *Journal of Memory and Language, 58*, 837–861.

O'Seaghda, P. G., Dell, G. S., Peterson, R., & Juliano, C. (1992). Models of form-related priming in comprehension and production. In R. G. Reilly & N. E. Sharkey (Eds.), *Connectionist approaches to natural language processing* (pp. 373–408). Hillsdale, NJ: Lawrence Erlbaum Associates.

Pashler, H. (1994). Overlapping mental operations in serial performance with preview. *Quarterly Journal of Experimental Psychology, 47*, 161–191.

Portier, S. J., van Galen, G. P., & Meulenbroek, R. G. J. (1990). Practice and the dynamics of handwriting performance: Evidence for a shift of motor programming load. *Journal of Motor Behavior, 22*, 474–492.

Perea, M., & Lupker, S. J. (2003). Does jugde activate COURT? Transposed-letter similarity effects in masked associative priming. *Memory and Cognition, 31*, 829–841.

Perea, M., & Lupker, S. J. (2004). Can CANISO activate CASINO? Transposed-letter similarity effects with nonadjacent letter positions. *Journal of Memory and Language, 51*, 231–246.

Plaut, D. C., McClelland, J. L., Seidenberg, M., & Patterson, K. (1996). Understanding normal and impaired word reading: computational principles in quasi-regular domains. *Psychological Review, 103*, 56–115.

Rastle, K., Croot, K. P., Harrington, J. M., & Coltheart, M. (2005). Characterizing the motor execution stage of speech production: Consonantal effects on delayed naming latency and onset duration. *Journal of Experimental Psychology: Human Perception and Performance, 31*, 1083–1095.

Rayner, K., & Posnansky, C. (1978). Stages of processing in word identification. *Journal of Experimental Psychology: General, 107*, 64–80.

Roelofs, A. (1997). The WEAVER model of word-form encoding in speech production. *Cognition, 64*, 249–284.

Roelofs, A. (1999). Phonological segments and features as planning units in speech production. *Language and Cognitive Processes, 14*, 173–200.

Roelofs, A. (2008). Tracing attention and the activation flow in spoken word planning using eye movements. *Journal of Experimental Psychology: Learning, Memory and Cognition, 34*, 353–368.

Schriefers, H., & Teruel, E. (1999). Phonological facilitation in the production of two-word utterances. *European Journal of Cognitive Psychology, 11*, 17–50.

Schriefers, H., de Ruiter, J. P., & Steigerwald, M. (1999). Parallelism in the production of noun phrases: experiments and reaction time models. *Journal of Experimental Psychology: Learning, Memory and Cognition, 25*, 702–720.

Seidenberg, M. S., & McClelland, J. L. (1989). A distributed developmental model of word recognition. *Psychological Review, 96*, 523–568.

Sevald, C. A., & Dell, G. S. (1994). The sequential cuing effect in speech production. *Cognition, 53*, 91–127.

Shattuck-Hufnagel, S. (1987). The role of word onset consonants in speech production planning: New evidence from speech error patterns. In E. Keller & M. Gopnik (Eds.), *Motor and sensory processing language.* Hillsdale, NJ: Lawrence Erlbaum Associates.

Snodgrass, J. G., & Vanderwart, M. (1980). A standardized set of 260 pictures: norms for name agreement, image agreement, familiarity, and visual complexity. *Journal of Experimental Psychology: Human Learning and Memory, 6*, 174–215.

Starreveld, P. A. (2000). On the interpretation of onsets of auditory context effects in word production. *Journal of Memory and Language, 42*, 497–525.

Stemberger, J. P. (1982). *The lexicon in a model of language production.* Unpublished doctoral dissertation, University of California, San Diego.

Stemberger, J. P. (1985). An interactive activation model of language production. In A. W. Ellis (Ed.), *Progress in the psychology of language* (Vol. 1, pp. 143–186). Hillsdale, NJ: Lawrence Erlbaum Associates, Inc.

Sternberg, S., Knoll, R. L., Monsell, S., & Wright, C. E. (1988). Motor programs and hierarchical organization in the control of rapid speech. *Phonetica, 45*, 175–197.

Sternberg, S., Monsell, S., Knoll, R. L., & Wright, C. E. (1978). The latency and duration of rapid movement sequences: Comparisons of speech and typewriting. In G. Stelmach (Ed.), *Information processing in motor control learning* (pp. 117–152). New York: Academic Press.

Sullivan, M. P., & Riffel, B. (1999). The nature of phonological encoding during spoken word retrieval. *Language and Cognitive Processes, 14*, 15–45.

Verwey, W. B. (1993). Effects of extended practice in a one finger keypressing task. *Acta Psychologica, 84*, 179–197.

Vitevitch, M. S. (2002). The influence of phonological similarity neighborhoods on speech production. *Journal of Experimental Psychology: Learning, Memory and Cognition, 28*, 735–747.

Wheeldon, L. (2003). Inhibitory form priming of spoken word production. *Language and Cognitive Processes, 18*, 81–109.

Yaniv, I., Meyer, D. E., Gordon, P. C., Huft, C. A., & Sevald, C. A. (1990). Vowel similarity, connectionist models, and syllable structure in motor programming of speech. *Journal of Memory and Language, 29*, 1–26.

APPENDIX A

Stimuli used in Experiment 1, 2, and 3

Phonologically related	Phonologically unrelated	Target
blue	green	ball
blue	green	bed
blue	pink	boot
blue	red	broom
blue	red	bus
green	blue	glass
green	blue	globe
green	pink	glove
green	red	goat
green	pink	gun
pink	blue	pen
pink	green	pill
pink	green	pin
pink	red	pipe
pink	red	purse
red	blue	rake
red	green	rat
red	pink	ring
red	blue	rope
red	pink	rug

APPENDIX B

Stimuli used in Experiment 4

Phonologically related	Phonologically unrelated	Target
INITIAL CONSONANT OVERLAP		
black	green	boat
black	green	broom
black	red	bus
black	red	bow
green	red	glove
green	black	goat
green	black	goose
green	red	glass
red	black	rug
red	green	rake
red	black	rat
red	green	rope

VOWEL OVERLAP

black	red	pan
black	green	tap
black	red	fan
black	green	hat
green	red	wheel
green	black	sheep
green	black	teeth
green	red	cheese
red	green	leg
red	black	vest
red	green	belt
red	black	tent

FINAL CONSONANT OVERLAP

black	red	monk
black	green	mask
black	red	sock
black	green	duck
green	black	chain
green	red	crown
green	black	pen
green	red	swan
red	black	sword
red	green	bird
red	green	cloud
red	black	squid

APPENDIX C

Stimuli used in Experiment 5

Phonologically related	Phonologically unrelated	Target
INITIAL CONSONANT OVERLAP		
blue	green	ball
blue	pink	bed
blue	pink	bell
blue	green	bowl
blue	pink	bus
green	pink	glass
green	blue	globe
green	pink	glove
green	blue	goat
green	blue	gun
pink	blue	pen
pink	green	pill
pink	blue	pin
pink	green	pipe
pink	green	purse

INITIAL-FINAL CONSONANT OVERLAP

blue	green	crab
blue	green	cab
blue	pink	knob
blue	pink	tub
blue	pink	web
green	pink	bag
green	blue	dog
green	blue	egg
green	pink	flag
green	blue	leg
pink	green	harp
pink	green	lamp
pink	blue	sheep
pink	blue	tap
pink	green	top

LANGUAGE AND COGNITIVE PROCESSES
2009, 24 (5), 713–734

Semantic context effects in language production: A swinging lexical network proposal and a review

Rasha Abdel Rahman

Humboldt-University Berlin, Germany

Alissa Melinger

University of Dundee, Scotland

The investigation of semantic context effects has served as a valuable tool in investigating mechanisms of language production. Classic semantic interference effects have provided influential support for and interest in a competitive lexical selection mechanism. However, recent interest in semantic facilitation effects has stimulated a discussion on whether context effects reflect competition during lexical selection. In this review we propose a framework of lexical selection by competition that is sensitive to the activation of lexical cohorts. We outline our proposal and then present a selective review of the empirical evidence, much of which has been central to the development of alternative non-competitive models. We suggest that by adopting the assumptions of our proposal we can parsimoniously account for a majority of the discussed semantic facilitation and interference effects.

Investigations of semantic context effects, a widely used tool to study the architecture of the speech production system, have considerably shaped our assumptions on the nature of lexical selection. Traditionally the term semantic context has referred primarily to the relationship between a target stimulus and some second stimulus within an experiment. In this paper, we intend semantic context to refer to any meaning-constraining context, i.e., discourse context, experimental context, situational context, within which a target word is uttered.

Correspondence should be addressed to Rasha Abdel Rahman, Humboldt-University Berlin, Rudower Chaussee 18, 12489 Berlin, Germany. E-mail: rasha.abdel.rahman@cms.hu-berlin.de

Preparation of this paper was supported by a grant (AB 277 1-2) from the German Research Council to Rasha Abdel Rahman.

http://www.psypress.com/lcp　　　　　　　　　　　DOI: 10.1080/01690960802597250

Until recently there has been a strong focus in the literature on *interference* effects that are typically induced by *categorical relations* between stimuli. These well-attested effects have long been taken as evidence for competition among co-activated entries during lexical selection, an assumption that is shared by many production models (e.g., Bloem & La Heij, 2003; Harley, 1993a, 1993b; Humphreys, Lloyd-Jones, & Fias, 1995; La Heij, 1988; Levelt, Roelofs, & Meyer, 1999; Roelofs, 1992; Starreveld & La Heij, 1996). Recently, however, reported polarity reversals and exceptions from classic interference effects have gained increasing attention. Several pieces of evidence suggest that semantic interference is a rather narrow phenomenon, seemingly restricted to categorical relations. The absence of semantic interference effects or the presence of facilitation for various types of non-categorical relations is problematic for competitive models of lexical selection because they generally do not stipulate or restrict the spread of activation within the conceptual system or between conceptual and lexical strata to categorically related items (for an alternative view, see Bloem & La Heij, 2003).

To resolve this contradiction, a recent proposal suggests that first, semantic interference does not reflect lexical selection mechanisms and that second, lexical selection is not by competition (Costa, Alario, & Caramazza, 2005; Finkbeiner & Caramazza, 2006; Janssen, Schirm, Mahon, & Caramazza, 2008; Mahon, Costa, Peterson, Vargas, & Caramazza, 2007; Miozzo & Caramazza, 2003).

According to Mahon and colleagues' (2007) response exclusion hypothesis, semantic facilitation reflects lexical priming (but see Costa et al., 2005 for a proposal that assumes a conceptual locus) of the target whereas interference effects arise post-lexically, in the articulatory buffer, to which distractor words are presumed to have privileged access. The output buffer constitutes a bottleneck stage which, once occupied by a distractor word, must be disengaged before articulation of the target word can start. The ease with which the non-target response can be excluded from production depends on its response relevance. If the distractor is a relevant response in a given experimental context, for instance because it shares semantic category with the target, exclusion of the non-target response is slower. However, when the distractor is not response relevant (for instance, because it is semantically unrelated or because of implicit task criteria such as naming whole objects rather than parts of objects; cf. Costa et al., 2005), exclusion is easier and therefore faster. While this proposal is seemingly intended as a model of picture-word-interference performance, the authors also claim that the same mechanism can account for multiple interference-like effects from a variety of paradigms (Mahon et al., 2007, p. 516).

The question of whether lexical selection is by competition is an important one for several reasons. As an explanatory mechanism, competition is broadly used across several different cognitive faculties. It plays a prominent role in various language functions, including word recognition (e.g., Gaskell & Marslen-Wilson, 1997; McClelland & Elman, 1986) sentence processing (e.g., Jurafsky, 1996; MacDonald, Pearlmutter, & Seidenberg, 1994; McRae, Spivey, & Tanenhaus, 1998), lexical ambiguity resolution (e.g., Duffy, Morris, & Rayner, 1988; Rayner & Duffy, 1986), Stroop conflicts (e.g., MacLeod, 1991), bilingual language processing (e.g., Green, 1986, 1998), as well as other components of the speech production process (e.g., syllable competition in the mental syllabary; Cholin, Levelt, & Schiller, 2006; Roelofs, 1997). Further-more, competition is not just a language-internal phenomenon; it is found as an explanatory device in various cognitive domains such as attentional processing (Duncan, 2001) and motor control (Georgopolous, Schwartz, & Kettner, 1986; Houghton & Tipper, 1994). Thus, determining whether competition is truly the mechanism underlying lexical selection in production has potential implications not just as a comprehensive explanation for a wide variety of experimental observations in production research but also for viewing the relationship between speech production and recognition, or other cognitive functions.

A SWINGING LEXICAL NETWORK ACCOUNT OF SEMANTIC INTERFERENCE

Here, we propose a theoretical account for semantic context effects that retains lexical competition. At the heart of this account are two assumptions that are either explicitly or implicitly incorporated in most current models of speech production. The first assumption is that the activation of an inter-related *cohort of lexical competitors* is a major determinant for lexical competition to be strong enough to result in detectable semantic interference effects. The activation of a single isolated competitor is typically not sufficient to induce measurable interference. This assumption is derived from models implementing selection mechanisms such as the Luce ratio (Levelt et al., 1999; Luce, 1959; Roelofs, 1992), however it may also be consistent with models that implement competition via inhibitory links between active representations (e.g., Caramazza, 1997; Harley, 1993a, 1993b; Howard, Nickels, Coltheart, & Cole-Virtue, 2006; Stemberger, 1985). According to the Luce ratio, the probability for selecting the target lemma at any given point in time depends on the state of its activation relative to (divided by) the *sum activation of all other* lemma nodes (cf. Roelofs, 1992, 1997). Consequently, we assume that the latency of target lemma selection varies as a function of the state of activation of the entire lexical network, and is proportionally delayed with an increasing number of active competitors.

The second assumption is that semantic context affects speech production at two processing levels. First, context affects conceptual processing due to semantic priming of the target concept. Second, semantic context influences lexical level processes due to competition between lexical entries for selection. These two effects yield a combination of facilitative and inhibitory influences (see Damian & Als, 2005; Navarette & Costa, 2005; Kuipers, La Heij, & Costa, 2006 for similar assumptions). The polarity of observed net effects in naming latencies is the result of a trade-off between conceptual facilitation and lexical competition. Which of the two opposing effects wins the game strongly depends on whether or not an inter-related lexical cohort of sufficient size is activated. Because lexical entries need to be selected from among competitors whereas concepts simply receive more or less activation, we assume that an increasing number of co-activated concepts and lexical nodes has a stronger influence on lexical interference than on conceptual facilitation.

Semantic facilitation effects are widely interpreted as contextual and conceptual. For instance, context-induced facilitation effects motivated the *message-congruency account* (Kuipers et al., 2006; Kuipers & La Heij, 2008) which holds that semantic facilitation is obtained when target and context converge on a single goal concept. In this account, convergence leads to conceptual facilitation, which can outweigh weaker lexical interference effects. Further support for the assumption that semantic contexts yield conceptual priming is found in a variety of studies revealing semantic facilitation effects (e.g., Bloem & La Heij, 2003; Bloem, van den Boogaard, & La Heij, 2004; Costa, Mahon, Savova, & Caramazza, 2003; Glaser & Düngelhoff, 1984; Kuipers & La Heij, 2008; Kuipers et al., 2006). For example, Bloem and La Heij (2003) observed faster translation times for words (e.g., translating English *dog* into Dutch *hond*) superimposed on semantically related pictures (e.g., cat) compared with unrelated pictures (e.g., tree). They interpreted this facilitation effect as evidence that the distractor picture primed the semantic representation of the target word, speeding concept selection. Null effects – when interference was expected – have also been taken as evidence for facilitation from a semantic context. Navarette and Costa (2005) failed to observe anticipated semantic inter-ference effects in a picture-picture interference study and argued that the interference had been neutralised by a comparably sized priming effect at the conceptual level. While the swinging network model adopts a conceptual-level explanation for these semantic facilitation effects, other models attribute the effects to lexical level processes that are mediated by conceptual activation (cf. Mahon et al., 2007; Roelofs, 2006, 2008a, 2008b).

To summarise, we assume that semantic contexts always induce both conceptual facilitation and lexical competition. The net effects will be facilitation-dominant when only a single or small number of competitors is activated, in which case conceptual priming outweighs lexical competition. In contrast, effects will be interference-dominant when a large number of inter-related competitors, a lexical cohort, is active, in which case cohort-induced lexical competition outweighs conceptual priming. One related but novel augmentation is the proposal that semantic and lexical activation spread is highly dynamic, flexible and adjustable to the specific context in which the utterance is produced. As a result, the activation of lexical cohorts in the course of word production is strongly modulated by contextual factors. This contextual sensitivity is in line with notions of ad hoc category formation (Barsalou, 1983). Specifically, Barsalou proposed that novel categories are constructed to achieve goals. For example, when stranded on a desert island one will quickly construct an ad hoc category of 'things that catch rain water'. We suggest that the same mechanisms that underlie goal-driven ad hoc category formation drive the flexibility we observe within the conceptual and lexical system.

Although lexical cohort activation is theoretically not a new concept, the consequences for semantic context effects and lexical selection latencies have not gained much attention. Particularly, recent debates about the locus of semantic interference effects have failed to take this factor into account. Discussions have focused on the relative activation levels of the target and a *single* lexical competitor. However, while this concentration may have started for expository purposes, it has crept into the theorising that underlies some research.

However, as we will argue below, the lexical cohort account has the potential to explain a range of semantic context effects – including polarity reversals associated with different types of semantic relation – without requiring additional assumptions to restrict lexical competition, and without the need to dismiss lexical competition. For example, in the model proposed by Bloem and La Heij (2003; Bloem et al., 2004), only the target concept and target co-hyponyms spread activation to their corresponding lexical representations. This assumption is adopted to account for the absence of predicted interference effects. In contrast, in the present model semantic context effects of different polarity and strength follow naturally from the two assumptions described above and do not have to be attributed to qualitatively different underlying processes. Furthermore, this account makes some unique predictions about when interference effects from non-categorically related contexts should be observed.

In the following we present the predictions derived from a lexical cohort account and provide a selective review of evidence supporting these predictions. The major part of this review will focus on findings that have recently been interpreted as evidence against lexical competition models – under the assumption that the activation status of a single competitor is the determining factor. We will re-evaluate this evidence in light of the cohort assumption.

EVIDENCE FROM THE PICTURE-WORD INTERFERENCE (PWI) PARADIGM

In the picture-word interference (PWI) paradigm a picture is presented for a naming response together with a to-be ignored word distractor. A classic and well-established finding in this paradigm is the semantic interference effect, that is, delayed naming latencies induced by categorically related, compared with unrelated words (e.g., Glaser & Düngelhoff, 1984; Glaser & Glaser, 1989; La Heij, 1988; Lupker, 1979; Lupker & Katz, 1981, 1982; Schriefers, Meyer, & Levelt, 1990).

Lexical competition models make two assumptions to account for this finding. First, in the course of picture naming, activation spreads at the conceptual level to the target and related concepts, which in turn activate their corresponding lexical nodes (e.g., Caramazza, 1997; Collins & Loftus, 1975; Collins & Quillian, 1969; Dell, 1986; Levelt et al., 1999; Roelofs, 1992, but see, e.g., Bloem & La Heij, 2003). Second, lexical nodes compete with the target for selection. When a categorically related distractor is presented, its associated lexical node receives converging activation from the picture and the word, and will therefore, as a highly active competitor, delay target selection. As discussed above, this often described variant of lexical competition models focuses on the activation level of one strong competitor – the lexical entry of the distractor word – without directly taking the activation status of the lexical cohort into account.

Recent evidence for polarity reversals of semantic distractor effects has challenged the assumption of competitive lexical selection. Specifically, semantically related distractor words that are not members of the target's semantic category seem to induce facilitation rather than interference. For instance, several studies have demonstrated no effects or facilitation when target and distractor are associatively related (e.g., Alario, Segui, & Ferrand, 2000; Bölte, Jorschick, & Zwitserlood, 2003; La Heij, Dirkx, & Kramer, 1990; Lupker, 1979). Facilitation has also been observed when targets and distractors have a part-whole relation (Costa et al., 2005).

Costa and colleagues (2005; see also Mahon et al., 2007) have interpreted such facilitation effects, including their own findings, as evidence against lexical competition because any semantic relation should induce interference, not just categorical relations. Instead, they argue that semantic contexts induce conceptual/lexical priming of the target, and that interference will only be observed when the distractors are potentially relevant responses that need to be discarded. If only whole objects are named in an experiment, then distractors that are parts of objects will be quickly dismissed as alternative responses. What remains is a semantic priming effect. A similar mechanism based on response relevance might hold for associative relations.

However, Abdel Rahman and Melinger (2007) have recently reported a study in which the associate distractors were also target pictures on other trials. They observed associatively induced facilitation despite the fact that the respective distractors were parts of the response set, and were therefore clearly relevant responses. Within one study, associatively related distractors induced facilitation whereas categorically related distractors induced classic interference effects. This finding cannot easily be explained purely in terms of the response relevant criteria. It would require the additional assumption that only categorical, but not associative, relations are processed and identified as relevant responses. Why this would be is not entirely clear.

Alternatively, the polarity reversals follow naturally from inherent differences between associative and categorical relations within the lexical cohort account. When target and distractor are members of the same category (e.g., bee and horse), they spread *converging* activation to a number of competitors, which share the category node and several semantic features (e.g., snake, mouse, fly, etc., cf. Figure 1). Thus, a whole cohort of inter-related competing lexical nodes is co-activated, and the network is swinging. With convergent activation, the interconnectivity of the cohort means that the bulk of the activation stays within the cohort, and each representation reinforces the activation of the whole set, resulting in comparatively high levels of activation, which in turn produce strong lexical competition effects.

In contrast, if target and competitor are associatively related but belong to different semantic categories (e.g., bee and honey), activation does not converge onto other related concepts because they do not share a common category node, and the number of other shared semantic features is low. Instead, activation from target and competitor concepts diverges onto mutually unrelated representations (e.g., bread, comb, and dessert). These activated concepts in turn pass their activation on to more and more unrelated concepts until the activation dissipates to insubstantial levels. This sort of divergent activation results in a wide-spread ripple of activation with two central loci of high activation at the origin, namely with target and distractor. This pattern of activation spreading gives rise to one-to-one competition within the lexical network, rather than one-to-many competition (cf. Figure 1).

As outlined above, the combined effects of conceptual priming and lexical competition will be facilitation-dominant when only one competitor is active (as is typically the case for associative relations), but interference-dominant when a lexical cohort is active (as is the case for categorical relations).

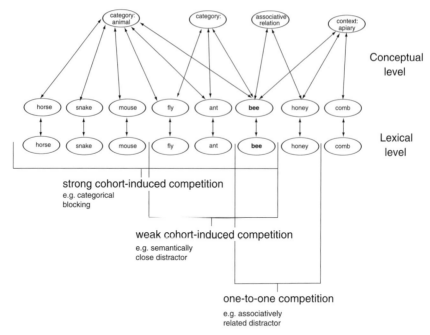

Figure 1. Schematic illustration of a cohort-based lexical competition model, adapted from Levelt et al. (1999). The fragment includes a conceptual and a lexical processing level. Arrows depict the bidirectional information transmission between the nodes of the network within and between the levels. For the sake of clarity, direct connections between conceptual nodes are not depicted. Depending on the semantic context, a target utterance (here: bee, in bold) can compete with a big or small lexical cohort or a single competitor.

Additionally, weak interference effects from a single competitor can also emerge when conceptual facilitation is absent (see below). The presentation of distractors that are parts of whole objects (e.g., car and bumper) might induce a one-to-one competition in a similar way as described for associates. This account for associative and categorical context effects receives further support from experiments with the semantic blocking paradigm (see below).

A further piece of evidence is that the presentation of semantically related verb distractors (e.g., target: bed, distractor: sleep) results in facilitation, rather than interference effects (Mahon et al., 2007). The authors have argued that this finding is at variance with lexical competition because such verb distractors are closely related to the target and should therefore receive strong converging activation, resulting in semantic interference, compared to unrelated verbs. However, in light of the cohort assumption again, this is not what would be expected. Just like associates, verb distractors such as 'sleep' and related targets (bed) systematically differ from categorically related noun distractors (chair) in that they tend to have a one-to-one semantic relation that will not yield significant converging activation within the lexical network. Consequently, conceptual priming will offset the one-to-one lexical competition.

Investigations of semantic distance effects are also relevant to the debate over lexical competition. The basic assumption here is again that the activation level of a single lexical competitor is the major determinant for semantic interference effects within lexical competition models. Based on this assumption, Mahon et al. (2007) have derived the prediction from lexical competition models that semantically close distractor words (e.g., target: horse, distractor: zebra) should interfere more with the naming response than semantically distant distractors (e.g., whale). However, what Mahon and colleagues observed was precisely the opposite: naming latencies associated with semantically distant distractors were slower than those associated with semantically close distractors. Other investigations of semantic distance have produced contrasting results, however. For example, Vigliocco, Vinson, Damian, and Levelt (2002a, 2002b) investigated effects of 'graded semantic similarity' using the semantic blocking paradigm. Because this paradigm differs from the PWI paradigm in important ways, particularly with respect to the activation of an inter-related lexical cohort, we will discuss this study in the following section on semantic blocking effects in more detail. We will include a discussion of the differences between the semantic distance effects observed by Mahon et al. and Vigliocco et al. in the section on blocking effects.

While the observation of slower naming latencies with increasing semantic distance might be viewed as being contrary to what a single-lexical competitor account would predict, it is in line with the above described trade-off account and competition induced by lexical cohorts. First, close distractors should yield stronger priming effects than distant distractors at the conceptual level. Second, one only needs to assume that semantically distant target–distractor pairs co-activate a lexical cohort with numerous different members belonging to this broadly defined category (e.g., animals: not only the target bee and distractor horse, but also other members of this category, such as ant, snake, mouse etc. are activated; cf. Figure 1). In contrast, semantically close target–distractor pairs (bee and fly) co-activate a much more confined and narrow category (e.g., insects: bee, fly, ant; cf. Figure 1). Such comparatively small semantic categories have fewer members than broad categories. Consequently, close distractors should induce less interference than distant distractors. While this claim is currently not supported by direct and independent empirical evidence, preliminary data point into this direction when the influences of semantic distance and category size effects are manipulated independently (Abdel Rahman & Melinger, 2008b).

The swinging network account proposed here incorporates the assumption that semantic activation spread can be modulated and adjusted in a situation-specific and flexible way. Support for this account, including some of the speculative aspects of the proposal, comes from studies that suggest a highly flexible architecture of the speech production system in terms of semantic activation spread. These studies show that meaning relations and contextually relevant categories can be formed, newly created, and even demolished by semantic context modulations (Abdel Rahman & Melinger, 2007; Abdel Rahman & Melinger, 2008b; see below). Thus, it is not unreasonable to assume that graded variations in target-distractor relations – such as semantic distance effects – strongly modulate the activation status of the whole lexical network. We will discuss this issue in more detail in the section on semantic blocking effects.

As mentioned above, the current proposal rests on two assumptions: activation of a cohort of lexical competitors and a trade-off between semantic facilitation and lexical interference effects. We suggest that a lexical cohort is necessary to produce sufficient competition to override conceptual facilitation effects; one-to-one competition will generally be insufficient to produce observable interference effects.

This proposal makes the prediction that even small interference effects from one-to-one competition should be observable if conceptual facilitation could be sufficiently reduced. Melinger and Abdel Rahman (2008) tested this hypothesis by investigating mediated semantic interference effects (Abdel Rahman & Melinger, 2008a; Hantsch, Jescheniak, & Schriefers, 2005; Jescheniak & Schriefers, 1998; Levelt, Schriefers, Vorberg, Meyer, Pechmann, & Havinga, 1991; Peterson & Savoy, 1998). Such mediated effects are observed for distractor words that are phonologically related to a semantic competitor of the target. Melinger and Abdel Rahman used pairs of associatively related competitors in their study (e.g., target: pyramid, distractors: camera, bagel (phonologically related to the associate camel).

The authors reasoned that an interference effect should be detected because the phonological distractor avoids strong conceptual activation of the associate competitor, while increasing its lexical activation level. The lexical representation of the competitor receives activation from two sources: the target, due to spreading activation, and the distractor, via phonological priming. Crucially, however, the presentation of a pair of words that is phonologically related to an associatively related competitor (camera, bagel) should not significantly activate the conceptual representation of the competitor (camel). Thus, semantic facilitation is bypassed. As predicted by the lexical cohort hypothesis, in this situation, one-to-one lexical competition was sufficient to observe interference effects because these effects are not offset by conceptual facilitation.

The present account is in line with similar effects for other types of relations such as near-synonyms (Jescheniak & Schriefers, 1998) or category members (Abdel Rahman & Melinger, 2008a). Because conceptual priming, semantic activation spread, and in turn lexical cohort activation is prevented by presenting distractors that are phonologically related to a competitor, a one-to-one lexical competition without concomitant conceptual facilitation should result in small but measurable interference effects.

Another common type of PWI polarity reversal that has received much attention is the so-called 'level of specificity' effect. In these studies, the target and distractor words describe objects at different levels of generality, i.e., animal (superordinate level), dog (basic level) or poodle (subordinate level). When the target and distractor differ in their respective levels of specificity, both facilitation (Costa et al., 2003; Glaser & Düngelhoff, 1984; Kuipers et al., 2006; Vitkovitch & Tyrrell, 1999) and interference (Hantsch et al., 2005; Glaser & Düngelhoff, 1984; Kuipers et al., 2006) have been observed. Several different proposals have been put forward to explain the polarity of the effects. Some evidence suggests that the modality of the distractor presentation matters to the direction of the effect, with written distractors more likely to produce facilitation and auditory distractors more likely to produce interference (Hantsch, Jescheniak, & Schriefers, 2006). It has also been argued that response congruency plays a role in determining the direction of these effects (Glaser & Glaser, 1989; Kuipers et al., 2006; Kuipers & La Heij, 2008; La Heij, Starreveld, & Kuipers, 2007; Lupker & Katz, 1981). While we do not believe that the entire pattern of results can be explained solely with reference to the current formulation of a swinging network and lexical cohort activation, we would like to speculate as to how the current approach could be extended to capture a large subset of the facilitation and interference effects.

A necessary assumption is that a semantic context, in this case the experimental naming instruction, can influence the dimensions along which activation resonates within the conceptual network. For example, when producing categorical labels such as 'animal' and 'furniture', semantic features that discriminate between members of each category should not be strongly activated. Rather, general features such as 'is a living thing', 'breathes', 'moves' will be active. Hence, the category node 'animal' will spread activation to other superordinate category nodes such as 'fish' and 'birds'. A basic level distractor, e.g., 'dog',will enhance the activation of the target 'animal' but it will not produce convergence because it is not related to the other categories (a dog is not a type of fish). As a result, the one-to-one competition at the lexical level will not be sufficient to overcome the semantic facilitation and the net result will be facilitative.

In contrast, interference effects are expected when the naming task is more specific than the distractor. In basic level naming, a target 'dog' will spread activation to competitors at the same level of specificity, e.g., 'cat', 'horse', 'tiger'. A superordinate distractor, e.g., 'animal', would be linked to many of the co-activated concepts, producing converging activation within the set of competitors, thus leading to enhanced cohort competition in the lexicon. Kuipers et al. (2006) reported exactly this predicted pattern of interference and facilitation effects. Furthermore, the same general approach explains several other level of specificity observations, but clearly not all of them (e.g., Costa et al., 2003, Experiments 1 and 2 but not 3; Glaser & Glaser, 1989; Hantsch et al., 2005, Experiments 3 and 5 but not 1, 2 and 4; Vitkovitch & Tyrrell, 1999, Experiments 1 and 3 but not 2).

EVIDENCE FROM THE SEMANTIC BLOCKING PARADIGM

In the semantic blocking paradigm pictures of objects are presented and named in blocks of trials containing either other members of a common semantic category (e.g., all objects are tools; homogeneous blocking condition) or unrelated objects from different categories (heterogeneous blocking condition; e.g., Belke, Meyer, & Damian, 2005; Damian & Als, 2005; Damian, Vigliocco, & Levelt, 2001; Kroll & Stewart, 1994; Vigliocco et al., 2002a, 2002b). When the objects are repeatedly presented, naming is slowed down in categorically homogeneous compared with heterogeneous blocks, paralleling the findings in the picture-word interference paradigm.

Just like the contextually induced interference effects in the PWI paradigm, blocking effects have long been thought to arise due to competition at the level of lexical selection. They are potentially also compatible with the non-lexical account described above, assuming that first, other objects in the homogeneous blocks are relevant responses – which they clearly are – and second, that 'previously named pictures will be available as potential responses' (Mahon et al., 2007, p. 516). Where precisely the potential alternative responses are available remains unclear. However, more difficult to explain along these lines is the observation of Damian and Als (2005), that semantic blocking effects are not affected by the presence of interspersed trials with unrelated objects or trials that contained non-language tasks such as mental rotation. According to the output buffer assumption, this should reduce or even abolish interference effects because many previous responses are either unrelated, and thus not response relevant, or are not even associated with speech production. Yet, interference effects are unaffected. Damian and Als suggest an incremental learning mechanism for such long-lasting effects: Competitors – or more precisely the links between concepts and names – might be strengthened due to learning, and will thus subsequently produce more potent competitors. Such long-lasting effects can be easily accommodated with our assumptions of dynamic network modulations. Therefore, and in line with Damian and Als (2005), we consider lexical competition as the most parsimonious explanation for semantic blocking effects.

Although the blocking paradigm can induce classic semantic interference effects, it differs from the PWI paradigm in important ways. Specifically, blocking allows for a flexible manipulation of semantic and lexical cohort activation. For instance, Belke and colleagues (2005) have demonstrated that semantic interference effects generalise to new, previously unnamed objects of the same semantic category. In line with the swinging network assumption, this finding suggests that blocking enhances the activation level of the whole semantic category, not just the activation of actually presented and named category members. Furthermore, the fact that the interference effects generalise to new category members supports the role of one-to-many competition over one-to-one competition.

Using the blocking paradigm, Abdel Rahman and Melinger (2007) have explored the specific mechanisms that underlie the polarity reversals observed for categorical and associative semantic relations. In these experiments, semantic interference was observed not only for homogeneous blocks consisting of category members (e.g., category: animals: bee, horse, mouse, etc.) but also for homogeneous blocks consisting of associates from different categories that belonged to a specific semantic context (e.g., context: apiary; bee, honey, comb, etc.), compared to heterogeneous blocks. Here, and in contrast to presenting an isolated distractor word, semantic blocking creates a situation in which related concepts and lexical entries synergistically activate each other. Thus, in the blocking paradigm lexical semantic interference effects are not restricted to category members but can also be found for associates from different categories because lexical cohorts can be activated for both types of relations. The observation that non-categorical relations can induce interference when a cohort of items is inter-related in a meaningful way supports the assumption that competition due to semantic contexts can be boosted by expanding one-to-one relations to one-to-many relations in a swinging lexical network.

Moreover, when the same material was presented in a classic picture-word interference situation, only categorically related distractors induced inter-ference whereas associatively related distractors induced facilitation (see above for a more detailed description of these distractor effects). As argued, the reversal of semantic effects for associates in the PWI and semantic blocking paradigm, and the constant effects of categorical relations across paradigms, is a direct consequence of the specific nature of categorical and associative relations. Whereas category members more or less automatically induce converging activation of other category members (cf. Belke et al., 2005; Schriefers et al., 1990; but see below, Abdel Rahman & Melinger,

2008b), associates often have an isolated one-to-one relation, particularly when presented as target–distractor pairs in the PWI paradigm.

As discussed above, the competition induced by a single competitor, even when this competitor receives converging activation from the picture and itself, will not offset conceptual priming and will therefore not emerge as an interference effect. It is only when associatively related objects can be inter-related by providing a semantic context that the converging activation of a lexical cohort results in interference effects that are comparable with categorically induced effects. Together, these findings strongly support the lexical cohort assumption and suggest that semantic context effects induced by different types of semantic relations with diverging polarities are based on the same underlying mechanism: a trade-off between conceptual priming and lexical competition.

Another investigation of graded semantic similarity that is directly related to the above discussed graded interference effects reported by Mahon et al. (2007) comes from Vigliocco and colleagues (2002b). In a semantic blocking paradigm, participants named blocks of pictures drawn either from a single homogeneous category (e.g., body parts), two related categories (e.g., body parts and clothing) or two unrelated categories (e.g., body parts and vehicles). In contrast to Mahon et al's findings, objects in homogeneous blocks were named slower compared with objects in the block with two related categories, which in turn were named slower than objects in the block with two unrelated categories (but see Lotto, Job, & Rumiati (1999) for potential effects of visual similarity on conceptual processing). Vigliocco et al.'s graded semantic effects also fall out from the assumptions of a highly flexible semantic network. Specifically, our proposal is that the semantic blocking paradigm mimics a constrained discourse context by increasing the relevance of links between contextually related concepts. The context can be thought of as an ad hoc category, e.g., 'things related to body parts', in which activation converges in a similar manner to taxonomic categories, thus inducing context effects that are not typically observed in paradigms such PWI. The result is an interference effect commensurate with the amount of lexical cohort activation.

Evidence that underscores the assumption that the spread of semantic activation during speech planning is highly flexible and adjustable to the semantic context comes from a recent blocking study (Abdel Rahman & Melinger, 2008b). In this study, pictures of objects were presented either in categorically homogeneous blocks consisting of semantic category members (e.g., coffee, milk, rice, etc.), in thematically homogeneous blocks consisting of seemingly unrelated objects that could potentially be assigned to a common theme (e.g., 'fishing trip': coffee, knife, bucket, etc.), or hetero-geneous blocks consisting of entirely unrelated objects (e.g., foods: coffee, shelf, bag, etc).

As would be expected, a classic semantic interference effect for the categorically homogeneous condition was found, whereas naming latencies did not differ between the thematically homogeneous and the heterogeneous condition. However, when the blocks were preceded by visually presented matching title words that contextualised or inter-related the objects according to their category or theme, interference was observed for both types of homogeneous blocks. Thus, seemingly unrelated objects can induce interference if they are inter-related in a meaningful way. We assume that the relationship suggested by the block title facilitates ad hoc category formation (Barsalou, 1983). This ad hoc adaptation proceeds quickly and easily given a congruent title word. Furthermore, all interference effects, both from the categorical and thematic homogeneous blocks, were largely reduced when the homogeneous blocks were preceded by titles that were incongruent to the objects in the block. These observations indicate a high degree of plasticity and situation-specific adaptation of the composition of meaning-related concepts and lexical cohorts. This demonstration of a flexible adjustment of semantic spread of activation provides supporting evidence for our claim that ad hoc adaptations can strongly modulate the strength and polarity of semantic context effects by recruiting different lexical cohort assemblies of varying size.

DISCUSSION AND CONCLUSIONS

In this paper we proposed a swinging lexical network account for semantic context effects in speech production and provided a selective review on experimental evidence supporting this account. The proposal combines two assumptions. First, the specific characteristics of semantic activation spread during language production are dynamically modulated by semantic context. The empirical evidence reviewed here suggests a high degree of plasticity in that situation-specific adjustments to conceptual and lexical network activation unfold: semantic contexts modulate the speed of lexical selection by flexibly recruiting context-specific lexical cohort assemblies of varying sizes (Abdel Rahman & Melinger, 2007; 2008b; Belke et al., 2005; Spalek & Damian, 2007).

The second assumption is that the strength and polarity of semantic context effects depend on the outcome of a trade-off between semantically induced conceptual priming and lexical competition. Most importantly, the crucial factor that determines whether facilitation or interference effects dominate is the activation of an inter-related lexical cohort that strongly competes with the target for selection. Only when such a context-sensitive cohort is active, that is, when the lexical network is swinging, will lexical competition outweigh conceptual priming – and semantic interference effects be observed. We have reviewed several pieces of evidence from the PWI and semantic blocking paradigms suggesting that the activation status of the entire lexical network is a major determinant for interference effects induced by various types of semantic relations (e.g., Abdel Rahman & Melinger, 2007; 2008b; Belke et al., 2005; Damian & Als, 2005; Melinger & Abdel Rahman, 2008). The circumstances where we predict interference to dominate facilitation are the following: (a) when a cohort of lexical candidates is active and/or (b) when conceptual facilitation is absent or strongly reduced. When neither of these criteria is satisfied, we expect facilitation. Here, as a basis for further empirical tests, we have discussed initial evidence supporting the above predictions. What further remains to be determined are the precise computational dynamics controlling the trade-off between interference and facilitation. For example, we do not know how large a lexical cohort must be before it can offset a conceptual facilitation effect. We also do not understand the full implications of assuming a conceptual, as opposed to a lexical, locus for semantic facilitation. It remains to be seen whether a lexical locus mediated by conceptual activation (as assumed by Roelofs, 2006, 2008a, 2008b) would also be consistent with the observed effects. Further specification will require computational modelling.

As discussed, the swinging network proposal is not an entirely new concept. Lexical cohort activation is an ingredient of many existing speech production models (most explicitly in Levelt et al., 1999; Roelofs, 1992, 1993, 2001, 2003, but also implicit in, e.g., Caramazza, 1997; Bloem & La Heij, 2003; Humphreys et al., 1995; Starreveld & La Heij, 1995, 1996). However, the impact of one-to-many competition induced by semantic contexts has not received much attention. The swinging network proposal does not require entirely new or qualitatively different assumptions for the effects of different types of semantic relations, (e.g., the assumption that the flow of activation between conceptual and lexical levels is restricted; Bloem & La Heij, 2003; Bloem et al., 2004; Kuipers et al., 2006; Kuipers & La Heij, 2008), and yet it covers a surprising range of data on semantic context effects, including many of the polarity reversals and exceptions from classic interference effects that have been interpreted as contra lexical competition models (e.g., Costa et al., 2005; Mahon et al., 2007). The gains in explanatory potential afforded by the swinging network proposal are achieved without the need to dismiss lexical competition, and without the need to attribute the underlying mechanisms to qualitatively different processes. Furthermore, although many of the reviewed context effects were facilitative, not inhibitory, the swinging network assumption can accommodate these observations while retaining lexical competition as an inherent element of lexical selection.

The review provided here is admittedly selective and clearly not exhaustive. It focuses strongly on recent evidence that has challenged lexical competition. The aim was to reinterpret this evidence in light of the cohort assumption, and in a broader sense to evaluate the scope of the assumption. Clearly, cohort competition cannot account for all reported polarity reversals. Specifically, it cannot explain recently reported reversed effects of masked distractor words (Finkbeiner & Caramazza, 2006) or the effects of distractor words on delayed naming (Janssen et al., 2008). Furthermore, alternative proposals, such as the role of response congruency between target and distractor (Glaser & Glaser, 1989; Kuipers et al., 2006; La Heij et al., 2007; Lupker & Katz, 1981), or differences in distractor modality (Hantsch et al., 2006) might play as much of a role in determining the direction of distractor effects at different levels of specificity as our speculative extension of the swinging network account does.

While some of the reviewed studies were directly designed to test for cohort activation, many observations were not. In the latter case, we provided speculations on how the data can be interpreted within a swinging network account. Although this approach has yielded an interesting new perspective on the microstructure of speech planning and how this microstructure is modulated by semantic context, more direct support, including independent empirical tests and computational simulations of the network structure, would facilitate further evaluation of the proposal. To this end, we can identify several unique predictions derived from the swinging lexical network proposal. Some of these predictions received support from the studies describe above while others are yet untested. These predictions should contribute to the future development of this research.

First, all types of semantic contexts (e.g., categorical relations, associative relations, and even unrelated items that are linked in a meaningful way) can in principle induce interference as well as facilitation effects. The polarity depends on whether conceptual facilitation or lexical cohort activation prevails. Thus, factors that enhance lexical cohort activation should cause interference. Factors that induce semantic priming but fail to induce cohort activation should cause facilitation. Factors that are designed to induce even strong activation of one isolated competitor while still priming the target concept should produce facilitation or null effects.

Further predictions pertain to speech errors, such as naturally occurring non-categorical semantic substitutions, or semantic paraphasia. We have argued that a semantic context can induce a cohort effect for various types of semantic relations. In natural discourse, constrained topics should suffice to create converging activation akin to what is observed in a blocked picture naming experiment. Specifically, in a constrained conversation about farms, concepts within that semantic field, e.g., barn, plow, field, etc. will be salient and convergent. Hence, we would expect semantic substitutions between these contextually related items, e.g., *barn* replaced by *plow*. In contrast, in an unconstrained conversation semantic substitutions of contextually related words would not be expected. This prediction has yet to be directly tested, although naturally occurring associatively related semantic substitution errors have been reported (Harley & MacAndrews, 2001). More detailed analyses of naturally occurring semantic substitution errors could be a valuable avenue for revealing additional evidence for the swinging network and lexical cohort activation.

We have presented a new framework for explaining both facilitative and inhibitory semantic effects in picture naming. Our proposal builds on assumptions that are implicit, but thus far largely neglected, in existing models. First, we reemphasised the importance of lexical cohorts to the competition mechanism underlying lexical selection. Second, we recognised that the semantic context affects word production both at the conceptual level, where priming effects arise, and at the lexical level, where interference arises. We also outlined the flexible manner with which the conceptual network can recruit various context-appropriate concepts into a lexical cohort; lexical cohorts can comprise concepts linked by common categories, contexts, and themes so long as the activation within the system is sufficiently convergent. We suggest that this notion of a flexible swinging network is crucial to an understanding of semantic context effects observed across a variety of experimental paradigms. In a selective review of recent key findings on semantic context effects we argued that the framework provides significant explanatory coverage, even of results previously thought to be incompatible with selection by competition, and makes unique testable predictions.

REFERENCES

Abdel Rahman, R., & Melinger, A. (2007). When bees hamper the production of honey: Lexical interference from associates in speech production. *Journal of Experimental Psychology: Learning, Memory and Cognition, 33*, 604–614.

Abdel Rahman, R., & Melinger, A. (2008a). Enhanced phonological facilitation and traces of concurrent word form activation in speech production: An object naming study with multiple distractors. *Quarterly Journal of Experimental Psychology, 61*, 1410–1440.

Abdel Rahman, R., & Melinger, A. (2008b). *The dynamic microstructure of speech production: Semantic interference built on the fly.* Manuscript submitted for publication.

Alario, F.-X., Segui, J., & Ferrand, L. (2000). Semantic and associative priming in picture naming. *Quarterly Journal of Experimental Psychology, 53A*, 741–764.

Barsalou, L. W. (1983). Ad hoc categories. *Memory and Cognition, 11*, 211–227.

Belke, E., Meyer, A. S., & Damian, M. F. (2005). Refractory effects in picture naming as assessed in a semantic blocking paradigm. *Quarterly Journal of Experimental Psychology, 58A*, 667–692.

Bloem, I., & La Heij, W. (2003). Semantic facilitation and semantic interference in word translation: Implications for models of lexical access in language production. *Journal of Memory and Language, 48*, 468–488.

Bloem, I., van den Boogaard, S., & La Heij, W. (2004). Semantic facilitation and semantic interference in language production: Further evidence for the conceptual selection model of lexical access. *Journal of Memory and Language*, *51*, 307–323.

Bölte, J., Jorschick, A., & Zwitserlood, P. (2003). Reading yellow speeds up naming a picture of a banana: Facilitation and inhibition in picture-word interference. *Proceedings of the European Cognitive Science Conference, Germany* (pp. 55–60). Mahwah, NJ: Lawrence Erlbaum Associates Inc.

Caramazza, A. (1997). How many levels of processing are there in lexical access? *Cognitive Neuropsychology*, *14*, 177–208.

Cholin, J., Levelt, W. J. M., & Schiller, N. O. (2006). Effects of syllable frequency in speech production. *Cognition*, *99*, 205–235.

Collins, A. M., & Loftus, E. (1975). A spreading-activation theory of semantic processing. *Psychological Review*, *82*, 407–428.

Collins, A. M., & Quillian, M. R. (1969). Retrieval time from semantic memory. *Journal of Verbal Learning and Verbal Behaviour*, *8*, 240–247.

Costa, A., Alario, F.-X., & Caramazza, A. (2005). On the categorical nature of the semantic interference effect in the picture-word interference paradigm. *Psychonomic Bulletin and Review*, *12*, 125–131.

Costa, A., Mahon, B., Savova, V., & Caramazza, A. (2003). Level of categorization effect: a novel effect in the picture-word interference paradigm. *Language and Cognitive Processes*, *18*, 205–233.

Damian, M. F., & Als, L. C. (2005). Long-lasting semantic context effects in the spoken production of object names. *Journal of Experimental Psychology: Learning, Memory, and Cognition*, *31*, 1372–1384.

Damian, M. F., Vigliocco, G., & Levelt, W. J. M. (2001). Effects of semantic context in the naming of pictures and words. *Cognition*, *81*, B77–B86.

Dell, G. S. (1986). A spreading-activation theory of retrieval in sentence production. *Psychological Review*, *3*, 283–321.

Duffy, S. A., Morris, R. K., & Rayner, K. (1988). Lexical ambiguity and fixation times in reading. *Journal of Memory and Language*, *27*, 429–446.

Duncan, J. (2001). An adaptive coding model of neural function in prefrontal cortex. *Nature Reviews Neuroscience*, *2*, 820–829.

Finkbeiner, M., & Caramazza, A. (2006). Now you see it, now you don't: On turning semantic interference into facilitation in a Stoop-like task. *Cortex*, *6*, 790–796.

Gaskell, M. G., & Marslen-Wilson, W. D. (1997). Integrating form and meaning: A distributed model of speech perception. *Language and Cognitive Processes*, *12*, 613–656.

Georgopoulos, A. P., Schwartz, A. B., & Kettner, R. E. (1986). Neuronal population coding of movement direction. *Science*, *233*, 1416–1419.

Glaser, W. R., & Düngelhoff, F.-J. (1984). The time course of picture-word interference. *Journal of Experimental Psychology: Human Perception and Performance*, *10*, 640–654.

Glaser, W. R., & Glaser, M. O. (1989). Context effects on Stroop-like word and picture processing. *Journal of Experimental Psychology: General*, *118*, 13–42.

Green, D. W. (1986). Control, activation and resource. *Brain and Language*, *27*, 210–223.

Green, D. W. (1998). Mental control of the bilingual lexico-semantic system. *Bilingualism: Language and Cognition*, *1*, 67–81.

Hantsch, A., Jescheniak, J. D., & Schriefers, H. (2005). Semantic competition between hierarchically related words during speech planning. *Memory and Cognition*, *33*, 984–1000.

Hantsch, A., Jescheniak, J. D., Schriefers, H., & Aßmann, S. (2006). Effects of distractor modality on semantic between-level effects in the picture-word-interference paradigm. *Abstracts of the 47th Annual Meeting of the Psychonomic Society, USA, 11*, 71.

Hantsch, A., Jescheniak, J. D., & Schriefers, H. (2006, August). *Semantic facilitation in the picture-word-interference paradigm: Implications for models of lexical access.* Paper presented at the International Workshop on Language Production, Chicago, IL, USA.

Harley, T. A. (1993a). Connectionist approaches to language disorders. *Aphasiology, 7,* 221–249.

Harley, T. A. (1993b). Phonological activation of semantic competitors during lexical access in speech production. *Language and Cognitive Processes, 8,* 291–309.

Harley, T. A., & McAndrews, S. B. G. (2001). Constraints upon word substitution speech errors. *Journal of Psycholinguistic Research, 30,* 395–418.

Houghton, G., & Tipper, S. P. (1994). A model of inhibitory mechanisms in selective attention. In D. Dagenbach & T. Carr (Eds.), *Inhibitory mechanisms in attention, memory and language* (pp. 53–112). San Diego, CA: Academic Press.

Howard, D., Nickels, L., Coltheart, M., & Cole-Virtue, J. (2006). Cumulative semantic inhibition in picture naming: Experimental and computational studies. *Cognition, 100,* 464–482.

Humphreys, G. W., Lloyd-Jones, T. J., & Fias, W. (1995). Semantic interference effects on naming using a postcue procedure: Tapping the links between semantics and phonology with pictures and words. *Journal of Experimental Psychology: Learning, Memory, and Cognition, 21,* 961–980.

Janssen, N., Schirm, W., Mahon, B. Z., & Caramazza, A. (2008). Semantic interference in a delayed naming task: Evidence for the response exclusion hypothesis. *Journal of Experimental Psychology: Learning, Memory, and Cognition, 34,* 249–256.

Jurafsky, D. (1996). A probabilistic model of lexical and syntactic access and disambiguation. *Cognitive Science, 20,* 137–194.

Kroll, J. F., & Stewart, E. (1994). Category interference in translation and picture naming: Evidence for asymmetric connections between bilingual memory representations. *Journal of Memory and Language, 33,* 149–174.

Kuipers, J.-R., & La Heij, W. (2008). Semantic facilitation in category and action naming: Testing the message-congruency account. *Journal of Memory and Language, 58,* 123–139.

Kuipers, J.-R., La Heij, W., & Costa, A. (2006). A further look at semantic context effects in language production: The role of response congruency. *Language and Cognitive Processes, 21,* 892–919.

Jescheniak, J. D., & Schriefers, H. (1998). Serial discrete versus cascaded processing in lexical access in speech production: Further evidence from the co-activation of near-synonyms. *Journal of Experimental Psychology: Learning, Memory, and Cognition, 24,* 1256–1274.

La Heij, W. (1988). Components of Stroop-like interference in picture naming. *Memory and Cognition, 16,* 400–410.

La Heij, W., Dirkx, J., & Kramer, P. (1990). Categorical interference and associative priming in picture naming. *British Journal of Psychology, 81,* 511–525.

La Heij, W., Starreveld, P. A., & Kuipers, J.-P. (2007). Structural complexity is not the (big) issue: A reply to Roelofs (2007). *Language and Cognitive Processes, 22,* 1261–1280.

Levelt, W. J. M., Roelofs, A., & Meyer, A. S. (1999). A theory of lexical access in speech production. *Brain and Behavioral Sciences, 22,* 1–38.

Levelt, W. J. M., Schriefers, H., Vorberg, D., Meyer, A. S., Pechmann, T., & Havinga, J. (1991). The time course of lexical access in speech production: A study of picture naming. *Psychological Review, 98,* 122–142.

Lotto, L., Job, R., & Rumiati, R. (1999). Visual effects in picture and word categorization. *Memory and Cognition, 27,* 674–684.

Luce, R. D. (1959). *Individual Choice Behavior.* New York: John Wiley & Sons.

Lupker, S. J. (1979). The semantic nature of response competition in the picture-word interference task. *Memory and Cognition, 7,* 485–495.

Lupker, S. J., & Katz, A. N. (1981). Input, decision, and response factors in picture–word interference. *Journal of Experimental Psychology: Human Learning and Memory, 7,* 269–282.

Lupker, S. J., & Katz, A. N. (1982). Can automatic picture processing influence word judgments? *Journal of Experimental Psychology: Human Learning and Memory, 8*, 418–434.

Mahon, B. Z., Costa, A., Peterson, R., Vargas, K. A., & Caramazza, A. (2007). Lexical selection is not by competition: A reinterpretation of semantic interference and facilitation effects in the picture-word interference paradigm. *Journal of Experimental Psychology: Learning, Memory and Cognition, 33*, 503–535.

McClelland, J. L., & Elman, J. L. (1986). The TRACE model of speech perception. *Cognitive Psychology, 18*, 1–86.

MacDonald, M. C., Pearlmutter, N. J., & Seidenberg, M. S. (1994). Lexical nature of syntactic ambiguity resolution. *Psychological Review, 101*, 676–703.

MacLeod, C. M. (1991). Half a century of research on the Stroop effect: An integrative approach. *Psychological Bulletin, 109*, 163–203.

McRae, K., Spivey-Knowlton, M. J., & Tanenhaus, M. K. (1998). Modeling the influence of thematic fit (and other constraints) in on-line sentence comprehension. *Journal of Memory and Language, 38*, 283–312.

Melinger, A., & Abdel Rahman, R. (2008). *Lexical competition induced by indirectly activated semantic associates during picture naming.* Manuscript submitted for publication.

Miozzo, M., & Caramazza, A. (2003). When more is less – a counterintuitive effect of distractor frequency in picture-word interference paradigm. *Journal of Experimental Psychology: General, 132*, 228–252.

Navarrete, E., & Costa, A. (2005). Phonological activation of ignored pictures: Further evidence for a cascade model of lexical access. *Journal of Memory and Language, 53*, 359–377.

Peterson, R. R., & Savoy, P. (1998). Lexical selection and phonological encoding during language production: Evidence for cascaded processing. *Journal of Experimental Psychology: Learning, Memory, and Cognition, 24*, 539–557.

Rayner, K., & Duffy, S. (1986). Lexical complexity and fixation times in reading: Effects of word frequency, verb complexity, and lexical ambiguity. *Memory and Cognition, 14*, 191–201.

Roelofs, A. (1992). A spreading-activation theory of lemma retrieval in speaking. *Cognition, 42*, 107–142.

Roelofs, A. (1993). A spreading-activation theory of lemma retrieval in speaking. In W. J. M. Levelt (Ed.), *Lexical access in speech productiom* (pp. 107–142). Cambridge, MA: Blackwell.

Roelofs, A. (1997). The WEAVER model of word-form encoding in speech production. *Cognition, 64*, 249–284.

Roelofs, A. (2001). Set size and repetition matter: comment on Caramazza and Costa (2000). *Cognition, 80*, 283–290.

Roelofs, A. (2003). Goal-referenced selection of verbal action: Modeling attentional control in the Stroop task. *Psychological Review, 110*, 88–125.

Roelofs, A. (2006). Context effects of pictures and words in naming objects, reading words, and generating simple phrases. *Quarterly Journal of Experimental Psychology, 59A*, 1764–1784.

Roelofs, A. (2008a). Tracing attention and the activation flow in spoken word planning using eye movements. *Journal of Experimental Psychology: Learning, Memory, and Cognition, 34*, 353–368.

Roelofs, A. (2008b). Dynamics of the attentional control of word retrieval: Analyses of response time distributions. *Journal of Experimental Psychology: General, 137*, 303–323.

Schriefers, H., Meyer, A. S., & Levelt, W. J. M. (1990). Exploring the time course of lexical access in production: Picture-word interference studies. *Journal of Memory and Language, 29*, 86–102.

Spalek, K., & Damian, M. F. (2007, August). *Limited attentional resources affect semantic facilitation effects in object naming.* Poster presented at the International Workshop on Language Production, Münster, Germany.

Starreveld, P. A., & La Heij, W. (1995). Semantic interference, orthographic facilitation, and their interaction in naming tasks. *Journal of Experimental Psychology: Learning, Memory, and Cognition, 21*, 686–698.

Starreveld, P. A., & La Heij, W. (1996). Time-course analysis of semantic and orthographic context effects in picture-naming. *Journal of Experimental Psychology: Learning, Memory, and Cognition, 22*, 896–918.

Stemberger, J. P. (1985). An interactive activation model of language production. In A. W. Ellis (Vol. Eds.), *Progress in the psychology of language,* (Vol. 1). Hove, UK: Lawrence Erlbaum Associates Ltd.

Vigliocco, G., Lauer, M., Damian, M. F., & Levelt, W. J. M. (2002a). Semantic and syntactic forces in noun phrase production. *Journal of Experimental Psychology: Learning, Memory, and Cognition, 28*, 46–58.

Vigliocco, G., Vinson, D. P., Damian, M. F., & Levelt, W. J. M. (2002b). Semantic distance effects on object and action naming. *Cognition, 85*, B61–B69.

Vitkovitch, M., & Tyrrell, L. (1999). The effects of distractor words on naming pictures at the subordinate level. *Quarterly Journal of Experimental Psychology, 52A*, 905–926.

LANGUAGE AND COGNITIVE PROCESSES
2009, 24 (5), 735–748

Why does lexical selection have to be so hard? Comment on Abdel Rahman and Melinger's swinging lexical network proposal

Bradford Z. Mahon and Alfonso Caramazza

Center for Mind/Brain Sciences (CIMeC), University of Trento, Italy, and Department of Psychology, Harvard University, USA

The semantic interference effect, in the picture-word interference paradigm, has played an important role in the development of certain models of lexical selection. However, and aside from the semantic interference effect, the typical pattern that is observed when contrasting semantically related and unrelated distractors in the picture-word paradigm is facilitation. We have argued that semantic facilitation, and not semantic interference, is informative about the dynamics of lexical selection. Semantic interference in the picture-word interference paradigm arises at a post-lexical level of processing. Abdel Rahman and Melinger (2009 this issue) defend the hypothesis of lexical-selection-by-competition and argue that when the hypothesis is supplemented with additional assumptions, it can be reconciled with findings that are otherwise difficult to explain. Here we explore Abdel Rahman and Melinger's proposal. We argue that it is not clear that the authors have in fact succeeded in explaining the findings they set out to explain. In conclusion, we suggest that the liabilities of retaining the hypothesis of lexical-selection-by-competition outweigh the explanatory scope of that view.

Keywords: Lexical competition; picture-word interference paradigm; response exclusion hypothesis; semantic interference; semantic facilitation.

Correspondence should be addressed to Bradford Z. Mahon, Center for Mind/Brain Sciences, University of Trento, Rovereto, Palazzo Fedrigotti – Corso Bettini 31, I-38068-Rovereto, Italy. E-mail: Mahon@fas.harvard.edu

The authors are grateful to Jorge Almeida, Stefano Anzellotti, Niels Janssen, Eduardo Navarrete, and Pienie Zwitserlood for their comments on an earlier version of this article. BZM was supported in part by an Eliot Dissertation completion grant; AC was supported in part by grant DC006842 from the National Institute on Deafness and Other Communication Disorders. Preparation of this article was supported by a grant from the Fondazione Cassa di Risparmio di Trento e Rovereto.

http://www.psypress.com/lcp   DOI: 10.1080/01690960802597276

INTRODUCTION

The semantic interference effect (SIE) refers to the observation that participants are slower to name pictures of objects (e.g., horse) in the context of semantic category coordinate distractor words (e.g., whale) compared with unrelated distractors (e.g., truck). It has been argued that the SIE arises due to increased competition for selection of the target word in the related compared with the unrelated condition (e.g., La Heij, 1988; Schriefers, Meyer, & Levelt, 1990). The hypothesis of lexical-selection-by-competition (unadorned) thus predicts that any semantically related distractor word should interfere more than an unrelated distractor word. This prediction follows from current models of semantic and lexical processing in which activation spreads among semantic representations in proportion to their semantic similarity (Bloem & La Heij, 2003; Caramazza, 1997; Collins & Loftus, 1975; Dell, Oppenheim, & Kittredge, 2008; Roelofs, 1992). However, and aside from the semantic interference effect, the typical pattern that is observed in the picture-word paradigm when comparing semantically related and unrelated distractor words is not interference: the typical pattern is semantic facilitation (see Mahon, Costa, Peterson, Vargas, & Caramazza, 2007 for review and discussion). We have thus argued for a model of lexical selection that takes semantic facilitation effects, in the picture-word interference paradigm, to be the critical empirical phenomenon that must be explained.

Distractor words, compared with pictures (or ink colours in the Stroop task) have a privileged relationship to articulatory processes. Thus, in order to produce the picture name, the articulators must first be disengaged from the distractor word. Excluding the distractor word as a candidate for articulation costs time, and when a distractor word shares criteria that must be satisfied by a correct response, it costs more time. The SIE, on this view, arises at a post-lexical level of processing and is not informative about the dynamics of lexical retrieval processes (Finkbeiner & Caramazza, 2006; Janssen, Schirm, Mahon, & Caramazza, 2008; Mahon et al., 2007; Miozzo and Caramazza, 2003; for review of earlier, related but not identical, proposals see Glaser & Düngelhoff, 1984). We refer to this account as the Response Exclusion Hypothesis.

The Response Exclusion Hypothesis predicts that if semantic category coordinate distractors are prevented from having privileged access to the articulators then no SIE should be observed; if anything, such distractors should lead to semantic facilitation. The Response Exclusion Hypothesis also predicts (all else equal) that if distractor words are slowed from having access to the articulators, then they will take longer to be excluded as potential responses; under those circumstances, the empirical prediction is made that naming latencies will be longer. Another prediction that follows from this view is that it should be possible to observe the SIE when naming latencies are no longer constrained by the bottleneck at lexical selection. All three predictions have been confirmed (Prediction 1: Damian & Bowers, 2003; Finkbeiner & Caramazza, 2006; La Heij, Heikoop, Akerboom, & Bloem, 2003; Navarrete & Costa, 2005; Prediction 2: Abdel Rahman & Melinger, 2007[1]; Burt, 2002; Miozzo & Caramazza, 2003; Prediction 3: Janssen et al., 2008; for review and discussion see Mahon et al., 2007).

The most direct way to determine whether the SIE reflects lexical-selection-by-competition is to manipulate the within-category semantic distance between distractor words and target pictures. As would be predicted by the view that lexical selection is not by competition, target naming latencies (e.g., horse) are faster in the context of within-category semantically close distractors (e.g., zebra) than in the context of within-category semantically far distractors (e.g., whale) (Mahon et al., 2007; see Ischebeck, 2003, for the same finding with Arabic numeral naming).

The challenge to the assumption of lexical-selection-by-competition is thus two-fold. First, the hypothesis must explain why there are polarity reversals from semantic interference to semantic facilitation. On the account that we have proposed, semantic facilitation effects reflect the dynamics of lexical selection, while the SIE arises at a post-lexical locus. The second challenge to the hypothesis of lexical competition is to explain why naming latencies to target pictures are faster for within-category semantically close distractors compared to within-category semantically far distractors. On the account we have proposed, the within-category distance effect follows from the contrasting effects of facilitation (at the lexical level, due to semantic distance) and interference at the response-level, due to the presence of category coordinate distractors.

In their article 'Semantic context effects in language production: A swinging lexical network proposal and a review', Abdel Rahman and Melinger (2009 this issue; hereafter AR&M) argue that both challenges can be met by a theory of lexical-selection-by-competition. AR&M make

---

[1] A number of studies have explored the effect on naming latencies of an associative relationship that points from distractor words to target pictures (see Mahon et al., 2007 for review and data). However, only recently (Abdel Rahman & Melinger, 2007) has the effect on naming latencies of having an associative relationship from the target toward the distractor been studied. When the associative relationship goes from the target picture to the distractor word, the hypothesis of lexical competition would predict greater interference for associatively related distractors than unrelated distractors. That prediction is at variance with the facilitatory effect that is empirically observed (Abdel Rahman & Melinger, 2007). That facilitatory effect can be interpreted within the framework of the Response Exclusion Hypothesis, following the same logic used for explaining the distractor frequency effect. Distractor words that are associates of the target pictures are available sooner for exclusion compared with distractor words that are not associates of the targets.

three principal claims: (1) That the arguments we have developed against the hypothesis of lexical-selection-by-competition fail to appreciate the role played by the number of activated non-target words; (2) There are trade-offs between facilitation at the semantic level and interference at the lexical level; and (3) There are strong biases (or even absolute constraints) on spreading activation in the semantic and lexical systems. Here we explore these three aspects of AR&M's proposal.[2]

COMMENTS ON AR&M'S SWINGING LEXICAL NETWORK PROPOSAL

What determines the amount of lexical competition?

The central claim of AR&M is that naming latencies to target pictures are affected by the level of activation of *all* words within the network: '... we assume that the latency of target lemma selection varies as a function of the state of activation of the entire lexical network, and is proportionally delayed with an increasing number of active competitors' (p. 715). There are at least two ways in which AR&M's proposal may be interpreted. On the one hand, and in the tradition of current models (e.g., Roelofs, 1992), AR&M may be taken to be (merely) emphasising the existing assumption that the (sum) level of activation of all words in the network is critical for determining the amount of competition for selection of the target word. On this interpretation, there is nothing about the 'number' (qua number) of activated words that is important, but only that the (sum) level of activation is computed over *all* words in the system. On the other hand, AR&M also at times seem to accord a special role to the 'number' of non-target words that are activated, without specification of their relative levels of activation. Here we explore both readings of AR&M's proposal. We argue that it is not obvious that either version provides a clear solution to the problems that are faced by the hypothesis of lexical-selection-by-competition. For exposition, we follow AR&M's lead in using the within-category semantic distance effect as the target phenomenon to be explained:

> While the observation of slower naming latencies with increasing semantic distance might be viewed as being contrary to what a single-lexical competitor account would predict, it is in line with the above described trade-off account

---

[2] AR&M cite unpublished data at several points in their argument; as there is no way to evaluate those findings, we focus here on the relation between the authors' theoretical claims and published findings.

and competition induced by lexical cohorts. First, close distractors should yield stronger priming effects than distant distractors at the conceptual level. Second, one only needs to assume that semantically distant target–distractor pairs co-activate a lexical cohort with numerous different members belonging to this broadly defined category (e.g., animals: not only the target bee and distractor horse, but also other members of this category such as ant, snake, mouse etc., are activated; cf. Figure 1 [AR&M]). In contrast, semantically close target–distractor pairs (bee and fly) co-activate a much more confined and narrow category (e.g., insects: bee, fly, ant; cf. Figure 1 [AR&M]). Such comparatively small semantic categories have fewer members than broad categories. Consequently, close distractors should induce less interference than distant distractors (Abdel Rahman & Melinger, 2008, p. 721; see Figure 1 therein).

Interpretation 1: What determines the amount of lexical competition is the (sum) level of activation of all words in the system (see e.g., Roelofs, 1992)

AR&M's construal of the activation state of the network in the within-category semantically close and far conditions highlights the point that a broader array of words may be activated in the semantically far than in the semantically close condition. Whether or not this is the case depends entirely on the semantic network architecture that is assumed to mediate how activation spreads among concepts. Is there a plausible semantic architecture that will guarantee that different sized cohorts of words will be activated in the within-category semantically close and far conditions? Perhaps the most straightforward way in which the semantic network might be organised in order to guarantee this (and which AR&M seem to indicate in their discussion – but see Figure 1 [AR&M], and footnote 3 and discussion below) is that distractor words and target pictures in the within-category semantically far condition do not share a common superordinate node. So for instance, the target 'bee' will activate other insects (through its super-ordinate concept INSECT) and the within-category semantically far distractor 'horse' will activate other animals, by virtue of its superordinate concept. In contrast, in the within-category semantically close condition, the target (bee) and the distractor (fly) will activate only insects, but not other living creatures (horse, snake, etc).

However, a suggestion along those lines would face an important difficulty. The within-category semantically far distractor shows semantic interference compared to the unrelated baseline. This would seem to compel the assumption that there is some common superordinate node that is shared by the target and the distractor in the within-category semantically far condition. This is because, on AR&M's proposal, the presence of semantic interference indicates that activation has converged on a cohort of words.

The potential difficulty faced by AR&M's proposal may, however, even be greater: given that the authors would be compelled to assume that there is a conceptual representation common to the target and distractor in the within-category semantically far condition, it follows that that representation will also be activated by the same items (distractors and targets) when they appear in the within-category semantically close condition.[3] Thus, it is not clear if there would be different sized cohorts of activated words in the within-category semantically close and far conditions.

There is another concern associated with AR&M's characterisation of the semantic network architecture. The authors do not (at least in the current deployment of their theory) consider the influences of other types of semantic relationships (see Figure 1 therein).[4] The onus is on the authors to show how such an impoverished semantic network can explain the range of semantic distance effects that historically, have formed a major impetus for current models of semantic memory (e.g., Collins & Loftus, 1975). For comparison, consider the semantic network in Roelofs (1992) model: there are a number of 'semantic features' (e.g., 'has-a', 'part-of', 'is-a', 'can-do', etc.) that are linked to lexical concepts, and which guarantee that the network will display the dynamic properties as a function of semantic distance that must be explained.

For discussion, it may be supposed that AR&M could adopt the lexical-conceptual space, present in for instance Roelofs (1992; see also Collins & Loftus, 1975). For discussion, one may also grant that there are different sized cohorts of activated words in the within-category semantically close and far conditions. The critical issue is then the relative (sum) levels of activation of those different cohorts. One must compare the activation levels of a relatively narrow cohort of words that is activated in common by both

---

[3] In Figure 1 (AR&M), the superordinate node ANIMAL is connected to basic level representations of insects (bee, fly, etc.) as well as to basic level representations of mammals (e.g., horse) and other living creatures (e.g., snake). Thus, the superordinate node ANIMAL would be activated in the within-category semantically close condition (target: bee, distractor: fly), and consequently all of the basic level items that are connected to that node would also be activated (e.g., horse, snake, etc.). Following the schematic in AR&M's Figure 1 thus leads also to the same conclusion: it seems that cohorts of the same size will be activated in the within-category semantically close and semantically far conditions, contrary to the authors' gloss in the excerpted passage.

It is also relevant here that in all of the experiments in which we studied within-category semantic distance effects, designs were used in which the same distractor words appeared in the two within-category conditions (close and far). This means that the (structurally fixed) semantic neighbourhoods (including superordinate category nodes) of distractors and targets in the within-category semantically close and far conditions are the same.

[4] In their schematic (Figure 1: AR&M) the authors stipulate the existence of other nodes that mediate how activation flows at the semantic level (e.g., 'associative relation'). It is not clear why such relationships should be afforded the status of a 'semantic node'.

the target concept and the within-category semantically close distractor, to a broad cohort of words that is diffusely activated by the target and the within-category semantically far distractor. AR&M are in agreement that the individual words within the narrower cohort will be more highly activated than those within the broader cohort. This is because words within the narrow, but not the broad, cohort will receive converging input from both the target and the distractor. It could thus be, and depending on the network parameters that were chosen, that the (sum) level of activation of the narrow cohort is greater than that of the broad cohort. Thus, even granting different sized cohorts of activated words in the two experimental conditions, the relative activation levels of the two cohorts remains unspecified (and in large measure, parameter dependent).

A similar issue arises in explaining the SIE itself in terms of lexical competition. That explanation assumes that in the related condition, a given word (e.g., a non-target coordinate of the distractor) receives activation from two sources (target and distractor); in contrast, in the unrelated condition, a given word (e.g., a coordinate of the distractor) receives activation from a single source (i.e., the distractor). Yet, it must be the case that the (sum) level of activation in the related condition is greater than in the unrelated condition, otherwise AR&M would not be able to explain the basic SIE. In other words, in order to explain the basic SIE, AR&M must assume that the sum level of activation of a relatively narrow cohort of words (in the related condition) is greater than the sum level of activation of a much broader cohort of words (in the unrelated condition). The only way in which this would be the case is if the individual elements that constitute the narrower cohort are more highly activated than the individual elements that constitute the broader cohort.

To this point we have followed AR&M's lead in *not* factoring in the relative levels of activation of words corresponding to the within-category semantically close and far distractors. The authors are in agreement that words corresponding to within-category semantically close distractors will be more highly activated than words corresponding to within-category semantically far distractors. When those activation levels are factored in, will it be the case that the (sum) activation level will be *less* in the within-category close than in the within-category far condition?

Interpretation 2: What determines the amount of lexical competition is the 'number' of activated non-target words

This interpretation of AR&M's claim is not exclusive of the interpretation in terms of (sum) activation levels. However, it is not clear that appealing to the 'number' of activated words, independently of the activation levels of those words, contributes toward explaining the amount of competition that is encountered at selection of the target word. It could not be that simply having 'more activated non-target words', independently of their activation levels, leads to more competition for target lexical selection. This is because the hypothesis could not then explain the basic SIE: an unrelated distractor word will activate an *entirely* different cohort of words than is activated by the target concept and the semantic coordinate distractor. Thus, *more* words will be activated in the unrelated than in the related condition. However, it is not the case that, for the SIE '... the latency of target lemma selection ... is proportionally delayed with an increasing number of active competitors' (AR&M, p. 715).[5]

Are there trade-offs between facilitation at the semantic level and interference at the lexical level?

AR&M argue that because the number of activated non-target words is important, there are tradeoffs between facilitation at the conceptual level and interference at the lexical level. In AR&M's terms, in situations of one-to-one competition a target word competes for selection with a single non-target word, while in situations of one-to-many competition, a target word competes for selection with a whole cohort of non-target words. AR&M stipulate that priming from the distractor to the target at the semantic level will be greater than interference at the lexical level in situations of one-to-one competition, but not in situations of one-to-many competition.

It is difficult to evaluate AR&M's proposal because as the authors acknowledge, they do not know '... how large a lexical cohort must be before it can offset a conceptual facilitation effect' (AR&M, p. 728). We also have no way of establishing this. It does seem clear, however, that some fine tuning will be required in order to determine the situations under which such cohorts are assumed to develop within the speech production system. For instance, AR&M argue that such a cohort can develop for contextually related nouns. Presumably, such a cohort should also develop for contextually related words that are not of the same grammatical class. For instance, when naming the picture 'bed' in the context of the distractor verb 'sleep',

---

[5] Another (conceivable) reading of AR&M's claim is that there is no gradation in the levels of activation of lexical nodes: lexical nodes are either activated (e.g., an activation state of '1') or are not activated (activation state of '0'). On such a theory, it would follow that what would truly matter is the sheer number of activated words, as that would be directly proportional to the amount of competition for selection of the target word. Such an account would be able, in principle, to explain why within-category semantically close distractors 'interfere less' than within-category semantically far distractor words. However, this version of the lexical-selection-by-competition hypothesis would not be able to explain the SIE: there will be more non-target words activated in the unrelated than the related condition. Furthermore, the theory would have no obvious way to implement the construct 'semantic distance'.

there is a clear set of items that should receive convergent activation (pillow, dream, mattress, etc.). Contrary to what AR&M's cohort account would predict however, facilitation and not interference is observed for semantically related verbs in noun naming (Mahon et al., 2007). Similar questions arise with respect to the facilitatory effect of distractor words that name parts of the target objects (Costa, Alario, & Caramazza, 2005; see also discussion below).

The arguments outlined in the preceding section about the relevance of the variable 'number of activated words' may undermine the notions of one-to-many and one-to-one competition. However, and independently of those arguments, it is not obvious that trade-offs, even as stipulated by AR&M, can explain polarity reversals from semantic interference to facilitation. Consider AR&M's explanation of the part-whole effect (Costa et al., 2005): Participants are faster to name objects when the distractors name a (non-visible) part of the object than when the distractor is unrelated. According to the network developed in Roelofs (1992), the presence of 'part-of' nodes (and their respective connections) will result in higher levels of activation for lexical nodes in the related than in the unrelated condition. It would then have to be argued on AR&M's account, that distractor-to-target priming facilitates target conceptual selection *more* than target words are slowed down due to competition at the lexical level.

Does such an explanation work? AR&M adopt the use of the Luce ratio as a means for determining when the target word will be selected (see Roelofs, 1992). The Luce ratio is a proportion that generates the probability (at each time step) of selecting the target word. The value of the Luce ratio is determined by dividing the level of activation of the target word by the (sum) level of activation of all words within the system, *including the target node.* Because the level of activation of the target word is included in the denominator of the Luce ratio, it must also be assumed that more activation spreads from the target representation to the distractor than from the distractor representation to the target. Critically, that asymmetry in spreading activation must be large enough to ensure that distractor-to-target priming *does not* outweigh the competition for selection of the target word. It is thus not obvious, that the trade-off account of AR&M, even as stipulated, can explain polarity reversals from semantic interference to facilitation.

Is spreading activation biased?

AR&M's suggestion of biases on spreading activation builds on previous proposals (e.g., Bloem & La Heij, 2003; see also discussion immediately above regarding asymmetries on spreading activation between targets and distractors). For instance, Bloem and La Heij (2003) proposed that activated concepts do not automatically spread activation to their corresponding lexical nodes, in order to explain why distractor pictures facilitate the translation of words that are semantic category coordinates. AR&M have not specified (e.g., as did Bloem & La Heij, 2003) the conditions that must obtain for such biases on spreading activation to be realised. The authors discuss the influence of contextual factors, such as the other items with which a given item is presented, and/or task-related instructions. Understood in that way, the idea of contextually induced 'biases' on the spreading of activation is not new: if a set of related concepts are co-activated, those concepts will tend to mutually activate one another. Furthermore, and as discussed by the authors, a new 'category' of items could be established by strongly activating those items within a specific task context.

A much more radical notion of biases on the spreading of activation could stipulate the presence of structural constraints that guarantee that only a subset of words are in fact activated, compared to the entire set of nodes that would otherwise be activated. For instance, it may be argued that lexical nodes corresponding to distractor words become activated only if those distractors are category coordinates of the target concepts. In this way, the proposal would redefine the construct of a 'lexical competitor' to only include words that are coordinates of the target concept. The motivation for such a revision is not clear. It is also not clear how such a constraint would be implemented, at either the semantic or lexical levels. Furthermore, the within-category semantic distance effect would remain to be explained.

'Semantic interference' is not synonymous with 'lexical competition'

A number of authors, including AR&M, have argued that 'semantic interference' effects observed in other naming paradigms constitute support for the assumption of lexical competition (Damian, Vigliocco, & Levelt, 2001; Belke, Meyer, & Damian, 2005; Kroll & Stewart, 1994). For instance, Brown (1981; see also Kroll & Stewart, 1994; Damian et al., 2001) observed that naming latencies to target pictures are slower if the pictures are blocked by semantic category than if they are intermixed with unrelated pictures. Damian and Als (2005) subsequently showed that naming latencies for target pictures from the same semantic category, all appearing in the same block, are slower even when unrelated picture naming trials are interspersed throughout the block. Similar to Damian and Als' observation, Howard, Nickels, Coltheart, and Cole-Virtue (2006; see also Brown, 1981) observed that naming latencies to each subsequently named within-category picture increase, independently of the number of intervening items from other categories (we refer to this as the Cumulative Within Category Cost; Navarrete, Mahon, and Caramazza, 2008).

As discussed by Damian and Als (2005; see also discussion in Dell et al., 2008; Howard et al., 2006) it is unlikely that either the semantic blocking effect or the related Cumulative Within Category Cost can be explained only by reference to (positive) spreading activation. As discussed by various authors, possible accounts may be developed in terms of a learning mechanism (Damian & Als, 2005; Dell et al., 2008), and/or memory related processes (Brown, Whiteman, Cattoi, & Bradley, 1985; see also Norman, Newman, & Detre, 2007), and/or a combination of excitatory and inhibitory connections (Dell et al., 2008; Howard et al., 2006). Regardless of the view that is adopted, it follows that those 'semantic interference effects' do not constitute evidence, either for or against, the hypothesis of lexical-selection-by-competition. Those phenomena also do not constitute evidence, either for or against, the Response Exclusion Hypothesis.[6]

In contrast, semantic facilitation effects are directly relevant for evaluating the dynamical principles that govern lexical retrieval processes. Belke and colleagues (2005; see also Damian et al., 2005) showed that semantic facilitation, and not semantic interference, is observed in the first presentation of items within a block. Abdel Rahman and Melinger (2007) found semantic facilitation (instead of semantic interference) for the first entire block. Such semantic facilitation effects are difficult to accommodate on the view that lexical selection is by competition. In contrast, on the model we have outlined, the 'normal' effect of semantic context on correct lexical selection events should be facilitatory. The pattern of how facilitation changes to interference is informative of the (perhaps, non-language relevant) processes that lead to interference (e.g., a learning mechanism, a memory related explanation, etc.).

CONCLUSION

The hypothesis of lexical-selection-by-competition faces two challenges: (1) to explain polarity reversals from semantic interference to facilitation in the picture-word naming task; and (2) to explain the facilitatory effect of

---

[6] In our first attempt to synthesise the various effects of semantic context on naming latencies in speech production (Mahon et al., 2007), we highlighted the similarity between the semantic blocking paradigm and the semantic interference effect in the picture-word interference paradigm. In both paradigms, semantic interference is induced by contextual stimuli that are semantic category coordinates of the target. We noted that '[p]reviously named pictures will be available as potential responses' (Mahon et al., 2007, p. 516). We no longer believe that aspect of the paradigm to be an integral part of a viable account of the semantic blocking phenomenon (see Navarrete et al., 2008). Regardless, the explanatory status of cumulative semantic effects is independent of the role of the Response Exclusion Hypothesis in explaining semantic interference in the picture-word paradigm.

decreasing semantic distance between distractors and targets. We have argued that AR&M's proposal does not succeed with respect to either challenge. Further assumptions can always be envisioned that would help to overcome these difficulties. Computational simulations can also be envisioned in which the parameter space might be searched in order to fit models to specific effects – our argument has not been that there is, in principle, no possible set of parameters that can explain specific findings that have been argued to be problematic for lexical-selection-by-competition. However, the additional assumptions that would be required in order to 'save' the assumption of lexical-selection-by-competition have their motivation only in that purpose. Is the assumption of lexical competition worth saving at *any* cost?

As AR&M acknowledge, their review of the experimental literature is selective, and the explanatory scope of the Swinging Lexical Network Proposal is even more restricted than the authors' review. For instance, the proposal does not address the findings that (1) SIE is observed in a delayed naming task (Janssen et al., 2008); (2) low frequency distractors interfere more than high frequency distractors (Burt, 2002; Miozzo & Caramazza, 2003); (3) either no SIE, or semantic facilitation is observed for picture distractors in picture naming (Damian & Bowers, 2003; La Heij et al., 2003; Navarrete & Costa, 2005); or (4) that masked semantic category coordinate distractors facilitate target naming compared with masked unrelated distractors (Finkbeiner & Caramazza, 2006).

Adopting the account that we have outlined would shift the focus of study in several different directions. For instance, one issue that becomes prominent concerns the dynamics of spreading activation at the semantic level, and how spreading activation facilitates processes involved in lexical access. Another change in focus concerns what the picture-word interference paradigm itself can tell us about language production: The Response Exclusion Hypothesis is, above all, a proposal about how conflicts that are induced by the picture-word (and Stroop) task are resolved within the speech production system. Thus, the issue arises of how the picture-word paradigm can be used to study the mechanisms of control that mediate the production of response-level representations.

REFERENCES

Abdel Rahman, R., & Melinger, A. (2007). When bees hamper the production of honey: Lexical interference from associates in speech production. *Journal of Experimental Psychology: Learning, Memory and Cognition, 33*, 604–614.

Abdel Rahman, R., & Melinger, A. (2009). Semantic context effects in language production: A swinging lexical network proposal and a review. *Language and Cognitive Processes, 24*, 713–734.

Belke, E., Meyer, A., & Damian, M. F. (2005). Refractory effect in picture naming as assessed in a semantic blocking paradigm. *Quarterly Journal of Experimental Psychology, 58A*, 667–692.

Bloem, I., & La Heij, W. (2003). Semantic facilitation and semantic interference in word translation: Implications for models of lexical access. *Journal of Memory and Language, 48*, 468–488.

Brown, A. S. (1981). Inhibition in cued retrieval. *Journal of Experimental Psychology: Human Learning and Memory, 7*, 204–215.

Brown, A. S., Whiteman, S. L., Cattoi, R. J., & Bradley, C. K. (1985). Associative strength level and retrieval inhibition in semantic memory. *American Journal of Psychology, 98*, 421–432.

Burt, J. S. (2002). Why do non-color words interfere with color naming? *Journal of Experimental Psychology: Human Perception and Performance, 28(A)*, 1019–1038.

Caramazza, A. (1997). How many levels of processing are there in lexical access? *Cognitive Neuropsychology, 14*, 177–208.

Collins, A. M., & Loftus, E. F. (1975). A spreading activation theory of semantic memory. *Psychological Review, 82*, 407–428.

Costa, A., Alario, F.-X., & Caramazza, A. (2005). On the categorical nature of the semantic interference effect in the picture–word interference paradigm. *Psychonomic Bulletin and Review, 12*, 125–131.

Damian, M. F., & Als, L. C. (2005). Long-lasting semantic context effects in the spoken production of object names. *Journal of Experimental Psychology: Learning, Memory, and Cognition, 31*, 1372–1384.

Damian, M. F., & Bowers, J. S. (2003). Locus of semantic interference in picture-word interference tasks. *Psychonomic Bulletin and Review, 10*, 111–117.

Damian, M. F., Vigliocco, G., & Levelt, W. J. M. (2001). Effects of semantic context in the naming of pictures and words. *Cognition, 81*, B77–B86.

Dell, G.S., Oppenheim, G. M., & Kittredge, A. K. (2008). Saying the right word at the right time: Syntagmatic and paradigmatic interference in sentence production. *Language and Cognitive Processes, 23*, 583–608.

Finkbeiner, M., & Caramazza, A. (2006). Now you see it, now you don't: On turning semantic interference into facilitation in a Stroop-like task. *Cortex, 42*, 790–796.

Glaser, W. R., & Düngelhoff, F.-J. (1984). The time course of picture–word interference. *Journal of Experimental Psychology: Human Perception and Performance, 10*, 640–654.

Howard, D., Nickels, L., Coltheart, M., & Cole-Virtue, J. (2006). Cumulative semantic inhibition in picture naming: experimental and computational studies. *Cognition, 100*, 464–482.

Janssen, N., Schirm, W., Mahon, B. Z., & Caramazza, A. (2008). The semantic interference effect in the picture-word interference paradigm: Evidence for the response selection hypothesis. *Journal of Experimental Psychology: Learning, Memory, and Cognition, 34*, 249–256.

Kroll, J. F., & Stewart, E. (1994). Category interference in translation and picture naming: Evidence for asymmetric connections between bilingual memory representations. *Journal of Memory and Language, 33*, 149–174.

Ischebeck, A. (2003). Differences between digit naming and number word reading in a flanker task. *Memory and Cognition, 31*, 529–537.

La Heij, W. (1988). Components of Stroop-like interference in picture naming. *Memory and Cognition, 16*, 400–410.

La Heij, W., Heikoop, K. W., Akerboom, S., & Bloem, I. (2003). Picture naming in picture context: Semantic interference or semantic facilitation? *Psychology Science, 45*, 49–62.

Mahon, B. Z., Costa, A., Peterson, R., Vargas, K., & Caramazza, A. (2007). Lexical selection is not by competition: A reinterpretation of semantic interference and facilitation effects in the picture-word interference paradigm. *Journal of Experimental Psychology: Learning, Memory, and Cognition, 33*, 503–535.

Miozzo, M., & Caramazza, A. (2003). When more is less: A counterintuitive effect of distractor frequency in picture–word interference paradigm. *Journal of Experimental Psychology: General, 132*, 228–252.

Navarrete, E., & Costa, A. (2005). Phonological activation of ignored pictures: Further evidence for a cascade model of lexical access. *Journal of Memory and Language, 53*, 359–377.

Navarrete, E., Mahon, B. Z., & Caramazza, A. (2008). *The cumulative within-category cost in picture processing*. Manuscript submitted for publication.

Norman, K. A., Newman, E. L., & Detre, G. (2007). A neural network model of retrieval-induced forgetting. *Psychological Review, 114*, 887–953.

Roelofs, A. (1992). A spreading-activation theory of lemma retrieval in speaking. *Cognition, 42*, 107–142.

Schriefers, H., Meyer, A. S., & Levelt, W. J. M. (1990). Exploring the time course of lexical access in language production: Picture–word interference studies. *Journal of Memory and Language, 29*, 86–102.

LANGUAGE AND COGNITIVE PROCESSES
2009, 24 (5), 749–760

Dismissing lexical competition does not make speaking any easier: A rejoinder to Mahon and Caramazza (2009)

Rasha Abdel Rahman

Humboldt-University Berlin, Germany

Alissa Melinger

University of Dundee, Scotland

The swinging lexical network proposal (Abdel Rahman & Melinger, 2009a this issue) incorporates three assumptions that are independently motivated and pre-existing in the literature. We claim that the combination of these three assumptions provides an account for a wide range of facilitation and interference observations. In their comment, Mahon and Caramazza question the success of our proposal by challenging the individual assumptions at its core. However, most of their criticisms are built on misconstruals of our proposal. Here, we revisit their points and clarify our position with regard to their specific concerns. We maintain that competition models do not necessitate an over-complication of lexical selection but rather provide an elegant and consistent mechanism to capture many empirical observations.

Keywords: Lexical cohort activation; Competition; Semantic interference effect; Speech production.

In our article (Abdel Rahman & Melinger, 2009a) we proposed a framework of lexical selection by competition that is sensitive to the activation status of lexical cohorts. We outlined a swinging lexical network proposal that builds on three assumptions. First, rather than concentrating on one-to-one competition as a major determinant for semantic interference effects, we focus on the activation status of whole cohorts of inter-related lexical items that mutually co-activate each other, thus creating a mass of highly active

Correspondence should be addressed to Rasha Abdel Rahman, Humboldt-University Berlin, Rudower Chaussee 18, 12489 Berlin, Germany. E-mail: rasha.abdel.rahman@cms.hu-berlin.de

Preparation of this paper was supported by a grants (AB 277 3-1 and 4-1) from the German Research Council to Rasha Abdel Rahman.

http://www.psypress.com/lcp   DOI: 10.1080/01690960802648491

units which together compete with the target entry for selection. Second, we assume a trade-off between contextually induced semantic facilitation and lexical competition. Context effects tend to be facilitation dominant when lexical competition is restricted to one-to-one relations and interference dominant when competition involves a cohort of active competitors (one-to-many competition). Third, we assume that the network dynamics are strongly affected by meaningful contexts gating the spread of activation at the conceptual level. Context-dependent dynamic adaptations of the conceptual system have a strong influence on lexical selection by flexibly recruiting cohorts of varying combinations and sizes.

We argued that the proposed framework explains a variety of reported facilitation and interference effects, some of which have been interpreted as evidence against lexical competition models. In their comment, Mahon and Caramazza (2009 this issue) questioned the explanatory scope of the proposal and criticised details of the swinging lexical network proposal. However, each of these criticisms is predicated on a flawed understanding of our three core assumptions. Therefore, in this response, we first discuss the criticisms and related misconceptions, clarifying out position along the way. We then discuss our proposal in light of two challenges Mahon and Caramazza identify for competition models. In the final section, we characterise some of the fundamental differences in our respective approaches in order to provide some backdrop for our differing views.

LEXICAL ACTIVATION LEVELS AND THE NUMBER OF ACTIVE COMPETITORS: WHAT DETERMINES THE AMOUNT OF COMPETITION?

Mahon and Caramazza offer two interpretations of our swinging lexical network proposal and discuss them as separate theoretical alternatives. However, contrary to their suggestion, the two interpretations are *not independent* of each other. According to one interpretation, the *number* of activated non-target words "... independently of the activation levels of those words" (p. 741) determines the amount of lexical competition. This is clearly not how we described lexical cohort activation in our article. The point we made is that the number of active competitors is an important factor because, due to contextual relations, these competitors *are mutually related and therefore co-activate each other*. The more inter-related competitors are active, the more strongly they activate each other, and the more competition they should induce. This is what we call the swinging lexical network. Thus, we do claim that the number of active competitors is an important factor for lexical selection latencies – not because of the number per se – but because of the strong influence that cohort size has on the individual activation levels of these competitors (that mutually activate each other), yielding in sum strong competition.

According to the second interpretation we are "... (merely) emphasising the existing assumption that the (sum) level of activation of all words in the network is critical for determining the amount of competition" (p. 738) (e.g., Levelt, Roelofs, & Meyer, 1999; Roelofs, 1992). We are indeed incorporating this assumption as the major determinant for semantic interference effects. However, as discussed in our article, we argue that the *size* of the cohort of active competitors is a critical factor. If the duration of target selection depends on the sum level of activation of all active nodes, then an increasing number of co-activated and contextually linked entries will increase the individual activation levels and, as a consequence, the sum level of competing activation considerably, thus delaying lexical selection of the target.

For an example, consider the picture-word interference (PWI) paradigm. Upon presentation of an object picture (for instance, a mouse), the target concept (MOUSE) and semantically related concepts (e.g., ANIMAL via 'is a' relations; FOUR LEGS via 'has' relations) are activated. As a consequence of this activation spread, categorically related concepts that share these features such as RABBIT, DOG, HORSE, CAMEL, etc., and associatively related concepts such as CHEESE, are activated. Due to continuous bidirectional information transmission between the conceptual and lexical levels, all active concepts pass activation to and receive activation from their respective lexical entries. As a result of this mutual between-level spread of activation, not only the target but also related non-target lexical entries such as rabbit, dog, horse, camel and cheese are activated and conjointly compete for selection according to the Luce ratio.

Now let's examine how different types of distractor words interact with the spread of activation instigated by the target picture. A categorically related distractor (e.g., rabbit) will activate the lexical entry rabbit and, via the bidirectional links between concepts and lexical entries, will also activate other concepts and lexical entries related to rabbit; mouse, dog, horse, camel, etc. Thus, not only will the competitor *rabbit* itself receive converging activation from the picture and the distractor word, but so will a whole cohort of shared category members. Because these related lexical entries co-activate each other, the network is now swinging. According to the Luce ratio, this semantically inter-related cohort of highly activated lexical competitors will induce strong one-to-many competition, resulting in sizable interference effects.

The situation is different when the distractor word is, for instance, associatively related to the target but drawn from a different semantic category (e.g., cheese). In this case, concepts and lexical entries such as grapes, red wine, ragout fin, etc. (categorically related to cheese), and mouse (associatively related) will receive activation from the distractor. In contrast to the scenario for categorically related distractors, however, the converging activation from picture and associate distractor is restricted to the target and a single competitor (the word itself) or a very small cohort; as most of the words related to the distractor are not also related to the target, activation does not resonate within a cohort of inter-related reciprocating items. Instead, activation from the two sources diverges onto mutually unrelated representations; the network is not swinging. Thus, in the case of associatively related distractors there is a comparatively weak one-to-one competition between the target and an isolated competitor. Naturally, in addition to the single strong competitor there are also many weakly active competitors, but this would also be the case when the distractor is unrelated to the target. The above described one-to-one account for facilitation-dominant semantic context effects is not restricted to associative relations. The same principles are assumed to hold for other types of distractors that tend to have a one-to-one relation to the target or co-activate a very small cohort, for instance semantically related verb distractors (e.g., bed, sleeping) or part-whole relations.

To summarise, neither of the interpretations of the swinging lexical network described and criticised by Mahon and Caramazza are accurate characterisations. Our cohort assumption hinges on both the size of the cohorts and the activation levels of the cohort members, which are intimately related with the cohort size. These two factors cannot be viewed separately or independently of each other. The more competitors from an inter-related semantic cohort that are co-activated, the more they will in turn activate each other (see also our discussion of the semantic distance effect, below). Thus, we explain effects of related distractors with the same mechanisms assumed to hold for one-to-one competition, namely, converging activation from target picture and distractor word. However, additionally, we take whole cohorts into account, not just single lexical competitors. We argue that this cohort activation has a much more powerful influence on competitive lexical selection than isolated competitors and their individual activation levels.

TRADE-OFFS BETWEEN CONCEPTUAL FACILITATION AND LEXICAL INTERFERENCE

The failure to appreciate the mechanics underlying cohort activation leads Mahon and Caramazza to challenge our assumption that there are trade-offs between contextually induced semantic facilitation and lexical competition. As an example, they discuss the facilitation observed in the PWI paradigm when distractors are parts of whole objects (Costa, Alario, & Caramazza,

2005). They argue that, according to Roelofs (1992) a part-of relation (e.g., target: car, distractor: bumper) should result in a higher activation level of the competitor compared to an unrelated word, and should therefore induce interference. A trade-off account, they argue, would have to assume stronger semantic priming than lexical competition effects. In fact, part-whole relations, as well as object-action relations, create the same competition scenario as associative relations (see discussion above), namely a situation in which the target and distractor do not activate a set of inter-related co-activating concepts. The flaw in their argument is the failure to incorporate a lexical cohort into the mix, thereby missing the crucial feature of the swinging lexical network proposal: It is the presence of a cohort that determines whether interference or facilitation wins out, not asymmetries in spreading activation, and not one-to-one relations.

Furthermore, it is interesting to note that the account advocated by Mahon and Caramazza also incorporates trade-offs. As they write, "On the account we have proposed, the within-category distance effect follows from the contrasting effects of facilitation (at the lexical level, due to semantic distance) and interference at the response-level, due to the presence of category coordinate distractors" (p. 737).

HARD-WIRED AND FLEXIBLE ASPECTS OF SEMANTIC NETWORK DYNAMICS

In their comment, Mahon and Caramazza misleadingly portray the semantic network's sensitivity to context as "biases on spreading activation" (p. 743) and argue that we have not specified the conditions for such biases. We reject this characterisation and take this opportunity to explain our view on dynamic lexical/semantic networks once more. In brief, we assume that the conceptual system and, mediated by the former, the lexical network, are shaped by meaningful associations and contexts extending beyond classic and hard-wired semantic relations that are stored in long-term memory (such as taxonomic categories). We assume that ad-hoc relations between concepts as well as ad-hoc categories that integrate related or unrelated concepts in a meaningful way (e.g., things to collect rain water when stranded on a desert island) can be flexibly formed as the context requires. Furthermore, we assume that these adaptations affect the activation status of lexical cohorts just as classic hard-wired relations do.

Although such flexible context adaptations have not yet gained much attention in speech production research, there is a rich research tradition examining the dynamics of contextual adaptations of the conceptual system on which we build our assumptions. This research strongly suggests that different facets of a concept's meaning are activated (or ignored) according to the specific situational requirement or goal (Barsalou, in press). Thus, activation in response to a stimulus is not fixed across all contexts but plastic and modulated by context (Barsalou, 1983, 1985, 1991; Chrysikou, 2006; Vallée-Tourangeau, Anthony, & Austin, 1998; for recent reviews, see Barsalou, 1993, 2007). For instance, Barsalou (1982) reported faster extraction of object features (e.g., flammability as an attribute of newspapers) in relevant contexts (e.g., building a fire) than in neutral contexts. Furthermore, while a piano has classic taxonomic category members such as trumpet and harp, it might alternatively form a much better-suited category with objects such as washing machine and wardrobe when thinking about moving heavy furniture (e.g., Barclay, Bransford, Franks, McCarrell, & Nitsch, 1974).

Together, the discussed evidence implicates a high degree of flexibility and dynamic adaptations of the conceptual system. What we suggest here is that these conceptual adaptations shape the microstructure of lexicalisation by dynamically recruiting context-specific cohorts of varying combinations and sizes. For instance, objects such as bee, honey and bee keeper are categorically unrelated but they are all situation relevant as associates of the context apiary, and therefore, in combination, induce interference (Abdel Rahman & Melinger, 2007); similarly, objects such as bucket, coffee and stool are categorically and associatively unrelated. However, in the context of a fishing trip, they can be meaningfully integrated into a common semantic theme and should thus, as an inter-active lexical cohort, induce lexical interference (Abdel Rahman & Melinger, 2009b). These adaptations at the lexical level are not necessarily instantaneous, however. They build up over time as more evidence of a relevant context is accrued and convergent activation accumulates on related items. Consistent with this view, interference effects induced in the semantic blocking paradigm are not reliable in early presentations but take time to stabilise (e.g., Abdel Rahman & Melinger, 2007; Belke et al., 2005). Thus, contrary to the contention of Mahon and Caramazza, this pattern of emerging interference in the blocking paradigm is completely consistent and predicted by the swinging lexical network model.

To summarise, we agree with Mahon and Caramazza that "... the idea of contextually induced 'biases' on the spreading of activation is not new: if a set of related concepts are co-activated, those concepts will tend to mutually activate each other" (p. 744). However, and critically, we additionally assume that this mutual co-activation extends not only to well-established categorical relations but also to associative and newly formed ad-hoc relations.

As an alternative interpretation, Mahon and Caramazza suggest that "A much more radical notion of biases on the spreading of activation could stipulate the presence of structural constraints that guarantee that only a subset of words are in fact activated, compared to the entire set of nodes that would otherwise be activated. For instance, it may be argued that lexical nodes corresponding to distractor words become activated only if those distractors are category coordinates of the target concepts. In this way, the proposal would redefine the construct of a 'lexical competitor' to only include words that are coordinates of the target concept" (p. 744). This is diametrically opposed to what we claim. We do not restrict spreading activation between levels, as Bloem and La Heij (2003) do. Indeed, our proposal depends upon continuous and bi-directional information transmission between the conceptual and lexical strata. As we suggest in our article, one of the advantages of our proposal is that it does not need any stipulations or constraints on specific types of semantic relations or structural constraints. Simply by incorporating existing and independently motivated components, such as the role of lexical cohorts and the flexibility of conceptual organization, we can account for facilitation and interference effects observed in a variety of experimental paradigms.

CHALLENGES TO THE ASSUMPTION OF LEXICAL SELECTION BY COMPETITION: POLARITY REVERSALS AND SEMANTIC DISTANCE EFFECTS

We will now turn to a discussion of the two challenges to lexical competition models proposed by Mahon and Caramazza. The authors focus on polarity reversals from interference to facilitation and on semantic distance effects. As discussed in the original article, we account for polarity reversals by assuming trade-offs between conceptual facilitation and lexical interference. If cohorts of inter-related lexical entries are invoked by contexts, we expect interference effects (e.g., when objects are named in blocks of categorically, associatively or thematically inter-related items or when categorically related distractor words are presented; Damian, Vigliocco, & Levelt, 2001; Abdel Rahman & Melinger, 2007, 2009b; Schriefers, Meyer, & Levelt, 1990). Alternatively, if conceptual facilitation is bypassed, competition in the absence of a cohort should be observable (e.g., when distractors are phonologically related to an associate; Melinger & Abdel Rahman, 2009). In contrast, conceptual facilitation in the context of one-to-one competition should result in null or facilitation effects (e.g., when activation from target and distractor converges to one or very few competitors; Abdel Rahman & Melinger, 2007; Costa et al., 2005; Mahon, Costa, Peterson, Vargas, & Caramazza, 2007, Experiments 1 and 2). These predictions are confirmed by observations in different experimental paradigms.

The second proposed challenge is graded semantic distance effects in the picture-word interference paradigm. Before turning to a detailed discussion we want to stress that we do not agree that the observation of faster response latencies for semantically close compared with more distant distractors is such a critical challenge for the assumption of lexical competition. This is mainly because there are few empirical observations of such effects which yield heterogeneous results (see discussion in Abdel Rahman & Melinger, 2009a this issue), Furthermore, the amount of semantic priming induced by semantically near and far distractors will differ and thus will contribute to the size and polarity of the effect.

To account for semantic distance effects, we have suggested that the distance between the two stimuli may be confounded not only with facilitatory semantic priming effects but also with the size of the recruited lexical cohorts. For instance, when picture and word are semantically close (e.g., carp and trout) they spread converging activation to members of a comparatively small and narrow natural class (other fish). This follows not from the taxonomic organisation of the network, as Mahon and Camamazza suggest, but from the high proportion of semantic features shared by target and distractor; both have gills, scales, fins, swim in schools, etc. Most other animals do not share these features and thus will not be recruited into the cohort. The resulting co-activation of a small cohort produces a comparatively small competition effect. Additionally, semantically close distractors should yield comparatively strong (facilitatory) semantic priming effects, again resulting from the high proportion of shared semantic features. In contrast, when picture and word are semantically distant (e.g., carp and sheep) the set of shared semantic features is comparatively general, e.g., both move, are alive, are edible, etc. These general features characterise the nature class of animals. Thus, the target and distractor spread converging activation to a large set of concepts and lexical entries. The large and activated lexical cohort produces a relatively large competition effect while semantic priming should be weaker than the priming effects of close distractors. Thus, we assume that the trade-off between more semantic priming and less lexical competition induced by within-category semantically near distractors compared with less semantic priming and more lexical competition induced by within-category semantically far distractors accounts for the semantic distance effects discussed by Mahon and Caramazza.

Importantly, it is the combination of picture and distractor (the common context) that determines semantic activation spread at the conceptual and lexical level, not the structural properties of the isolated stimuli as such. This combination defines a common context, in this case based on the shared semantic features, that gates the activation flow at the conceptual and lexical level.

Future experiments will have to reveal whether our speculations on graded semantic distance effects are correct or not. In any case, they are not triggered by the assumption that "... distractor words and target pictures in the within-category semantically far condition do not share a common superordinate node" (p. 739). Furthermore, assuming a common super-ordinate node in the semantically far condition, it is not the case that, as Mahon and Caramazza put it, "... it follows that that representation will also be activated by the same items (distractors and targets) when they appear in the within-category semantically close condition" (p. 740). We assume that part of this misconception of our proposal is related to different views on how semantic activation spread is realised and on the failure to take dynamic context-dependent adaptations into account.

GENERAL COMMENTS AND CONCLUSIONS

Finally, we want to stress some fundamental differences in our approach to studying lexical selection compared to the approach adopted by Mahon and Caramazza in their response exclusion hypothesis (REH), particularly with regard to how the extant literature is considered. A key point for the REH is that "... the typical pattern that is observed in the picture-word paradigm when comparing semantically related and unrelated distractor words is not interference: the typical pattern is semantic facilitation" (p. 736). This sentence reveals that Mahon and Caramazza are primarily concerned with explaining polarity reversals observed with the PWI task. As the authors state, 'The Response Exclusion Hypothesis is, above all, a proposal about how conflicts that are induced by the picture-word (and Stroop) task are resolved within the speech production system" (p. 746). By focusing primarily on the PWI literature, they conclude that semantic facilitation, but not semantic interference, is informative to lexical selection processes.

In contrast, we view the insights from other paradigms as pertinent and we believe they support our position that both interference and facilitation effects are relevant to understanding lexical selection processes. We maintain that if one considers other tasks equally, the claim of non-competitive lexical selection becomes untenable. Numerous studies using a variety of production tasks, such as (cyclic and non-cyclic) semantic blocking (Abdel Rahman & Melinger, 2007; Belke, Meyer, & Damian, 2005; Damian & Als, 2005; Howard, Nickels, Coltheart, & Cole-Virtue, 2006), semantic substitution elicitation (e.g., Vigliocco et al., 2004), and tip of the tongue resolution (Abrams & Rodriguez, 2005), report results that implicate lexical competition.

Mahon and Caramazza consider these data as orthogonal to the current debate. We disagree with this assumption but recognise the need for further research to confirm or disconfirm the involvement of lexical competition in these effects (e.g., see Aristei, Abdel Rahman & Melinger, 2009, for ERP evidence for a tight functional and temporal coupling of distractor and blocking effects).[1]

The REH locates semantic interference effects at the articulatory output buffer, where distractor words need to be discarded to make room for the target word. As Mahon and Caramazza explain "when a distractor word shares criteria that must be satisfied by a correct response, [excluding the distractor word] costs more time" (p. 736). However, even within the PWI literature there are reports of facilitation and interference effects that are problematic on this account. For example, associative facilitation has been reported even when distractors are valid naming responses in the experiment and thus share relevant response criteria with the target (Abdel Rahman & Melinger, 2007). Furthermore, slower naming latencies have been reported for semantically unrelated distractor words that differ from the target picture name in grammatical gender (e.g., Cubelli et al., 2005), or are phonologically related to a categorical or associate competitor (e.g., Jescheniak & Schriefers, 1998; Abdel Rahman & Melinger, 2008; Melinger & Abdel Rahman, submitted). These competitors should be easy to exclude from the response buffer because they are semantically unrelated. Yet, they slow naming times.

Finally, Mahon and Caramazza claim that one of the merits of their proposal is that it shifts the focus away from semantic interference toward the "dynamics of spreading activation at the semantic level, and how spreading activation facilitates processes involved in lexical access" (p. 746). We recognise the value of this shift in focus, which is why one of the three assumptions of the swinging lexical network proposal is that the spread of conceptual activation is sensitive to meaningful contexts in which a word is uttered. Dynamicism and flexibility in the conceptual system are core components here. This assumption motivates our investigations into, for example, the relationship between ad hoc category formation and lexical selection (Abdel Rahman & Melinger, 2009b). We therefore entirely agree that understanding the dynamics of conceptual activation and organisation is crucial to a deeper understanding of conceptually mediated lexical selection.

In conclusion, we reject Mahon and Caramazza's charge that we have *unnecessarily complicated* the production process merely for the sake of salvaging lexical competition. Competition provides an elegant and comprehensive explanation for a host of empirical observations. Rather than throwing the baby out with the bath water, we believe our proposal provides

---

[1] Despite their implication to the contrary, the majority of proposals put forward to account for these effects incorporate some aspect of lexical competition (e.g., Abdel Rahman & Melinger, 2008; Damian & Als, 2005; Dell, Oppenheim, & Kittredge, 2008; Howard et al., 2006; Kroll & Stewart, 1994; Oppenheim, Dell, & Schwartz, 2007; Vigliocco et al., 2004).

an integrative account that covers a variety of effects from multiple experimental paradigms.

REFERENCES

Abdel Rahman, R., & Melinger, A. (2007). When bees hamper the production of honey: Lexical interference from associates in speech production. *Journal of Experimental Psychology: Learning, Memory and Cognition, 33*, 604–614.

Abdel Rahman, R., & Melinger, A. (2008). Enhanced phonological facilitation and traces of concurrent word form activation in speech production: An object naming study with multiple distractors. *Quarterly Journal of Experimental Psychology, 61*, 1410–1440.

Abdel Rahman, R., & Melinger, A. (2009a). Semantic context effects in language production: A swinging lexical network proposal and a review. *Language and Cognitive Processes, 24*, 713–734.

Abdel Rahman, R., & Melinger, A. (2009b). *The dynamic microstructure of speech production: Semantic interference built on the fly.* Manuscript in preparation.

Abrams, L., & Rodriguez, E. L. (2005). Syntactic class influences phonological priming of tip-of-the-tongue resolution. *Psychonomic Bulletin and Review, 12*, 1018–1023.

Aristei, S., Abdel Rahman, R., & Melinger, A. (2009). *Electrophysiological chronometry of semantic context effects in language production.* Manuscript submitted for publication.

Barclay, J. R., Bransford, J. D., Franks, J. J., McCarrell, N. S., & Nitsch, K. (1974). Comprehension and semantic flexibility. *Journal of Verbal Learning and Verbal Behavior, 13*, 471–481.

Barsalou, L. W. (1982). Context-independent and context-dependent information in concepts. *Memory & Cognition, 10*, 82–93.

Barsalou, L. W. (1983). Ad hoc categories. *Memory and Cognition, 11*, 211–227.

Barsalou, L. W. (1985). Ideals, central tendency, and frequency of instantiation as determinants of graded structure in categories. *Journal of Experimental Psychology: Learning, Memory, and Cognition, 11*, 629–654.

Barsalou, L. W. (1991). Deriving categories to achieve goals. In G. H. Bower (Ed.), *The psychology of learning and motivation: Advances in research and theory* (Vol. 27, pp. 1–64). San Diego, CA: Academic Press. [Reprinted in A. Ram & D. Leake (Eds.). (1995). *Goal-driven learning* (pp. 121–176). Cambridge, MA: MIT Press/Bradford Books.]

Barsalou, L. W. (1993). Flexibility, structure, and linguistic vagary in concepts: Manifestations of a compositional system of perceptual symbols. In A. C. Collins, S. E. Gathercole, & M. A. Conway (Eds.), *Theories of memory* (pp. 29–101). Hove, UK: Lawrence Erlbaum Associates Ltd.

Barsalou, L. W. (in press). Ad hoc categories. In P. C. Hogan (Ed.), *The Cambridge encyclopedia of the language sciences.* New York: Cambridge University Press.

Belke, E., Meyer, A. S., & Damian, M. F. (2005). Refractory effects in picture naming as assessed in a semantic blocking paradigm. *Quarterly Journal of Experimental Psychology, 58A*, 667–692.

Bloem, I., & La Heij, W. (2003). Semantic facilitation and semantic interference in word translation: Implications for models of lexical access in language production. *Journal of Memory and Language, 48*, 468–488.

Chrysikou, E. (2006). When shoes become hammers: Goal-derived categorization training enhances problem-solving performance. *Journal of Experimental Psychology: Learning, Memory, and Cognition, 32*, 935–942.

Costa, A., Alario, F.-X., & Caramazza, A. (2005). On the categorical nature of the semantic interference effect in the picture-word interference paradigm. *Psychonomic Bulletin and Review, 12*, 125–131.

Cubelli, R., Lotto, L., Paolieri, D., Girelli, M., & Job, R. (2005). Grammatical gender is selected in bare noun production: Evidence from the picture-word interference paradigm. *Journal of Memory & Language, 53*, 42–59.

Damian, M. F., & Als, L. C. (2005). Long-lasting semantic context effects in the spoken production of object names. *Journal of Experimental Psychology: Learning, Memory, and Cognition, 31*, 1372–1384.

Damian, M. F., Vigliocco, G., & Levelt, W. J. M. (2001). Effects of semantic context in the naming of pictures and words. *Cognition, 81*, B77–B86.

Dell, G. S., Oppenheim, G. M., & Kittredge, A. K. (2008). Saying the right word at the right time: Syntagmatic and paradigmatic interference in sentence production. *Language and Cognitive Processes, 23*, 583–608.

Howard, D., Nickels, L., Coltheart, M., & Cole-Virtue, J. (2006). Cumulative semantic inhibition in picture naming: experimental and computational studies. *Cognition, 100*, 464–482.

Kroll, J. F., & Stewart, E. (1994). Category interference in translation and picture naming: Evidence for asymmetric connections between bilingual memory representations. *Journal of Memory and Language, 33*, 149–174.

Jescheniak, J. D., & Schriefers, H. (1998). Serial discrete versus cascaded processing in lexical access in speech production: Further evidence from the co-activation of near-synonyms. *Journal of Experimental Psychology: Learning, Memory, and Cognition, 24*, 1256–1274.

Levelt, W. J. M., Roelofs, A., & Meyer, A. S. (1999). A theory of lexical access in speech production. *Brain and Behavioral Sciences, 22*, 1–38.

Mahon, B. Z., & Caramazza, A. (2009). Why does lexical selection have to be so hard? Comment on Abdel Rahman and Melinger's swinging lexical network proposal. *Language and Cognitive Processes, 24*, 735–748.

Mahon, B. Z., Costa, A., Peterson, R., Vargas, K. A., & Caramazza, A. (2007). Lexical selection is not by competition: A reinterpretation of semantic interference and facilitation effects in the picture-word interference paradigm. *Journal of Experimental Psychology: Learning, Memory and Cognition, 33*, 503–535.

Melinger, A., & Abdel Rahman, R. (2009). *Lexical competition induced by indirectly activated semantic associates during picture naming*. Manuscript submitted for publication.

Oppenheim, G. M., Dell, G. S., & Schwartz, M. F. (2007). Cumulative semantic interference as learning. *Brain and Language, 103*, 175–176.

Roelofs, A. (1992). A spreading-activation theory of lemma retrieval in speaking. *Cognition, 42*, 107–142.

Schriefers, H., Meyer, A. S., & Levelt, W. J. M. (1990). Exploring the time course of lexical access in production: Picture-word interference studies. *Journal of Memory and Language, 29*, 86–102.

Starreveld, P. A., & La Heij, W. (1995). Semantic interference, orthographic facilitation, and their interaction in naming tasks. *Journal of Experimental Psychology: Learning, Memory, and Cognition, 21*, 686–698.

Vallée-Tourangeau, F., Anthony, S. H., & Austin, N. G. (1998). Strategies for generating multiple instances of common and ad hoc categories. *Memory, 6*, 555–592.

Vigliocco, G., Vinson, D. P., Indefrey, P., Levelt, W. J. M., & Hellwig, F. (2004). Role of grammatical gender and semantics in German word production. Journal of Experimental Psychology: Learning, Memory. and Cognition, 30, 483–497.

LANGUAGE AND COGNITIVE PROCESSES
2009, 24 (5), 761–775

Competing conceptual representations trigger co-speech representational gestures

Sotaro Kita

University of Birmingham, Birmingham, UK

Thomas Stephen Davies

University of Bristol, Bristol, UK

Various interconnections between the processing of speech and gesture have been demonstrated in the literature. However, it is not well understood what cognitive factors influence intra-speaker variation of the gesture frequency. This study investigates the hypothesis that provides a unifying explanation for the previous findings on this issue; namely, competing representations in the conceptualisation process for speaking trigger representational gestures. Twenty adult participants described complex geometric figures. In the easy condition, the organisation of the lines necessary for conceptualisation were highlighted by making some lines darker, but in the hard condition, unnecessary competitor conceptualisations were highlighted. The descriptions in the two conditions were lexically comparable. However, the rate of representational gestures (but not that of beat gestures) was higher in the hard condition than in the easy condition. This finding is compatible with the idea that gestures may play a role in the conceptualisation process for speaking.

Keywords: Gesture; Speech production; Space; Conceptualization.

Speaking and speech-accompanying (i.e., co-speech) gestures are integral parts of our communicative practices. These gestures come in different types (Efron, 1972; Ekman & Friesen, 1969; McNeill, 1992). In emblems such as the ok-gesture and the thumb-up gesture, the form and meaning of gestures are fixed by cultural conventions. In beat gestures, which are small

---

Correspondence should be addressed to Sotaro Kita, School of Psychology, University of Birmingham, Birmingham B15 2TT, UK. E-mail: s.kita@bham.ac.uk

We thank Flora Wilson for collecting and coding a part of the data, and Katerina Kantartzis, Pienie Zwitserlood, and anonymous reviewers for their valuable comments on various versions of the manuscript.

http://www.psypress.com/lcp   DOI: 10.1080/01690960802327971

bidirectional movements, the form does not systematically change according to the linguistic content they highlight (McNeill, 1992). In representational gestures ('iconic' and 'deictic' gestures in McNeill, 1992), the relationship between the form and meaning is established at the moment of speaking by iconicity and deixis. As representational gestures can change their forms flexibly depending on the communicative and linguistics contexts, representational gestures have drawn much attention from researchers. The link between processing of speech and representational gestures has been intensively studied not only in comprehension (e.g., Beattie & Shovelton, 1999; Cassell, McNeill, & McCullough, 1999; Goldin-Meadow & Sandhofer, 1999; Krauss, Morrel-Samuels, & Colasante, 1991) but also in production.

The production processes for speech and representational gestures are tightly inter-linked. Co-speech representational gestures emerge early in development. Children already combine speech and representational gestures in a coordinated way at the one-word stage (e.g., Goldin-Meadow & Butcher, 2003). Co-speech representational gestures are a resilient feature of our communicative behaviour in the sense that they develop with minimal input. For example, congenitally blind individuals produce such gestures (Iverson & Goldin-Meadow, 1997). Also, production of representational gesture is co-ordinated with speech at the level of generation of a message for utterance formulation. For example, how gestures depict events varies in accordance with how information about the events is distributed over clauses in different languages (Kita & Özyürek, 2003; Özyürek, Kita, Allen, Furman, & Brown, 2005; Özyürek, Kita, Allen, Brown, Furman, & Ishizuka, 2008) or in different constructions within a language (Kita, Özyürek, Allen, Brown, Furman, & Ishizuka, 2007).

Despite the tight link between speech and gesture production, it is not the case that speakers produce representational gestures equally often in all speaking situations. Communicative contexts modulate frequency of gestures. The rate of gesturing is higher in a face-to-face situation than in a situation in which the listener cannot see the speaker, for representational gestures (Cohen, 1977) but not for beat gestures (Alibali, Heath, & Meyers, 2001). Contents of speech influence the rate of representation gestures. Speakers produce more gestures when talking about spatial contents than when talking about non-spatial contents (Rauscher, Krauss, & Chen, 1996). This suggests that some gestures may be generated from underlying spatial representations (but see Wagner, Nusbaum, & Goldin-Meadow, 2004, for an alternative view).

Speakers also produce more representational gestures when the speaking task is more difficult. Based on such findings, three different underlying mechanisms for gesture production have been proposed (Kita, 2000), depending on the types of difficulty manipulation.

First, visual access to the stimuli affects the rate of representational gestures. Speakers produce more representational gestures when describing stimuli from memory than when describing stimuli in front of the speaker (de Ruiter, 1995; Morsella & Krauss, 2004; Wesp, Hess, Keutmann, & Wheaton, 2001). The researchers proposed that representational gestures enhance the spatial imagery during speaking (the Image Activation Hypothesis), and thus when spatial imagery is 'degraded' in the memory condition, representational gestures are triggered. However, the degraded spatial representation in the memory condition may not have been the proximal cause of a higher gesture rate. The degraded spatial representation might have caused difficulties in speech production processes that rely on the spatial representation, and these speech production difficulties might have triggered representational gestures.

Second, the complexity of planning necessary for speech production affects the rate of representational gestures. For example, speakers produced more representational gestures in spontaneous speech than in scripted speech (Chawla & Krauss, 1994). The researchers proposed that gestures facilitate retrieval of words from the mental lexicon (the Lexical Retrieval Hypothesis; see also Krauss, Chen, & Chawla, 1996; Krauss, Chen, & Gottesman, 2000), and thus spontaneous speech with a higher load on the lexical access process triggers more representational gestures. However, as Chawla and Krauss (1994) also acknowledge, the above experiment may have manipulated speech difficulty not only at the lexical level, but also at the 'conceptualisation' level (Levelt, 1989).

Third, the difficulty in conceptualisation for speaking triggers more representational gestures. The conceptualisation process determines what information to be linguistically encoded in each utterance (Levelt, 1989). Thus, conceptualisation is difficult, for example, when it is not easy to decide what information is relevant for the communicative goal (e.g., unsure as to what the appropriate answer to a question is) or how to package relevant but complex information into chunks that can readily be encoded in an utterance or how to order relevant information in discourse (i.e., 'the linearisation problem' in Levelt, 1989). Studies have demonstrated that these types of difficulties trigger representational gestures, even when the lexical output is held relatively constant. For example, 5-year-old children produced more representational gestures that expressed physical features of task objects when they explained a solution to Piagetian conservation tasks than when they simply described the task objects (Alibali, Kita, & Young, 2000). In the description of patterns of dots, adult speakers produced more representational gestures when dots were presented with lines connecting them, which suggested possible ways for grouping the dots in the description, than when no such lines were provided (Hostetter, Alibali, & Kita, 2007). In the description of routes through a network of dots connected by lines, adult speakers produced more representational gestures in the non-deterministic part of the route where the dots can be visited in multiple ways than in the deterministic part (Melinger & Kita, 2007). In a similar description task, speakers produced more representational gestures when a secondary task was spatial in nature and interfered with the primary spatial description task than when the secondary task was non-spatial (Melinger & Kita, 2007). The researchers proposed that gesture facilitates conceptualisation for speaking (the Information Packaging Hypothesis, Kita, 2000), and thus a higher load on the conceptualisation process triggers more representational gestures. More specifically, it was proposed that representational gestures are triggered by the load on the 'parsing' of a complex spatial array into verbalisable units (Hostetter et al., 2007) or on selective attention necessary in focusing and linearisation during conceptualisation for speaking (Melinger & Kita, 2007). One way of bringing together these two specific proposals is to hypothesise that when multiple representations compete during conceptualisation for speaking, speakers produce more gestures.

The current study tests this specific prediction with adult speakers. They described complex diagrams as shown in Figure 1. They were instructed to describe the contents of each component box of the diagram. The dark lines in the hard condition created shapes that spanned multiple boxes, and these shapes created grouping of lines that competed with the box-by-box organisation of the lines as required by the instruction. In the easy condition, the dark lines divided the diagram in the way compatible with the instruction. Furthermore, the participants were instructed to ignore the dark lines in their descriptions, and thus they gave essentially the same description in the two conditions, which controlled the lexical output in the two conditions.

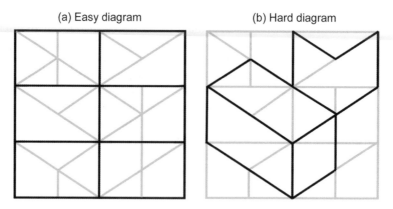

(a) Easy diagram   (b) Hard diagram

Figure 1.   The example of stimulus diagrams for the easy and the hard conditions.

One important limitation of Hostetter et al. (2007) and Melinger and Kita (2007) was that participants described stimuli from memory. Thus, it is difficult to rule out the possibility that the manipulation of conceptualisation difficulty is confounded with the difficulty in maintaining spatial imagery during speaking. In other words, their results could be interpreted on the basis of the Image Activation Hypothesis, according to which the load on image activation should trigger representational gestures (de Ruiter, 1995; Morsella & Krauss, 2004; Wesp et al., 2001). Thus, in the current study, the stimulus figures remained visible to the speaker during description in order to remove any memory component from the task.

The prediction is that the rate of representational gestures should be higher in the description of the hard diagrams than in the description of easy diagrams. Furthermore, we examined if the increase in the representational gesture rate from the easy to the hard condition correlates with the increase in the indices of speech production difficulty. Finally, none of the above-mentioned theories predict a difference in the rate of beat gestures between the easy and hard conditions.

METHOD

Participants

Twenty-eight students of the University of Bristol participated in the study. They were all were fluent English speakers and had normal or corrected-to-normal vision. Eight of the participants did not produce gestures, and were therefore excluded from the analysis.

Stimuli

The stimuli were six grid-like diagrams (10 cm × 10 cm). Four of the diagrams had six equal-sized boxes (e.g., Figure 1) and two had four equal-sized boxes. Each box contained horizontal, vertical and diagonal lines. No two boxes consisted of identical patterns. In order to minimise the difficulty in lexical choice, the spatial locations of the lines within boxes were easily definable relative to the other elements within the box. For example, the lines started and ended at a halfway point of another line or a crossing point of other lines, or a corner of the box. In the easy condition the boundaries of each box within the grid were emphasised with dark lines, so that they stood out compared with the grey lines inside each box. In the hard condition, various geometric figures that span across multiple boxes were fore-grounded by dark lines.

Design

The independent variable was a within-participant factor, conceptualisation difficulty, which contained two levels: easy and hard. The dependent variables for crucial analyses of gestures were two measures of gesture rates: the number of gestures per minute (the description duration) and number of gestures per 100 words in the description. The diagrams in each condition had a structurally identical partner in the other condition that differed only in patterns of dark lines (e.g., Figure 1a and 1b). In order to prevent the recognition of 'common structures', all three diagrams in one condition were the 180° rotated forms of the structurally identical partners in the other condition. Thus, the participant who saw Figure 1a in the easy condition saw the 180° rotated form of Figure 1b. Note that the rotation does not substantially change the content of description: what was right becomes left, what was up becomes down.

Two sets of stimuli were created, depending on whether the easy stimuli or the hard stimuli were 180° rotated. Half the participants described one set and the other half described the other set. (All participants described six diagrams in total. Among the six diagrams, four of them (two easy and two hard diagrams) contained six equal-sized boxes as in Figure 1, and two of them (one easy and one hard diagram) contained four equal-sized boxes.) In each set, easy and hard diagrams were presented alternately, with the structurally identical partners from the two conditions being farthest apart in the sequence. Within sets, the stimuli were presented in one order to half the participants, and in the reverse order to the other participants. Thus, there were a total of four counterbalancing groups, to which the participants were randomly allocated.

Procedure

Participants were tested individually. They were seated on one side of a large screen (about $1.5 \text{ m} \times 1.5 \text{ m}$) that blocked visual contact between the participant and the addressee (a confederate). The participants were told that the study concerned how people describe geometric shapes, and that their task was to describe geometric figures to another person seated on the other side of the blocking screen. The addressee provided the occasional sign of acknowledgement such as 'ok', 'uh uh', 'yes', but did not engage in an extended exchange. The participants were instructed to first divide the stimulus diagrams into either 4 or 6 equally sized boxes (depending on whichever the picture would allow) and describe the contents of each box. The participants were instructed to ignore the difference between dark and light lines in their description. After describing two practice diagrams, the participants described six experimental diagrams. The diagrams were pinned-up at eye-level onto the blocking screen (which stood at about 30 cm away from the knees) one at a time and remained present until the participants had completed their description. The participants were not subject to any time restrictions. The description was recorded with a PAL DV video recorder, for later analysis.

Gesture coding

On the basis of both visual and auditory information, gestures were categorised into the following types according to McNeill's (1992) classification system. In *iconic gestures*, gestural movement resembled the part of the diagram (mostly lines) being described (e.g., the hand moves diagonally, when describing a diagonal line). In *deictic gestures*, gestural movement indicated a location in the diagram or in the gestural representation of the diagram. The gestural movement with a pointing hand shape that traced a line to represent a line in the diagram was not counted as a deictic gesture, but it was counted as an iconic gesture. Note that all iconic and deictic gestures were related to the contents of the diagram, thus had a spatial content such as lines in a particular orientation, the contour of a shape, and (relative) location of various elements of the diagrams. In *beat gestures*, the hand with a natural relaxed hand shape makes a small bi-directional movement, typically near the resting position of the hand.

In order to establish the intercoder reliability of gesture classification, all gestures produced for one randomly selected diagram for each participant were independently classified by a second coder (total 748 gestures). The two coders agreed 89.7% of the time, Cohen's $kappa = 80.9$, $p < .001$.

RESULTS

Speech

We compared the speech output between the easy vs. hard diagrams in order to confirm that the hard diagrams were more difficult to describe than easy diagrams. More specifically, we compared the two conditions with respect to four variables that capture the difficulty difference: the duration of descriptions, the number of words used in the description, and the speech rate (number of words per second). As representational gestures are assumed to be generated from underlying spatio-motoric representations (Feyereisen & Havard, 1999; Kita, 2000; Krauss et al., 2000; but see Wagner et al., 2004), we distinguished spatial words (e.g., spatial preposition, spatial adverbs,

TABLE 1
The mean (*SD*) duration, number of spatial and non-spatial word tokens, and speech rate in the descriptions of the Easy and Hard diagrams, plus the mean (*SD*) difference between the two conditions

	Easy	*Hard*	*Hard–Easy*
Duration (seconds)	387 (105)	418 (119)	30.4 (47.2)
Number of spatial word tokens	506 (114)	522 (125)	16.7 (32.6)
Number of non-spatial word tokens	431 (143)	455 (163)	24.1 (53.4)
Speech rate (words/second)	2.36 (0.24)	2.44 (0.27)	−0.079 (0.15)

dimensional and directional adjectives, nouns referring to concrete objects and shapes) and non-spatial words.[1] (See Appendix for the exhaustive lists of the two type of words.). The participants took a longer time, used more word tokens, and spoke more slowly in the hard condition than in the easy condition: duration, $t(19) = 2.88$, $p < .05$; number of spatial word tokens, $t(19) = 2.28$, $p < .05$; number of non-spatial word tokens, $t(19) = 2.02$, $p = .058$; speech rate, $t(19) = 2.32$, $p < .05$, indicating that the hard diagrams were indeed more difficult to describe. (See Table 1 for the means and *SD*s.)

Next, we sought evidence that the participants gave descriptions with essentially the same contents in the easy and hard conditions (as instructed). If the descriptions in the two conditions were comparable in the content, then we would expect that the relative frequencies of various words in the description should be similar between the two conditions. For example, if a speaker used the word 'left' very often and the word 'square' only a few times in the easy condition, then the same pattern of should hold also in the hard condition. In order to verify this, we compared the number of times each word was used in the two conditions. The token frequency of each word was aggregated over all participants and morphological variants (e.g., cross vs. crossed vs. crossing). The token frequencies of each word in the two conditions (separately for spatial and non-spatial words) are shown in Figure 2. The token frequencies of words in the two conditions were highly correlated for both spatial words and non-spatial words (Spearman correlation for the raw token frequencies, spatial words $N = 99$, $rho = .910$, $p < .001$, non-spatial words, $N = 143$, $rho = .823$, $p < .001$; Pearson correlation after log transformation, spatial words, $N = 72$, $r = .972$, $p < .001$, non-spatial words, $N = 88$, $r = .964$, $p < .001$). These analyses indicate that the words that were used often in one condition were also used often in the other condition, confirming that the participants gave descriptions with comparable contents in the easy and hard conditions, as instructed.

---

[1] As the stimuli to be described were purely spatial, we did not have motor contents in the verbal response.

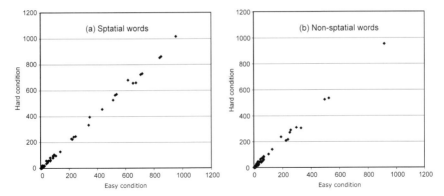

Figure 2. The token frequencies of spatial words (a) and non–spatial words (b) in the easy and hard conditions. Each dot represents a word (type). The plot (b) does not include the frequencies for 'the' (2738 for easy and 2839 for hard) so that the frequencies of other words can be shown

Gesture

We examined whether the gesture rates differed between the easy and hard conditions. The rate of gesturing (per 100 words) in the hard condition was higher than in the easy condition for iconic gestures, $t(19) = 3.62$, $p < .01$, and deictic gestures, $t(19) = 2.44$, $p < .05$, but not for beat gestures, $t(19) = 1.65$ (see Figure 3).[2] The analysis based on the rate of gesturing per minute yielded basically the same pattern of results. The gesture rate in the hard

---

[2] One of the reviewers suggested to examine if the participants who showed a stronger sign of speech difficulty in the hard condition also produced much more representational gestures in the hard condition. Such a finding would further support the idea that the higher rates of iconic and deictic gestures in the hard condition were due to relative conceptualisation difficulty. For the correlational analysis, we computed new variables that captured the increase in speech difficulty and in the gesture rate from the easy condition to hard condition, by subtracting the value for the easy condition from that for the hard condition (i.e., hard–easy). Because some of the variables had outliers, we used non-parametric (Spearman) correlation (Pearson correlation would give the same results). The increase in the iconic gesture rate did not significantly correlate with the increase in the duration ($rho = .136$), the number of spatial word tokens ($rho = -.073$), the number of non-spatial word tokens ($rho = .045$), and the speech rate ($rho = -.194$). The increase in the deictic gesture rate did not significantly correlate with any of the speech variables either: the increase in the duration ($rho = -.259$), the number of spatial word tokens ($rho = -.139$), the number of non-spatial word tokens ($rho = 0.259$), and the speech rate ($rho = .029$).One possible reason for the lack of significant correlation is that the speech variables did not have sufficiently large variability between participants, relative to the size of the group means, and thus could not capture the relationship to the variability in the increase of the gesture rates. Note that the three speech variables were significantly different from zero. That is, duration, the number of spatial words, and speech rate differed between the easy and hard conditions significantly (marginally significantly for non-spatial words), which is possible only if the variability between participants was sufficiently small relative to the means. Thus, the three speech variables (hard–easy) may not have been optimal for the correlation analyses.

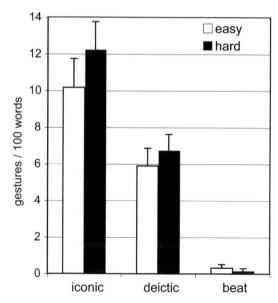

Figure 3. The rates of iconic, deictic, and beat gestures (per 100 words) in the easy and hard conditions. The error bars indicate standard errors.

condition is significantly higher than in the easy condition for iconic gestures, $t(19) = 3.13$, $p < .01$, and marginally higher in deictic gestures, $t(19) = 1.76$, $p = .094$, but not for beat gestures, $t(19) = 1.64$. Thus, iconic and deictic gestures, but not beat gestures, were produced more frequently in the hard condition than in the easy condition.

DISCUSSION

This study investigated how conceptual difficulty for speaking influences the rate of gesturing. In the easy condition, the dark lines separated a figure into boxes in the way congruent with the way the participants were instructed to describe the diagrams. In the hard condition, the dark lines formed shapes that competed with the grouping of the lines necessary for the description task. The difficulty of description indeed differed between the two conditions as the participants took a longer time, used more word tokens, and spoke more slowly in the hard condition than in the easy condition.[3] It was also found that

---

[3] These variables only index general difficulty in speaking, and do not directly tap into conceptualisation difficulty. However, the nature of the manipulation (Figure 1) strongly suggests that the difficulty in speaking arose from the competing representations in the hard condition, which made it more difficult to decide exactly which part of the diagram to verbally describe in each utterance. Note also that there are no agreed-upon variables that distinguish difficulties in conceptualisation vs. lexical access in spontaneous connected speech (Kita, 2000).

there is a very strong correlation of word token frequencies between the two conditions; that is, the words used often in one condition was also used often in the other. This indicates that the participants gave descriptions with comparable contents in the two conditions.[4] Crucially, the speakers produced representational gestures at a higher rate in the hard condition than in the easy condition, whereas the rate of beat gestures did not significantly differ between the two conditions. This supports the hypothesis that competing representations during the conceptualisation for speaking trigger the production of representational gestures.

The competition hypothesis also has a theoretical advantage in that it can provide a unified account for many of the previous findings. Representational gestures were triggered by the load on parsing complex spatial arrays into verbalisable units (Hostetter et al., 2007). The complex figures can be parsed in multiple ways, and different alternatives presumably competed with each other, which may trigger representational gestures. Representational gestures were also triggered by the load on selectional attention when linearising spatial information (Melinger & Kita, 2007). Linearisation of information also entails organising competing representations activated simultaneously. A similar interpretation can be given to the finding that more representational gestures were produced in the spontaneous speech than in the scripted speech (Chawla & Krauss, 1994). In spontaneous speech, complex information needs to be linearised so that it can be verbalised in a sequence of utterances. The competing representations in the linearlisation process might have triggered more representational gesture in the spontaneous speech condition.

One interesting question for future research is whether the competition of *any* type of representations triggers gestures. The current study investigated a case of competing spatial information. It has been noted that representational gestures are produced particularly often during speech with spatial contents (Rauscher et al., 1996) and motoric contents (Feyereisen & Havard, 1999). Thus, it is possible that representational gestures originate from spatio-motoric imagery, and only the competition between spatio-motoric images triggers representational gestures. However, it has also been proposed that representational gestures originate from amodal propositional representations (Wagner et al., 2004). If that is the case, any type of competing

---

[4] Participants used more words in the hard condition than in the easy condition, while maintaining the high correlation between the token frequencies at which various words were used in the two conditions. This suggests that, in the hard condition, the participants may have sometimes repeated descriptions. Repeated descriptions would increase the number of word tokens used in the hard condition, while maintaining the relationship that the words frequently used in the easy condition are also frequently used in the hard condition.

conceptual representations activated during conceptualisation for speaking should trigger representational gestures.

Though the current experiment does not directly test whether gesture has a facilitatory effect on speaking, the results have implications for theories about self-oriented functions of gestures. More specifically, the results of this study are compatible with the idea that gesture facilitates conceptualisation processes for speaking, which determines what information needs to be encoded in each utterance (Information Packaging Hypothesis; Kita, 2000). With the current results and the findings from previous gesture prohibition studies, we may be able to triangulate how gesture influences speech production. When gesture is prohibited, the participants spoke less fluently about space (Rauscher et al., 1996), and they performed worse in a concurrent memory task in which they had to retain a letter sequence or a visual pattern (Goldin-Meadow, Nusbaum, Kelly, & Wagner, 2001; Wagner et al., 2004). Animated cartoons that the participant described in Rauscher et al.'s experiment lend themselves to multiple competing ways of description, and the dual task situations in Goldin-Meadow, Wagner and their colleagues' studies also require management of competing representations in competing tasks. The picture that emerges from this set of studies and the current study is that representational gestures may be triggered *because* gestures facilitate certain cognitive processes, in particular, management of competing representations in the conceptual planning for speaking.

It is difficult to accommodate the current results within the account based on the theory that gesture facilitates access to the syntactic or phonological lexical representation (Lexical Retrieval Hypothesis; Krauss et al., 1996, 2000) as essentially the same set of words were used at a comparable relative frequency in the two conditions. The current results cannot be easily explained either by the account based on the theory that gestures enhances spatial imagery constructed from long-term memory (Image Activation Hypothesis; de Ruiter, 1995; Morsella & Krauss, 2004; Wesp et al., 2001) as the stimuli were always visible during description. It has to be noted, however, that the current results do not provide any evidence *against* these two hypotheses, and that more than one hypothesis could be correct. Finally, explanations based on communicative functions of gestures (see Kendon 1994 for a review) are also difficult for two reasons. First, the speaker and the addressee were not in visual contact, and thus the gestures were not meant to be seen by the addressee. Second and more importantly, the communicative goal of the speaker was identical in the two conditions as they were instructed to communicate the same content to the addressee. It has to be noted again that our results do not refute the idea that communicative factors modulate the gesture rate. Given the results from the studies on the role of gesture in communication (e.g., Alibali et al., 2001; Beattie & Shovelton, 1999; Cassell et al., 1999; Cohen, 1997; Goldin-Meadow &

Sandhofer, 1999), both communicative and cognitive factors are likely to modulate the gesture rate.

This study furthered our understanding of why speakers do not produce gestures equally often in all situations, and what kind of underlying mechanism can account for the uneven distribution of gestures. The idea that competing conceptual representations trigger gestures dovetails with the findings that gestures can be an indicator of different stages of learning (Church, & Goldin-Meadow, 1986), and that body movements play an important role in cognition in general (e.g., Alibali, Kita, Bigelow, Wolfman, & Klein, 2001; Cacioppo, Priester, & Berntson, 1993; Chu & Kita, in press; Glenberg & Kaschak, 2002; Schwartz & Black, 1999; Wohlschlager & Wohlschlager, 1998). Representational gestures seem to have deeply rooted interconnections with the processes of learning, thinking, and speaking.

REFERENCES

Alibali, M. W., Heath, D. C., & Myers, H. J. (2001). Effects of visibility between speaker and listener on gesture production: Some gestures are meant to be seen. *Journal of Memory and Language, 44,* 169–188.

Alibali, M. W., Kita, S., Bigelow, L. J., Wolfman, C. M., & Klein, S. M. (2001). Gesture plays a role in thinking for speaking. In C. Cavé, I. Guaïtella, & S. Santi (Eds.), *Oralité et gesturalité: Interactions et comportements multimodaux dans la communication* (pp. 407–410). Paris: L'Harmattan.

Alibali, M. W., Kita, S., & Young, A.J. (2000). Gesture and the process of speech production: We think, therefore we gesture. *Language and Cognitive Processes, 15,* 593–613.

Beattie, G., & Shovelton, H. (1999). Mapping the range of information contained in the iconic hand gestures that accompany spontaneous speech. *Journal of Language and Social Psychology, 18,* 438–462.

Cacioppo, J. T., Priester, J. R., & Berntson, G. G. (1993). Rudimentary determinants of attitudes. II. *Journal of Personality and Social Psychology, 65*(1), 5–17.

Cassell, J., McNeill, D., & McCullough, K.-E. (1999). Speech-gesture mismatches: Evidence for one underlying representation of linguistic and nonlinguistic information. *Pragmatics and Cognition, 7,* 1–33.

Chawla, P., & Krauss, R. (1994). Gesture and speech in spontaneous and rehearsed narratives. *Journal of Experimental Social Psychology, 30,* 580–601.

Chu, M., & Kita, S. (in press). Spontaneous gestures during mental rotation tasks: Insights into the microdevelopment of the motor strategy. *Journal of Experimental Psychology: General.*

Church, R. B., & Goldin-Meadow, S. (1986). The mismatch between gesture and speech as an index of transitional knowledge. *Cognition, 23,* 43–71.

Cohen, A. A. (1977). The communicative functions of hand illustrators. *Journal of Communication, 27,* 54–63.

de Ruiter, J. P. (1995). Why do people gesture at the telephone? In M. Biemans & M. Woutersen (Eds.), *Proceedings of the center for language studies opening academic year '95–96* (pp. 49–56). Nijmegen, the Netherlands: Center for Language Studies.

Efron, D. (1972). *Gesture, race, and culture.* The Hague: Mouton.

Ekman, P., & Friesen, W. V. (1969). The repertoire of nonverbal behavioral categories: Origins, usage, and coding. *Semiotica, 1,* 49–98.

Feyereisen, P., & Havard, I. (1999). Mental imagery and production of hand gestures while speaking in younger and older adults. *Journal of Nonverbal Behavior, 23*, 153–171.

Glenberg, A. M., & Kaschak, M. P. (2002). Grounding language in action. *Psychonomic Bulletin and Review, 9*, 558–569.

Goldin-Meadow, S., Alibali, M. W., & Church, R. B. (1993). Transitions in concept acquisition: Using the hand to read the mind. *Psychological Review, 100*, 279–297.

Goldin-Meadow, S., & Butcher, C. (2003). Pointing toward two-word speech in young children. In S. Kita (Ed.), *Pointing: Where language, culture, and cognition meet* (pp. 85–107). Mahwah, NJ: Lawrence Erlbaum Associates Inc.

Goldin-Meadow, S., & Sandhofer, C. M. (1999). Gestures convey substantive information about a child's thoughts to ordinary listeners. *Developmental Science, 2*, 67–74.

Goldin-Meadow, S., Nusbaum, H., Kelly, S. D., & Wagner, S. M. (2001). Explaining match: Gesturing lightens the load. *Psychological Science, 12*, 516–522.

Hostetter, A. B., Alibali, W. M., & Kita, S. (2007). I see it in my hand's eye: Representational gestures are sensitive to conceptual demands. *Language and Cognitive Processes, 22*, 313–336.

Iverson, J., & Goldin-Meadow, S. (1997). What's communication got to do with i: Gesture in blind from birth children. *Developmental Psychology, 33*, 453–467.

Kendon, A. (1994). Do gestures communicate? A review. *Research on Language and Social Interaction, 27*, 175–200.

Kita, S. (2000). How representational gestures help speaking. In D. McNeill (Ed.), *Language and gesture* (pp. 162–185). Cambridge, UK: Cambridge University Press.

Kita, S., & Özyürek, A. (2003). What does cross-linguistic variation in semantic coordination of speech and gesture reveal? Evidence for an interface representation of spatial thinking and speaking. *Journal of Memory and Language, 48*, 16–32.

Kita, S., Özyürek, A., Allen, S., Brown, A., Furman, R., & Ishizuka, T. (2007). Relations between syntactic encoding and co-speech gestures: Implications for a model of speech and gesture production. *Language and Cognitive Processes, 22*, 1212–1236.

Krauss, R. M., Morrel-Samuels, P., & Colasante, C. (1991). Do conversational hand gestures communicate? *Journal of Personality and Social Psychology, 61*, 743–754.

Krauss, R. M., Chen, Y., & Chawla, P. (1996). Nonverbal behavior and nonverbal communication: What do conversational hand gestures tell us? In M. Zanna (Ed.), *Advances in experimental social psychology* (Vol. 28, pp. 389–450). Tampa, FL: Academic Press.

Krauss, R. M., Chen, Y., & Gottesman, R. F. (2000). Lexical gestures and lexical access: A process model. In D. McNeill (Ed.), *Language and gesture* (pp. 261–283). Cambridge: Cambridge University Press.

Levelt, W. J. M. (1989). *Speaking*. Cambridge, MA: The MIT Press.

McNeill, D. (1992). *Hand and mind*. Chicago: University of Chicago Press.

Melinger, A., & Kita, S. (2007). Conceptualization load triggers gesture production. *Language and Cognitive Processes, 22*, 473–500.

Morsella, E., & Krauss, R. M. (2004). The role of gestures in spatial working memory and speech. *American Journal of Psychology, 117*, 411–424.

Özyürek, A., Kita, S., Allen, S., Furman, R., & Brown, A. (2005). How does linguistic framing of events influence co-speech gestures? Insights from crosslinguistic variations and similarities. *Gesture, 5*, 219–240.

Özyürek, A., Kita, S., Allen, S., Brown, A., Furman, R., & Ishizuka, T. (2008). Development of cross-linguistic variation in speech and gesture: Motion events in English and Turkish. *Developmental Psychology, 44*, 1040–1054.

Rauscher, F. H., Krauss, R. M., & Chen, Y. (1996). Gesture, speech, and lexical access: The role of lexical movements in speech production. *Psychological Science, 7*, 226–231.

Schwartz, D. L., & Black, T. (1999). Inferences through imagined actions: Knowing by simulated doing. *Journal of Experimental Psychology: Learning Memory and Cognition, 25*, 116–136.

Wagner, S. M., Nusbaum, H., & Goldin-Meadow, S. (2004). Probing the mental representation of gesture: Is handwaving spatial? *Journal of Memory and Language*, *50*, 395–407.

Wesp, R., Hess, J., Keutmann, D., & Wheaton, K. (2001). Gestures maintain spatial imagery. *American Journal of Psychology*, *114*, 591–600.

Wohlschlager, A., & Wohlschlager, A. (1998). Mental and manual rotation. *Journal of Experimental Psychology: Human Perception and Performance*, *24*, 397–412.

APPENDIX
EXHAUSTIVE LISTS OF WORDS UTTERED

The following are the exhaustive lists of spatial and non-spatial words uttered by the participants. The words in capital letters were those in which morphological variants (e.g., big vs. bigger, square vs. squares) were collapsed in the correlational analyses of frequencies.

List of non-spatial words

APOSTROPHE & S (e.g., 's' in 'that's'), A, about, actually, again, all, already, also, although, and, another, any, as, ask, basically, BE, before, bit, bold, both, but, by, can, completely, complicated, confirm, cool, could, DESCRIBE, different, directly, DO, each, EASY, effectively, either, END, EQUAL, essentially, even, exactly, excuse, FINAL, first, FIVE, for, forgotten, FOUR, full, GET, good, guess, HAVE, how, I, if, ignore, imagine, in, it, itself, just, kind, know, last, light, like, LOOK, main, me, mean, mention, mixed, more, my, next, no, not, nothing, now, number, of, oh, ok, on, ONE, only, or, ORIGINAL, other, overall, PART, perfect, plus, PREVIOUS, question, realised, repeat, same, say, see, sense, should, similar, SIX, so, sorry, START, STOP, that, the, them, then, there, they, think, though, THREE, time, told, twelve, twenty, two, using, very, way, WE, well, what, when, where, whether, which, whichever, whole, will, with, without, woah, word, yeah, yes, YOU.

List of spatial words

above, across, along, at, back, base, below, between, BIG, BISECT, BLOCK, bottom, BOX, BREAK, CARRY, centre, clock, COME, CORNER, CROSS, CUT, DIAGONAL, diagram, DIAMETER, diamond, DISSECT, DIVIDE, down, downwards, draw, edge, envelope, evenly, far, figure, flag, FORM, from, GO, half, hand, heading, HIT, HORIZONTAL, INTERCEPT, intersect, into, joining, LARGE, LEAD, LEFT, leftwards, LINE, little, LOW, MAKE, MEET, MIDDLE, midpoint, moving, off, opposite, out, over, parallel, PASS, POINT, quadrants, reaches, RECTANGLE, right, round, ROW, RUN, SECTION, SEGMENT, separate, SHAPE, shooting, SIDE, sized, SMALL, SPLIT, SQUARE, straight, symmetry, TAKE, THESE, through, tiny, to, top, TOUCH, towards, TRIANGLE, union, jack, UP, VERTICAL, within.

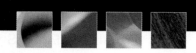

AUTHOR SERVICES

Publish With Us

The Taylor & Francis Group Author Services Department aims to enhance your publishing experience as a journal author and optimize the impact of your article in the global research community. Assistance and support is available, from preparing the submission of your article through to setting up citation alerts post-publication on **informa**world™, our online platform offering cross-searchable access to journal, book and database content.

Our Author Services Department can provide advice on how to:

- direct your submission to the correct journal
- prepare your manuscript according to the journal's requirements
- maximize your article's citations
- submit supplementary data for online publication
- submit your article online via Manuscript Central™
- apply for permission to reproduce images
- prepare your illustrations for print
- track the status of your manuscript through the production process
- return your corrections online
- purchase reprints through Rightslink™
- register for article citation alerts
- take advantage of our i*OpenAccess* option
- access your article online
- benefit from rapid online publication via i*First*

See further information at:
www.informaworld.com/authors

or contact:
Author Services Manager, Taylor & Francis, 4 Park Square, Milton Park, Abingdon, Oxon OX14 4RN, UK, email: authorqueries@tandf.co.uk